The
Three Families
of
H. L. Hunt

ALSO BY ARDIS BURST

The Management Game

The
Three Families
of
H. L. Hunt

Ardis Burst

WEIDENFELD & NICOLSON
New York

Published by Weidenfeld & Nicolson, New York
A Division of Wheatland Corporation
841 Broadway
New York, New York 10003-4793

Published in Canada by General Publishing Company, Ltd.

Library of Congress Cataloging-in-Publication Data

    Burst, Ardis.
        The three families of H. L. Hunt / Ardis Burst. — 1st ed.
          p.   cm.
        Includes index.
        ISBN 1-555-84142-2
        1. Hunt, H. L.   2. Businessmen—United States—Biography.
    I. Title.
    HC102.5.H86B87   1988
    338.092′4—dc19
    [B]

                                      88-21098
                                            CIP

Manufactured in the United States of America

This book is printed on acid-free paper

Designed by Irving Perkins Associates

First Edition

10 9 8 7 6 5 4 3 2 1

To my patient husband

CONTENTS

THE THREE HUNT FAMILIES

H. L. Hunt and Lyda Bunker
(1889–1974)   (1889–1955)

Margaret (Hill)	H. L., Jr. "Hassie"	Caroline	Lyda
(1915–)	(1917–)	(1923–)	(1925)

Nelson Bunker	William Herbert	Lamar
(1926–)	(1929–)	(1932–)

H. L. Hunt and Frania Tye (Lee)
(1889–1974)   (1904–   )

Howard	Haroldina (Franch)	Helen (Cartledge)	Hugh
(1926–1975)	(1928–)	(1930–1962)	(1934–)

H. L. Hunt and Ruth Ray
(1889–1974)   (1917–   )

Ray	June	Helen	Swanee
(1943–)	(1944–)	(1949–)	(1950–)

INTRODUCTION

IN April 1948, Haroldson Lafayette Hunt made his debut before the American people, when two of the most widely read magazines in the country, *Life* and *Fortune*, identified him as "probably the richest single individual in the U.S."[1] *Fortune* went on to describe Hunt as a man "whose quiet habits and abhorrence of cameras make him an unknown even to most of his fellow Texans."

H. L. Hunt was fifty-nine years old, in the prime of his life. He shared a lovely home with his wife of many years and already had several grandchildren. His primary businesses—oil and gas exploration and production—were generating a gross weekly income of more than $1 million. He had also begun investing in tangible assets that were certain to increase in value long into the future: farm and ranch property, cattle, and urban real estate in the booming cities of Texas. He was even starting to channel some of his six-day-work-week energy into such nonfinancial areas as politics and social commentary.

In 1987, almost forty years later, Nelson Bunker Hunt, the most prominent of H. L. Hunt's sons, was fifty-nine years old. By rights, Bunker should have been poised, like his father before him, to enjoy twenty-five more years of good living. He, too, enjoyed excellent health, a successful marriage, and was blessed with several grandchildren. His primary businesses were oil and gas exploration and production; he was heavily invested in tangible assets. But a *Fortune* feature on Bunker was quite different from the earlier piece about his father. Headlined "Fighting to Rescue the Family Fortune," the article described how Bunker and his two younger brothers were struggling to salvage the steadily eroding Hunt assets.[2] The situation was critical: recent events threatened the entire basis of the family millions.

Even in an American economic landscape littered with offspring who could not match the greatness of their financially successful fathers, the contrast between H. L. Hunt and his son Bunker is arresting. And how Bunker and his two brothers lost more than a billion dollars is only one part of the larger Hunt story, a surprising tale that spans a hundred years and has a cast that includes three completely independent families, in which Hunt fathered a total of fifteen offspring.

The saga of the Hunt families hinges on the legacies Hunt's children, and later his grandchildren, inherited from the enigmatic oilman. H. L. Hunt was a complex and often contradictory individualist. Whereas the financial fortunes he left to the second and third generations were relatively straightforward, the psychological legacies he bequeathed to them, often unwittingly, are as complicated and tangled as the darkest subconscious underpinnings of the man himself. It was Hunt's psychological legacy, for example, that in the final assessment constituted one of the most significant factors in the financial downfall of Bunker.

It was also Hunt's psychological legacy that was significant in the financial *success* of Caroline Hunt, the woman *Fortune* dubbed "Bunker Hunt's Savvy Sister," and whom the *New York Times* identified in 1986 as the wealthiest woman in the United States.[3] Hunt's complex legacy was even significant in the decision of his two youngest daughters, Helen and Swanee, not to capitalize on their riches, but, rather, to live simple lives while setting up a foundation that supported social causes that Hunt himself would have opposed violently.

How could one man's legacy lead to so many varied outcomes? In part, the differences stem from the fact that each of Hunt's children was wholly individual, born with different strengths and weaknesses, different inclinations, a different temperament. Furthermore, while six of the children grew up in a traditional family with legally married parents, four were part of a secret family, raised by a mother who, quite in error, believed that *she* was Hunt's legally wedded wife. In addition, there were Hunt's four youngest children, born many years after his first two families, whose mother Hunt married only when the oldest child was already into his teens. And as the Hunt family story will reveal, despite the many differences family members exhibited, they all seemed to draw from similar legacies, which led them to act in ways that were often surprisingly similar from family to family and generation to generation, even when the settings for their actions were very different.

The story of Hunt's families and the legacies he left to them is both fascinating and, in many respects, unique. Few American dynasties have gained, much less lost, such enormous sums of money. Fewer yet have been so complex in structure that they provide constant opportunities for the kinds of conflicts that fuel soap operas: dramatic courtroom confrontations; ever-changing alliances between siblings, half-siblings, in-laws, and generations; behind-the-scenes business dealings that influence the New York Stock Exchange, the Chicago commodities market, and even the London silver market.

Rarely have there been families in which so many children were forced to struggle so deeply in their search for their own identities. In the face of their often oppressive legacies, Bunker, Caroline, Helen, Swanee, and the rest have confronted their heritage over and over again as they tried to create a meaningful future out of a troubled past. It is this struggle, as well as the outward drama, that makes the Hunt story so intriguing.

I

H. L. Hunt,
Progenitor

ONE

THE circumstances of H. L. Hunt's early life were a curious mixture of the oppressively ordinary and the highly unusual. Like many other people in the late 1800s, he grew up on a farm, where he was involved with the work of the family from the time he was a young child. The family's values were centered on working hard, going to church on Sunday, and getting ahead in the world. Throughout Hunt's life, these basic Middle American values were those that were to guide him. But there was also a quality of isolation in his family's situation that, combined with his individualistic temperament and precocious intelligence, set him far apart from the people around him. Ironically, these aspects of Hunt's childhood formed the basis of both his greatest strengths—intellectual curiosity, a willingness to take decisive action—and his greatest weaknesses—the unusual and limiting emotional needs that drove him to lead a life that, in certain respects, was extremely unconventional.

Haroldson Lafayette Hunt, Jr., was born in 1889 near a small farming town in southern Illinois called Vandalia. His parents had met and married there after the Civil War, his father having settled in Illinois to escape the volatile environment of Reconstruction.[1] Haroldson Lafayette Hunt, Sr., had fought for the Confederacy, lost his father and brother, and been incarcerated in a prisoner-of-war camp. When the war was over, he and the remainder of his family left Arkansas, where he had grown up, and went looking for a more peaceful place to begin farm life again.

Hunt's mother, in contrast, had grown up in Illinois and had been a nurse in the Civil War on the Union side, working with her father, a doctor. Ella Rose Myers had been born in St. Louis but had spent

3

her late childhood in Murphysboro, Illinois, where she lived with a friend of the family after her mother died. She was well educated, having gone to college, and had taught school for a number of years.

H. L. Hunt himself has given us the facts of his upbringing and family history in the two autobiographical works he wrote in his eighties. He does not describe how his parents met and married or speculate on their relationship, but he does say that when they met, both Hash, as his father was known, and Ella had been married before, their spouses had died, and each had a child. Perhaps this was what brought the well-educated young woman and the farmer together.

They were married in 1872. In addition to the two previous children, they produced eight more together. H. L. Hunt, Jr., was the last of these, born when his parents were both forty-six years old. His nearest sibling was his brother Leonard, who had been born three years before. Hash and Ella seem to have been convinced that they had finally produced their last son, because they chose to name this child after his father, implying that this was the last chance they would have for a Junior. "Junior" became Hunt's nickname; his family shortened it to June or Junie.

Hash Hunt was an ambitious, rather entrepreneurial man. After beginning postwar life in Illinois as a farmer, with eighty acres of land, he gradually expanded his economic interests. First, he began acting as a middleman for other farmers in the area. He bought produce and farm animals from local farmers and trucked their products, along with his own, to the nearest town, where he sold them at whatever profit he could obtain. He also began dealing in farm products and agricultural futures in the much larger market in Chicago, sometimes taking his sons with him. He reinvested the profits he made in farmland and eventually held 500 acres. He maintained a cash flow adequate to open a bank.

Hash also solidified his standing in the community. He became an active Republican and obtained appointments to local positions of power, such as county supervisor. Later, he ran for office and was elected county sheriff.

H. L. Hunt's descriptions of his father are generally matter-of-fact, and he does not provide his readers with great insights into their relationship. However, he does make certain statements about his youth that imply that his father held traditional values and expected his children to participate in the world he was building. "I quickly discovered that recognition for achievements had to be earned through constructive accomplishments and industriousness," he wrote. It seems likely that the person demanding these accomplishments was his father, who, he said, "could administer discipline when it was required." Most of what Hunt has to say about his father chronicles his successes in business or politics, impersonal areas in which his son played only a peripheral role.

Ella Hunt is described in more detail by her son, and the picture of her and her relationship with him is more complex. Ella seems to have concentrated her energies on her home and family after her second marriage. In part this was undoubtedly demanded by the fact that she bore eight children. But even after the last child was born and began to grow up, she appears to have been reluctant to step out of the role of deeply involved, perhaps even doting, mother.

Two things in particular indicate Ella's desire to maintain an unusually close and protective role for herself in her youngest son's life. The first is that until he was around school age, she kept him physically very close to her. Not only did she spend a great amount of time with him, but also she chose to maintain an aspect of physical dependence that is usually ended much earlier: Ella did not wean her last son until he was seven years old.

The stories of Hunt's nursing are drawn from his oral reminiscences, but he wrote in detail about other aspects of his close relationship with his mother. He described them sitting on a log waiting for Hash to return from selling a load of chickens, eggs, and other produce, and Ella reading from the Bible in "Greek, Latin, German, and French," translating for her son as she went along. Hunt also recalled baking bread with his mother and running into the house to ask for her help on little projects he was doing for his father.

The second indication that Ella was reluctant to let her youngest son grow up was the fact that she never sent him to school. Rather than encourage him to establish himself in his own world, with children his own age, she decided to keep him at home and teach him herself.

Hunt recalled his mother's decision to keep him from attending school as being well founded, though his brothers and sisters had all attended the school located about one and a half miles from the Hunts' house.

There was no reason for me to attend public schools, since my
elder brothers and sisters had brought home the Primer and the
First, Second, Third, Fourth, and Fifth Readers, and my
mother was the wisest and smartest person and the best teacher
I ever knew. . . . I barely remember when I began reading but I
remember listening to my mother, who was highly educated,
incessantly reading to me.[2]

Ella no doubt had her own reasons for keeping her young son close
to her. She may, for example, have been compensating for her own
childhood losses: after the death of her mother, when she was nine,
and after her father remarried and had other children, she continued
to live with another family. Or Ella may have enjoyed molding and
shaping her "youthful prodigy," using her own education and experience as a teacher. She may also have been hoping to create a
sophisticated and well-read companion for herself, someone to balance her capable but work-oriented farmer husband. Regardless of
her motivations, she seems to have been happy to prolong her son's
childhood.

The son himself, however, eventually concluded that he was ready
to get out on his own. In 1905, Hunt was sixteen years old. It was
then that the teen-ager rejected the family's suggestion that he begin
clerking in their bank in Vandalia, and, instead, embarked on his
own version of a young man going west. Perhaps unable to find the
chance to become more independent at home, he simply packed up,
hopped a train, and set out alone.

The following period of Hunt's life, which ended with the death
of his father in 1911, was characterized by an enormous amount of
change and uncertainty. He lived in Kansas, Colorado, Utah, north-
ern and southern California, Texas, and Arizona. He topped sugar
beets, drove mule trains, built highways, planted grain, and washed
dishes. He narrowly escaped being robbed, being shanghaied for a
tramp steamer, and being an eyewitness of the San Francisco earthquake of 1906.

During the six years Hunt was on the road, most of the jobs that
he held were manual labor. Although, in his autobiography, he tells
of a few instances where he was put in charge of other men, he was
usually just another worker.

However, early on Hunt began to differentiate himself from the other men he worked with by honing a skill that he had displayed ever since he was a young child: an ability to play cards and to play to win.

In an interview Hunt granted in 1967, he discussed at great length the card games he had engaged in during that and subsequent periods of his life. One story he told illustrates well all the elements of Hunt's approach to life, as it was evolving at this time.

Although he was living in a camp for railroad laborers, where he could undoubtedly have gotten a poker game together, he chose to go off alone to play cards in a camp of Mexican laborers some miles away—to gamble with people who were strangers and whose behavior was unpredictable. He also decided to play a game that was not as familiar to him as was poker: a game called *cancoon*, played with a Spanish deck of forty cards. For Hunt, his opponents' advantage seems only to have increased the appeal of the game.

Hunt began to play. After a while, he began to win and, in his words, "to win sensationally." More men joined the game, and the players began running out of money and going back to their living quarters to get more. Hunt neither stopped playing while he was ahead nor had any pangs of conscience regarding the amount of hard-earned money he was taking from his opponents.

Finally, according to his recollections, he had won $4,000; by then, "it seemed like the money began to dry up." Hunt took his winnings and ran six or so miles back to his camp, cutting through the woods so the losers could not follow his route along the tracks by handcar and take their winnings back.[3]

After a restless night, he got up early and, saying nothing to anyone, left camp, completely alone. He had proven himself the better man in the game itself and the luckier man in that he got out of the situation alive and with his winnings intact. H. L. Hunt had tempted fate—in as many different ways as he could devise in a single evening—and won. He was on his way to a lifetime of taking chances, on his own, that continued to grow in magnitude and complexity.

During this period, both through his gambling and through the chances he took in leading a peripatetic life, Hunt also developed a great deal of faith in what he called "Hunt Luck." He later described one situation where his luck was very important to him. He had returned to San Francisco from Los Gatos, a town to the south, a few days before.

I was staying and sleeping on the third story of a hotel alongside one of the two tall buildings in San Francisco. Fortunately for me a semi-pro baseball team was being organized in Reno, Nevada, which took me away from San Francisco for a try-out for the team. My right shoulder had been hurt in a runaway on a farm and I could not make the team, but perhaps that baseball try-out saved my life, because I soon read in the newspapers about the huge loss of life and property in the great city which I had just left on an afternoon train in the Chicago area.[4]

Hunt offers no evidence that the building in which he had been staying was destroyed: he might have escaped injury anyway. But his timing, the fact that he went to try out for a team even though he had to travel many miles and was unlikely to play his best because he was injured, and the detail that he had been staying next to one of the tallest buildings clearly show that he believed luck had played a major role in saving his life.

This early period of roaming and gambling came to an end when, within a short period, both his brother Leonard, to whom he was close, and his father died. Hunt, after returning home for his father's funeral and finding that he had inherited $5,000, decided, at age twenty-two, to settle down.

He bought 960 acres of farmland near the town of Lake Village, Arkansas, an area that was part of the rich Mississippi River flats and was considered very productive cotton land. During the first few years he lived in Lake Village, he made a concerted attempt to succeed as a cotton farmer. However, the Mississippi flooded two years in a row, virtually wiping out his crops. He dealt with the resultant financial crisis primarily by pursuing a "business" he had succeeded in before: gambling.

Hunt's alternative business dealings were well known to the people in Lake Village, a small town of about 1,500 people. He played cards there during the day, and in the evening he crossed the lake to play for bigger stakes in the larger town of Greenville, Arkansas, a Mississippi cotton port. Periodically, he and some of his gambling friends from Greenville would take a trip down the river to play big-time cards in New Orleans, where high-stakes card games were readily available.

Even though it was obvious that most of Hunt's money came from his winnings at cards, he was socially accepted in Lake Village. An old man who knew him during the 1920s remembered Hunt as essentially honest and reliable. "Although he was a poker player, he never did anything dishonest," the man recalled in the 1970s. "Somehow he just managed to inspire confidence. People trusted him."[5]

H. L. Hunt, rolling stone and high-stakes card player, was on his way to becoming part of the community that would provide him with a wife and the financial means to make his next move.

TWO

BY 1914, H. L. Hunt had matured into a tall, well-built, imposing young man who dressed stylishly and had a winning way with the ladies. Blond and rather handsome, he had established an active social life for himself in his small town. That summer, he met Lyda Bunker, a young woman who had been away from home teaching school, but whose family lived in Lake Village. Although Hunt had been romantically involved with Lyda's sister, and Lyda was considering an engagement to another man, the two married less than six months after they met. Perhaps the fact that Hunt's mother had died in September of that year, while Hunt was courting Lyda, influenced his decision to become a family man.

Lyda came from a good family. Her father was a successful businessman, and the Bunkers could trace their heritage back to English royalty. She and Hunt were married in a small home ceremony on November 26, 1914. Eleven months later, in October 1915, they had their first child, a girl, whom they named Margaret. For several years, beginning in 1914, Hunt had been successful in raising cotton and was making a good living as a planter. Margaret was, therefore, born during the first period of economic stability that Hunt had known since he had gone out on his own at age sixteen.

Two years later, in November 1917, the young couple had their second child, a son they named Haroldson Lafayette Hunt, Jr., and called "Hassie." Some months before Hassie's birth, however, Hunt suffered an economic setback; the Mississippi again overflowed, wiping out his year's crop. Lyda, who had also had a recent loss, when her younger brother, Floyd, died in 1916, returned to teaching to provide a steady income for the family. She and Hunt did not have any more children for some time, perhaps because of the precariousness of their financial situation.

After the 1917 crop loss, Hunt began to look for new ways to earn money. He began by parlaying his own farmland into a larger real-estate position. Prices for land on which cotton, in particular, could be grown were rising sharply, and Hunt eventually succeeded in leveraging his position into holdings of 15,000 acres. He also became involved in futures trading, particularly of cotton.

Hunt apparently was fairly successful in speculating until 1920. Believing that the cotton boom that had been pushing up land prices was coming to an end, and a drop in the price of cotton was imminent, he quickly sold his own crop in New Orleans. Then he upped the ante by taking what would have been a high payout investment if prices dropped; he sold short in the cotton futures market. However, the price of cotton went up. "I posted margins until my cash was gone," Hunt said, "and I was closed out." Some months later, the market broke, but it was too late to do Hunt any good: he had lost what he described as a small fortune.

Despite his losses in the gambles of risky business ventures, Hunt continued what might be called his "recreational and social gambling." At times, his need to gamble seems to have outweighed his need to take care of his family and spend time with them. Hunt later recalled a trip to New Orleans with Lyda and Margaret; Margaret was to have her tonsils out. Leaving Lyda with the sick child, he went to a hotel and got involved in a high-stakes poker game. He began with $100 worth of chips; by the time he "had to leave for dinner," presumably to rejoin Lyda, he had won an additional $600.

Leaving Lyda again after dinner, he returned to the hotel and sat in on a no-limit game that included some of the most famous poker players in the country. Because, by his report, he knew more about them than they knew about him, he was able to parlay his winnings into $10,200. As was his habit, he quit at midnight.[1]

By 1921, Hunt was becoming disenchanted with land as an investment. He had lost a great deal of money in the cotton market through his commodity ventures. His land holdings were heavily leveraged and land prices were heading downward. He was thirty-two years old and the father of two children. His wife was, for all practical purposes, providing the basic economic support for the family. It was during this year that Hunt reached what was, in effect, the turning point in his business and economic life.

He had been negotiating all day for a position in a 25,000-acre piece of property. The deal was near completion, and the sellers had asked Hunt to give them a few minutes alone with their lawyers to work out some final details. Hunt stepped outside and began walking up and down a boardwalk near the office. He asked himself what it was he really wanted. Are you going to bury yourself here for the remainder of your life? he later recalled thinking. If his current holdings regained their value, he would have enough property to be a rich man. Meanwhile, rather than take on additional holdings in real estate, he could rent his acreage and investigate the oil business everyone was talking about. When he was called back in, he told the assembled group that he had changed his mind and wished to withdraw from the negotiations. The deal went no further.

The oil boom that was attracting Hunt's attention was taking place near Lake Village, in a town called El Dorado. In a way, what is surprising is not that Hunt decided to investigate the oil boom at this time, but that he had not done it sooner.

The Arkansas boom was part of a larger series of oil-field developments, which also took place throughout Texas, Oklahoma, and Louisiana. The boom had started in 1901, with a gusher in a South Texas field called "Spindletop." The set of six wells that were drilled there could produce as much oil as the rest of the world combined at the time. Spindletop was followed by the exploration of many other fields throughout the south-central area, and the whole romance of oil-field boom and bust, of fortunes made and lost, began.

In their book *Life in the Oil Fields*, Roger and Diana Olien describe the situation that existed: "The oil fields offered attractions apart from money. Exploration, with elements of high risk and high stakes, with fortunes made and lost overnight, was more exciting than the plodding routine of country life. It was fast-moving, unpredictable, and constantly challenging."[2]

Hunt saw getting into the oil business as an adventure. During the hours after he backed out of the land deal, he recalled, his mind raced with thoughts of El Dorado, "just as the Spanish *Conquistadores* must have thought, anxiously, about their *El Dorado*, the legendary place of gold which was the object of their relentless quest." He imagined oil as black gold gushing out, "spraying not just the chiefs but

everyone with an ebony gilt and creating lakes of the liquid trea-
sure." He had succumbed to "black gold fever" and could only think,
"On to El Dorado."[3]

Hunt went into this high-risk situation in 1921 in a style now
clearly his own. To the uncertainty of entering a new business about
which he knew nothing—he had never even seen an oil well—he
added the fact that he had no money to invest. At the time, his only
assets were highly illiquid real estate holdings, so he borrowed fifty
dollars "expense money" to use in getting started.

As a lone operator, rather than in partnership with an experienced
oilman, throughout 1921 and 1922 he bought and sold small leases,
often completing deals in a single day. He managed to rebuild his
capital base enough to begin drilling his own wells. He became more
skilled in the technology, learning how to locate oil, drill a well, and
keep a well producing once it was drilled. He started to expand into
other areas of oil production, building simple pipelines, which carried his oil to depots where he could sell it profitably. Sometimes he
made mistakes, but he learned from them and gradually improved
his financial position.

Hunt also continued to play poker, sometimes reportedly using
his winnings to pay his drilling crews. He later said that during this
time he came to appreciate just how good at poker he was by playing
against "high-powered talent from all over the country."[4] In describing the secrets of his success from the vantage point of old age, Hunt
said he had a photographic memory, which enabled him not only to
remember what cards had been played, but also to anticipate approx-
imately where the cards would come up in the next game, since most
dealers shuffled the cards only cursorily between hands.

While Hunt was developing his oil interests, he was frequently
separated from his family, who continued to live in Lake Village.
Eventually these semibachelor days came to an end. He made
enough money—or it was managed prudently enough by Lyda, to
whom Hunt often attributed "ninety percent of [his] financial success"—to buy a small house and move his family, which then consisted of Lyda and the two children, ages six and four, to El Dorado.
Lyda did not resume teaching there. In January 1923, she gave birth
to a third child, a girl they named Caroline.

For several years, everything appears to have gone well. Hunt
continued to expand his oil interests outside land dealing and to drill

wells himself. By 1924, he had substantial holdings, including a number of producing wells. In February 1925, Lyda had another child, a girl, who was named for her. The family had just moved into a larger house, which the Hunts had had built for themselves.

Then in March, only a month later, misfortune struck the family: baby Lyda died. One of the older children apparently left an unlighted gas jet turned on in the new house. The gas asphyxiated the infant.[5]

At first, Hunt's behavior was more or less what one would expect. Shortly after baby Lyda's death, Hunt and his wife took a trip to New York, leaving the other children at home. There they tried to overcome their bereavement by going to Broadway plays and fancy restaurants. They also conceived another child, to replace the daughter they had lost.

But after returning from New York, Hunt did not settle back into his business and proceed with his life as before. Rather, he made arrangements to take himself out of the oil business, where he was doing quite well. He sold almost all his oil-field holdings.

Hunt then went one step farther. He discounted the $600,000 note he had received for his holdings for cash. He was then cut off from the future of the oil business almost completely. At age thirty-six, with three children and a pregnant wife, he was cash-rich, but his professional future was a completely blank slate. Taking the money he had raised, he left his family and got on a train for the lengthy journey to Florida, where a land boom was underway, but where he knew no one and had no business connections.

THREE

H. L. HUNT's arrival in Florida marked the beginning of a new era in his life. Although his stay there was brief, totaling only a few months, a series of events took place that was to alter his and his children's futures irreversibly.

Shortly after he arrived in Florida, he began looking at land-purchase opportunities, apparently in the hope of getting in on the ground floor of the developing land boom. Quite early in his search, he visited some property in the company of a young real-estate agent named Frania Tye.[1]

Frania was not a native Floridian. She had recently moved to Florida from Buffalo, New York, where she had grown up as the ninth child in a family of ten children. Her parents had immigrated from Poland prior to her birth. Although the family was not indigent, it was hardly well off, and Frania had been supporting herself since her late teens.

She had held jobs in Buffalo and in Cleveland, to which she had moved to be near her fiancé. After he broke off their engagement, in 1925, Frania decided to try working in Florida. She, too, had heard about the land boom there and believed there might be good work opportunities for a young woman.

The Tye family was Catholic and very traditional. Her father, acting as a kind of chaperone, accompanied his daughter, who was twenty-one years old, to Tampa, Florida, and helped her get settled in a small hotel there. Leaving her in the care of the owners of the hotel, whom he had come to know and trust, he returned to New York. With a modest nest egg from her father, Frania bought a tea shop and ran it briefly. She soon decided, however, that real estate

offered a better opportunity for economic progress. She sold the tea
shop and became a real-estate sales agent.

How Frania met Hunt and exactly how their relationship evolved
was never discussed publicly by Hunt himself. After Hunt's death,
however, Frania made a claim against his estate. In court proceedings subsequent to her claim, she testified in detail about what
happened in 1925. Frania met the man who introduced himself as
Major Franklin Hunt in the course of showing him an orange grove
that was for sale. Although the man did not buy the property, he did
ask Frania out. The two began dating shortly after they met.

Within a brief time, Major Hunt indicated a desire to change the
nature of their relationship, to extend beyond simply seeing each
other. He asked Frania to "come to his room," but she refused. It
never occurred to her at the time that Hunt might already be married; in her upbringing, married men did not become involved with
other women.

Shortly after this rebuff of his advances, Hunt left Tampa for
several weeks, telling Frania he had to attend to other business. He
had described himself to her as working in the oil fields of Louisiana,
adding that he was originally from Illinois and still had family there.
When he returned to Tampa, he and Frania began seeing each other
again, with increasing frequency.

It was on one of their dates during this period that Hunt again
proposed a change in their relationship, telling Frania that he
couldn't even work because he was thinking of her constantly. That
night the couple had dinner together, then drove around for hours
discussing the possibility of getting married. At dawn, they decided
they would marry that day.

A few hours later, Hunt bought a wedding ring in a pawnshop and
told Frania that one of his friends, the man who had introduced
them, would take care of the marriage license. Hunt and Frania were
married by a justice of the peace that afternoon. Hunt's friend and
the justice's wife were their witnesses.

Within a few weeks of the marriage, Hunt left to return to his
work. He and Frania corresponded, and he asked her to move to
Shreveport, so they could be closer to his work and together more.
By the time she moved, in February 1926, Frania was pregnant with
their first child. During the next four years, while two more children
were born to the couple, Frania lived in Shreveport. Although she

later said she did not meet any of Hunt's family, nor was he around for many holidays, he did spend a great deal of time in Shreveport and he continued to provide her with enough money to live comfortably.

While Hunt was establishing and sustaining what was, in effect, his second family, he continued to live with Lyda and their children as if nothing had changed.[2] The child who had been conceived as a replacement for the lost baby was born in February 1926. He was a boy, whom the Hunts named Nelson Bunker.

Hunt also returned to building his oil business in El Dorado and began expanding his interests throughout East Texas and into Louisiana, with his holdings there administered in Shreveport. His geographic diversification tied in conveniently with his juggling of two families and apparently provided him with the flexibility he needed to keep both Frania and Lyda from becoming aware of one another.

That Hunt was successful in sustaining two households is evidenced by the fact that he fathered children over the next eight years with both women. Frania's first child, Howard, was born almost eight months after Bunker's birth to Lyda, in October 1926. Frania had a second child, Haroldina, two years later. Lyda, who was thirty-seven at the time of Bunker's birth, had another child, William Herbert, in March 1929. In October 1930, Frania had her third child, a girl named Helen. Two years later, Hunt had another and final child, Lamar, with Lyda, who was then forty-three. Frania's last child, Hue, was born in October 1934.

In the course of this eight-year period, while Hunt fathered seven children and sustained two families, a number of economic changes were taking place in his life. One of the most important was in his oil business. In September 1930, he got involved in what could have been just another of his dozens of high-risk undertakings. He was forty-one years old. He had been in the oil business for a total of nine years, continuing, most of the time, to find that business to his liking.[3]

Although Hunt always claimed that he simply followed his instincts in identifying productive oil fields, he was, even then, looking at a number of technological innovations finding their way into the oil business. One such innovation was a drill-stem testing tool that enabled those drilling to take a sample of what was at the bottom of the well before it was completed. If a well was drilled all the way to a strike, whatever was at the bottom of the hole—oil, gas, salt water—would, under its own pressure, erupt through the top of the well. Valuable oil could be lost this way; at the very least, it produced a terrible mess and made it much harder to "cap" the well and bring its flow under control. The drill-stem testing tool was designed to provide information before the well "came in."

A man Hunt had been working with on this tool called him one day and said that another independent who'd been interested in the tool seemed to have a promising well in process and might be looking around for capital to complete it.

As it turned out, "might be looking" was an understatement. The wildcatter, an old man named Columbus Marion "Dad" Joiner, had been in the oil business since 1897. Despite years of exploration over an extended area throughout the West and the Central states, Joiner was, at age seventy, one of the many independent oilmen who always managed to miss striking it big.

At the time Hunt looked into Joiner's drilling operation, the old man was at the end of a string of seventeen dry wells. The site of his current well had been chosen because he was able to obtain the right to drill on the land free, from a widow, Mrs. Daisy Bradford. The decision to drill there was based on a geological report by a man who was not really a geologist.

"Doctor" A. D. Lloyd had changed his career several times before hitting on geologist; he had studied medicine, worked as a chemist and a mining engineer, searched for gold, and sold patent medicine. He had also changed his name, from Joseph Idelbert Dunham, apparently to escape harassment from six wives and a large number of children.

Lloyd's report seemed to have been inspired by the copy on the patent medicine he had once peddled. "Gentlemen," it concluded, "all these major oil trends, intersecting as they do here in East Texas, bring about a state known in the oil business as the apex of the apex, a situation not found anywhere else in the world." The report was accompanied by a map of the United States with lines drawn from most of the known major oil fields in such a way that they intersected in East Texas.

Regardless of the questionable scientific integrity of Lloyd's report and Joiner's decision, many people, especially those living in the deeply impoverished farmland where Joiner was drilling, wanted desperately to believe that they were sitting on top of an oil patch. Joiner was able, though only slowly and with many stops and starts, to raise enough money to put together the skimpiest kind of rig possible and start drilling. Most of his investors bought twenty-five-dollar "certificates," which entitled them to some share of the proceeds from the strike, should it ever come. At the same time, Joiner leased thousands of acres surrounding his drilling site on the basis of legal documents that more or less rivaled the certificates in their lack of specificity and reliability.

Although Joiner's well looked irresistible to his small investors, major oil companies, with more sophisticated geological staffs, believed that Joiner's cause was hopeless. When one man visited the well and saw a sample of oil-rich sand that had been pulled from the bottom of the well (indicating that a strike was likely), he reported that he believed the well had been "salted," meaning that the sand displayed as proof of the presence of oil was actually from another site.

Finally, after a daunting series of unlucky events, financial crises, and various misfortunes, the well did come in. Even so, it looked in many ways like just as chancy an investment as anything else that bore the mark of that perennial failure Dad Joiner.

As Hunt became familiar with the site, the high-risk situation did not deter him. He believed he was the one man capable of beating the expertise of the big-company geologists. Although the well behaved in a "peculiar" way, producing a limited amount of oil quickly and then drying up until the next day, Hunt was experienced in following his instincts about potentially productive areas. In fact, as he pointed out in his autobiographies, no one had the kind of expertise in assessing geological conditions that later became commonplace, so his guess was at least as good as anyone else's.

Hunt concluded that Joiner's well was on the edge of a major field, which spread in a different direction from that he and others had initially assumed. About half of the leases Joiner held were in the area where Hunt now expected production to be high. The other half, Hunt believed, would prove to be in dry territory.

By this time, Joiner's success in bringing in the Daisy Bradford #3 was beginning to prove his downfall. Not only were many of his leases of questionable legality, based as they were on a handshake and lacking clear title; but also many of his investors now wanted their money back at once. Hunt described Joiner's creditors as "a pack of hungry wolves," and predicted that those who benefited most from the strike would not be Joiner and his small investors but the lawyers who gathered to litigate titles and contract terms.

Many observers have concluded that by the time Hunt got involved in serious discussions about acquiring Joiner's holdings, he had access to information concerning the long-term value of the holdings that he had, through subterfuge, prevented Joiner from also obtaining. There are tales of Hunt more or less locking Joiner in a hotel room, plying him with liquor and women, and forcing him to enter into an unfavorable contract.[4]

Regardless of the truth of these stories, the fact remains that *any* financial interest Hunt took in Joiner's holdings was at this point high-risk. Hunt, believing, as he often did, in a combination of his own inherent luck and his natural abilities to do better than most people, was more than willing to take this risk, however. He talked about his assessment of Joiner's situation this way: "Notwithstanding his lack of good titles and mounting legal problems, I decided to make an offer to Joiner to buy him out lock, stock and barrel. . . . [W]ith the friendship that had developed between us, Joiner told me directly: 'Boy, you would be buying a pig in a poke!' "[5]

Hunt recalled that he had only $109 available to invest in the field's development. He approached representatives of several of the big oil companies, inviting them to join him in developing Joiner's property, but they all found the situation too risky.

Here again was H. L. Hunt, lone operator, looking at a situation that appears almost unrivaled in terms of its low likelihood of success. The field was uncharted. Joiner did not hold clear title to what Hunt was buying. Hunt had no money to invest in the operation. It was the height of the Great Depression. If Hunt did, by some miracle, strike it big, he would still have to settle with Joiner's creditors.

In a burst of creative risk-taking, Hunt defied common sense completely by introducing one last element of uncertainty into the venture. He wrote the agreement he finally forged with Dad Joiner in a completely new legal form, which involved paying for leases out of the reserves of the field itself, with the payment schedule evolving as various percentages of wells drilled and brought in. Hunt mentions quite casually that "the validity of the production-payment idea was tested in court in many cases and was uniformly sustained by the Texas Supreme Court and, later, by courts in other states."[6]

In order to develop his interest in the East Texas field, Hunt had, once again, to move out of the house, leaving his wife and family, which at this point included five children: Margaret, fifteen, Hassie, thirteen, Caroline, eight, Bunker, five, and Herbert, two. Since he also had a household with Frania and their first two children, Howard, four, and Helen, two, his new home was actually his third. He established himself in Henderson, Texas, taking his son Hassie with him. Hunt explained his decision to have the child live with him by noting that "Hassie, who was only thirteen . . . had grown up in the oil fields and knew as much about the oil business as anyone."

There may have been more to Hunt's decision to have Hassie live with him than Hunt allowed. Hunt and Lyda had named their oldest son Haroldson Lafayette, after his father. As was to be expected in the time Hunt lived in and given the kind of man he was, he apparently took great pride in this son and had great expectations of his joining the business and furthering the Hunt name and fortunes.

Unfortunately, Hassie did not grow into the ideal son that Hunt probably envisioned. Apparently, even as a young child, Hassie exhibited a certain amount of antisocial behavior. His sister Caroline recalled many years later that Hassie was always a "nonconformist child." Harry Hurt, Hunt's biographer, went further in describing Hassie as Lyda's "problem child," who was spoiled by his father and consequently believed he could do what he pleased, including breaking things and causing trouble for the rest of the family. Lyda's attempts at disciplining Hassie were unproductive; he continued to do as he liked.[7]

Perhaps as appeasement to Lyda, or perhaps because he thought he could help Hassie if they were living together, Hunt took the young boy with him to Henderson.

During the two years he and Hassie lived in Henderson, Hunt obtained clear rights to Joiner's holdings through the successful litigation of 300 lawsuits. He began drilling productive wells and confirmed his intuition about the direction of the fields he had bought. Financial security did not immediately follow oil production, however. At the very time Hunt was bringing in his fields, both the Depression and the surge in total U.S. oil output, owing to the volume of oil from the East Texas fields, depressed oil prices heavily. The high volume of oil Hunt was finally able to bring in sold on the open market for as little as ten cents a barrel.

FOUR

IN 1930 and 1931, H. L. Hunt was living an unusually complex and demanding life. His entire financial future was tied up in a complicated and high-risk business deal. Even if he gained clear title to property he believed he had obtained fairly, the productive capability of that property in terms of dollars generated by barrels of oil was in serious doubt due to the oil glut and the Depression. Hunt was also leading a complicated personal life. His own home was in Henderson, Texas, where he had the primary responsibility for a difficult and troubled teen-age son. He had a wife and four other children in a town in Arkansas. He had a second woman who thought she was his wife living with what soon became three children, first in a town in Louisiana, then, after late 1930, nearer by, in Dallas, Texas.

Hunt, however, still had energy left to get involved in one more area: setting social policy. He considered his actions there important to his economic well-being, and also felt that he could have an impact on the financial situation of the entire U.S. economy.

The scene of his activities was his own oil-drilling operation in the recently acquired East Texas oil fields; the provoking factor was the enormous increase in unemployment that developed as the Depression spread across Texas.

Industry practice was to run drilling rigs twenty-four hours a day, with the drilling crew working in two twelve-hour shifts. Hunt decided to spread the work around by going to six-hour shifts six days a week. Partially to compensate for each man's reduced income, he raised wages ten percent per hour. The net outcome was an increase of between 150 and 200 jobs on his rigs alone; all of these jobs presumably went to men who would have been totally unemployed otherwise. [1]

Over the next year or so, Hunt made a major effort to have his plan, which he dubbed the "Flexible Work Week," adopted across the country. He contacted various politicians he knew or who represented his area, by writing letters and meeting them when feasible. He abandoned his efforts to promulgate this approach only after the passage of the National Industrial Recovery Act in 1933.

During this same period, Hunt was also looking for government support for several other programs he favored. Unlike his plan to put men back to work, which featured a lack of intervention by government, these programs required that government agencies become involved in certain aspects of private enterprise.

The first thing Hunt, along with many other oilmen, wanted was the enactment of an oil-depletion allowance. [2] This allowance, which was eventually made into law, would permit a certain amount of the profits from oil production to be excused from taxation. Theoretically, these untaxed profits could then be used for further exploration. Hunt believed that if oil profits were taxed at the same rate as profits from what he perceived to be lower-risk economic enterprises, there would not be sufficient economic incentive to look for oil, since the risks of losing all the exploration money in a given deal were substantial.

The second area in which Hunt hoped to see government action was the production of oil and gas. As the situation in his East Texas fields demonstrated only too clearly, when an area proved to be a good source of oil, many wells were drilled at once, and the price of the produced oil and gas subsequently fell sharply. No driller was willing unilaterally to limit his own output: while his pumps were turned off, his competitors would keep theirs running, depleting the same oil he was tapping. At the very least, continued drilling would lower underground pressure, and all drillers would have to install more costly pumping equipment to dispose of foreign matter such as salt water that was pumped up as underground pressure dropped. Hunt kept working for government control of production until a federal law passed in 1935 put such a program in place.

Although Hunt and his fellow oilmen were not successful in getting federal legislation passed until 1935, prices for oil did begin to stabilize after 1931. By October 1932, Hunt had enough economic stability to buy "the fine Mayfield home . . . in the heart of an area of large and fine homes in Tyler," a Texas town about twenty-five miles from his major fields. Lyda's and his last child, Lamar, had been born in El Dorado in August of that year, and Hunt chose a home he described as large and "well suited to my growing and lively family."[3]

The years the family spent in Tyler were important. Hunt was becoming a wealthy man during this period; Lyda was developing ways of coping with his frequent absences. She became active in various community affairs and began traveling with some of the children, taking trips to California, New England, and even to Alaska, trips without Hunt.

Lyda and Hunt apparently also became interested in making sure that their children had social skills and found places for themselves in society. In 1935, their oldest daughter, Margaret, who was then nineteen, was chosen to be queen of the third annual Tyler Rose Festival, an important event in the Texas social calendar. After the festival, according to one account, "the Hunts gave a lavish party," which 600 people attended.[4] They sent their other daughter, Caroline, to the exclusive Hockaday Academy in Dallas as a boarder.

Hunt later said that "the time we lived in Tyler may have been some of the best days we had as a family." The children were growing up, the family was involved in the community, and Hunt was making a great deal of money, as well as taking his first steps in the arena of social and political action. Even the nonconformist child, Hassie, was fitting in; one of Hunt's fondest memories of the period in Tyler was of the time he and Hassie won the father-and-son look-alike contest sponsored annually by Tyler High School.

While things were going smoothly for the H. L. Hunt family in Tyler, life continued for the Franklin Hunt family in Dallas, only ninety-nine miles away. Frania had moved to Dallas at Hunt's urging in the fall of 1930, around the time the couple's third child, Helen, was born. The family seems to have lived a satisfactory life for a while, but this stability came to an abrupt end in 1934.[5] It was then, probably around the time that Margaret was becoming heavily involved in the Tyler social scene, that Frania attended a party at which Margaret was also a guest. According to Frania's recollection many years later, someone pointed out Margaret as the daughter of the rich oilman H. L. Hunt. At about this time, too, a friend in

Dallas told her that Hunt was married to another woman and had another family.

Frania asked Hunt about his other life. He told her the truth, and Frania, who was pregnant with their fourth child, decided she should leave Dallas and move with her children back to the part of the country where she had grown up. Consequently, Hunt bought a house in upper-middle-class Great Neck, Long Island, to which Frania and her three children moved. There, the fourth child, Hue, was born.

A troubled time followed for Frania. She did not break off her relationship with Hunt completely; correspondence from Hunt to Frania during this time indicates that they were still romantically involved and that Hunt wished to sustain their closeness. This may have been especially difficult for Frania, who throughout her life was a practicing Catholic. She continued to spend time with Hunt when he came to New York and to take trips with him and the children, but according to one biography of Hunt, Frania was sick—though whether physically or emotionally is not specified—for about three years after Hue's birth. In 1936, she moved, ostensibly for reasons of health, to New Orleans, but she lived there only briefly before returning to Great Neck. Her children were then ages two, six, eight, and ten.

Throughout this period, Hunt's financial fortunes continued to improve. In 1935, he set up trusts for his and Lyda's children, with holdings in Placid Oil, the oil-and-gas-property arm of his evolving empire, as the primary asset. By 1938, he was beginning to diversify his ever-increasing holdings in several ways.[6] He began again buying real estate, particularly farm and ranch properties, which he continued to accumulate until he eventually held millions of acres. He also became involved for the first time in some international energy transactions. Because of the increasing complexity of his business dealings, he decided to move his business organization to a larger city, where he could have ready access to better transportation, banking, and communications facilities.

In Dallas, Hunt found a house that was perfect for his family. It was large and comfortable, consisting of fourteen rooms. Situated on ten acres and standing on top of a small hill overlooking White Rock Lake, a lovely reservoir surrounded by a park in a nice residential section of the city, it was impressive. It was even in political harmony with Hunt's world view, as that was evolving during this time, because the house was a replica of Mount Vernon, right down to, according to Hunt, "a glassed-in cupola set atop the roof just as in General Washington's home."

When the family moved to Dallas, two of the children were already young adults and were living outside the family home. Margaret, twenty-three, had recently married a man named Albert Galatyn Hill, who was working for Hunt Oil. Hassie, twenty-one, had, because of his stormy relationship with his father, at one point changed his name legally to Hassie Hunt; he had also established his own successful oil-drilling business, completely independent of his father's operations.

Lyda, now forty-nine, welcomed the opportunity to move from Tyler. In Dallas, she gradually joined some of the most important social organizations, such as the Dallas Women's Club, a prominent garden club, and the Daughters of the American Revolution. She devoted more of her energy to her church, the Highland Park Presbyterian Church. She continued to care for her growing boys and to travel, usually accompanied by several of the children.

While Hunt found continuing stability for most of his first family in Dallas and constant good fortune in his growing business enterprises, his life by the late 1930s was not completely free of problems. Frania and her children again left Great Neck, in 1939, and moved to Houston. There she was confronted by unfriendly people, with the fact that she was living as Hunt's wife but was not legally married to him. Although Frania and the children spent some time in Los Angeles, where they did not have to deal with the reality of Hunt's other family, from this point on, the relationship's days were numbered. Finally, Frania provoked a confrontation with Hunt by leaving the four children in a hotel room in Dallas while she returned to Houston. When Hunt convinced her to return to talk things over, he was there with his daughter Margaret.

Why he chose to bring his daughter, who was eleven years younger than his secret "wife," to this meeting is an interesting question. Perhaps Hunt, who was now fifty-two and had been leading a double life for sixteen years, hoped to integrate his two families. If this was the case, perhaps he chose to begin to reveal the truth by discussing the situation with Margaret, rather than Lyda. He had developed a special relationship with his oldest daughter. She had worked as his assistant prior to her marriage, and consequently he treated her as something more than just a pretty, well-behaved girl. He obviously valued her judgment; perhaps in his need to confide in someone, she seemed the most likely to be sympathetic yet realistic.

Regardless of his motivation, Hunt's action succeeded, temporarily, in pacifying or intimidating Frania. She returned to Houston with the four children. Afterward, Hunt apparently began facing the reality that his days with Frania were ending. A short time later, he asked Frania to return to Dallas to meet Lyda. The three met together; later, Lyda invited Frania to lunch alone.

Frania regarded Lyda as a very gracious and understanding person, "the finest woman I ever met."[7] Lyda, for her part, made what she saw as a magnanimous offer to the troubled Frania. At age fifty-two, with her own children finally reaching independence, Lyda offered to adopt Frania's four children and raise them as if they were her own.

Although she turned down Lyda's offer, Frania did not sue Hunt for bigamy and did not publicize her problems in such a way that any of Hunt's family would be hurt. She later said that it was because of the impression Lyda had made on her that she decided at the time to leave Hunt and his other family alone.

Several months after the meeting with Lyda, Frania and Hunt worked out a legal agreement that formalized their economic relationship. Hunt had previously set up modest trusts for their children, and these remained in place. Although he continued to see his and Frania's children until his death, the January 1942 agreement apparently also signified the end of the emotional relationship. Twelve days later, Frania married John Lee.

FIVE

BY now Hunt was fifty-three years old, a very rich man, and a person who commanded respect from those with whom he had business dealings. More and more, however, he was realizing that his family would never offer everything he had hoped for. Hassie, in particular, was displaying continuing signs of what the family defined as "being different," and Hunt's dreams of an ideal father-son relationship were increasingly hard to sustain. Hunt therefore looked for a new approach to life, one that could make up for some of the insoluble problems he faced at home. It was at this time that he met the next woman with whom he was to have a long and complex relationship.

Ruth Ray, twenty-five, was a secretary at the offices of Hunt Oil Company in Shreveport.[1] She, of course, knew who H. L. Hunt was and had formed a high opinion of his integrity from what she heard about how he conducted his business. Reportedly, Hunt first noticed Ruth one day when she was waiting for a bus after work. He offered her a ride home. This evidently was the beginning of a relationship that relatively quickly included sexual intimacy.

In the fall of 1942, Ruth left her job, telling her co-workers that she was going to marry a man named Raymond Wright. She even sent wedding announcements to them. Apparently, Ruth had become pregnant in July, and Hunt's response was to move her to New York and establish a separate household with her, just as he had with Frania eight years earlier. The first of four children the two were to produce together was born in New York in April 1943. A few months after the baby, Ray Lee Wright, was born, Ruth moved to Dallas, into a nice but modest house Hunt had bought for her. It was quite near the much larger house where he lived with his legal wife and their unmarried children.

From the beginning, not only was Hunt's relationship with the third woman who would bear him children different, but the woman herself was different. In contrast to Frania's and Lyda's drive and relative sophistication, Ruth was a sweet and unspoiled country girl.[2] She had grown up in a small town in Oklahoma, the youngest of six children. Her father had died when she was an infant, and the family had little money. Ruth had attended college briefly and then taken a job as a secretary. Although she had enough drive to leave her town and find a good job for herself, she never planned a career or, indeed, seemed to feel the need for one.

The stories about and interviews with Ruth, as well as the descriptions of her by her children, all paint a consistent picture. Ruth was a sweet and loving person who was supportive of Hunt and believed he had many fine qualities. She was religious and believed that the spiritual world was more important than the material world. She felt that a woman's place was in the home and she raised her children to believe the same thing.

If Ruth Ray had simply married Hunt, the life she, her husband, and her children led might have been simpler and more straightforward. The father, a bit absentminded and overly involved with his work, would be king. What he said went, and when he came home from a hard day at work, the children would bring his slippers and his wife would put his favorite meatloaf on the table. The children would behave themselves, go to church, and grow up to lead lives that might be characterized as boring in their goodness and predictability. The wife would lovingly take care of everybody, sacrificing herself and any aspirations outside the home she might have had, but would find herself amply rewarded by her loving and caring family.

In fact, in some ways this is how things were. Ruth had a son, Ray, followed by three daughters: June, born in 1944; Helen, born in 1949; and Swanee, born in 1950. All four of Ruth's children remembered the family as very normal and middle-class in many respects.[3] June recalled that her parents were strict and demanding but focused on giving the children an understanding of how to take responsibility and get along in the world. Helen said that, growing up, she "felt as normal as apple pie." There was a sense of economy in the house; Hunt would walk around turning off lights and reminding the children of the cost of electricity. At Christmas, the children would go to Oklahoma to be with their mother's family.

Some of this sense of normalcy can be explained by the fact that from shortly after the time their first child was born, Ruth and H. L. Hunt lived in the same city, and near each other. Furthermore, their relationship was not nearly as clandestine as the one with Frania had been. By this time, Hunt's marriage to Lyda had weathered one extra family, and he probably expected it to weather another. Because Hunt's other children were older, he felt less torn between spending time with Ruth's children and with Lyda's.

Even as Hunt and Ruth were beginning their "normal" life together, however, Hunt could not completely escape the problems and challenges of his first family, as well as the continuing responsibility of sustaining some kind of relationship with the children he had fathered with Frania.

The most painful problem he encountered with his older children had to do with his son Hassie. In 1943, even as he was fathering a new son, Hunt was, in some respects, finally losing his beloved oldest son, his namesake, who had inherited his genius for finding oil.

During high school in Tyler, Hassie had occasionally lapsed into inappropriate and even antisocial behavior, reportedly making suggestive comments to nice young women in Tyler and engaging in physical confrontations with his father. As time went on, his behavior had become more erratic. One Hunt biographer describes an incident in which Hassie, wanting a car he saw in a dealer's showroom, picked up a rock and broke the huge picture window in the front of the building. When an alarmed salesman appeared behind the broken glass, Hassie simply said, "I want that car." He paid for the car and the window, and drove away in his new purchase.[4]

Many years later, Hassie's sister Caroline explained that the family, which she described as very tolerant, had simply accepted Hassie as he was.[5] Hunt apparently took steps to protect his son, making sure that Hassie had people around him who could take care of his basic needs and deal with any irregular behavior. Things might have continued this way for years if it had not been for the Second World War.

As a physically healthy twenty-five-year-old, Hassie was highly eligible for the draft. He probably could have obtained a medical exemption based on his emotional problems, but documenting these problems would have forced the Hunts to face the extent of his illness. Although Hunt managed to keep Hassie from being drafted for some months, eventually the military caught up with him. He served first in Washington, then in Louisiana. It was there that Hassie finally suffered a major breakdown. He was discharged from the military a seriously ill young man, and his condition led Hunt to embark on a project that involved him for the rest of his life: trying to find a cure for the problems of the son he now was forced to admit was quite sick.

Although Hassie was clearly the family's major concern, Hunt's next son, Bunker, also was involved in a somewhat worrisome situation. Bunker had followed the tradition that was then prevalent among wealthy Texas families: he had gone east to school, where he could flourish in a better academic environment, but where he could also gain a rudimentary knowledge of the world outside Texas. Whereas the young women usually went to Virginia for the first two years of college, the young men often went earlier, to military or prep school. Bunker had attended Culver Military Academy and a prep school in Pennsylvania. After graduation, he returned to Texas to go to the University of Texas, in Austin. However, Bunker, as his sister Caroline later recalled, was "not a person who was going to sit down and study."[6] Incensed by a geology professor's remark that natural resources should be controlled by the federal government, Bunker quit school and joined the Navy.

Lyda's other children continued to live more conventional lives. Caroline attended Mary Baldwin College, in Virginia, for the obligatory two years and then transferred to the University of Texas. There she met a handsome naval officer; shortly after her graduation in 1943, they were married. Herbert and Lamar, who in 1945 were thirteen and sixteen years old, continued their schooling quietly.

Meanwhile, Hunt's and Frania's children were also maturing. Haroldina, their second child, was now in her teens. Like Hassie, she grew up to suffer from serious mental illness. Although no biographies have been able to detail the progression of Haroldina's illness, it is possible that by this time Hunt was becoming aware that he had fathered not one but two mentally troubled children.

A final source of disquiet for Hunt during this period may have been the social environment in which he now found himself and his first family. When he moved to Dallas in 1938, the foundations of his great fortune were already in his pocket. At that time, the city's social set was quite intent on maintaining their distinction between "old money" and "new money." Though by the standards of most of the rest of the world *all* money in Dallas was new, Dallasites had forged their own guidelines.

Oil people, in particular, were considered *nouveau riche* and socially unacceptable. When Hunt moved to Dallas, he had apparently tried to gain some acceptance in the established social circles. He applied to the most prestigious country club in the city, a club whose initiation fees and membership dues he could well afford. The club, however, already had its quota of gauche Texas oilmen. Without any hesitation, they refused him admission.[7]

During this time, as Hunt moved, began a new family, and attempted to join Dallas social circles, one thing remained the same for him: his love of gambling. In fact, he upped the ante in his nonbusiness activities by gambling in areas outside those where his own skill could play a major role, for example, in poker; he concentrated instead on putting large sums of money into areas governed more by chance or by the vagaries of other people. With big money coming in from the East Texas fields he had obtained from Dad Joiner, he began to bet large sums on horse races.[8]

In an interview many years later, Hunt recalled a typical horse-race story from this period. He had chosen to place his bets on a horse which started the day at a hundred to one. He put $1,000, at forty to one, for the horse to place, and $1,000, at twenty to one, for it to show. When a man he knew requested that he engage in a personal bet with him at the same odds, Hunt did so. He then had $4,000 riding on a horse that nobody else expected to win, show, or place.

The horse came in third, but the winner was disqualified. Hunt consequently won $120,000, and he undoubtedly relished the fact— enough so that he told the story thirty-five years later. Despite this win, it appears that Hunt's "gambling profile"—here manifested by putting a lot of money on a horse nobody else thought much of— hadn't changed since his days in the West alone. He was still essentially the big risk taker, the man who would bet all and go back for more.

Although Hunt always liked to talk about the Hunt luck, he did nonetheless hedge his bets during this period. He developed an elaborate handicapping system, which consisted of complex mathematical formulas into which was factored a huge variety of data, including weather forecasts, stable gossip, and other people's handicap statistics. He even hired mathematicians to work out the odds for different horses in different races using his system.

Hunt stopped gambling briefly during the war, reportedly for patriotic reasons—to avoid tying up scarce resources such as telephone lines. Then, in the postwar period and into the 1950s, he started betting at a completely new level. One description characterizes his bets as "bizarre, archducal."[9] He reportedly bet $300,000 on a single World Series game and frequently bet $100,000 on a Southwest Conference football contest. Jimmy the Greek claimed to have won $243,000 playing gin with Hunt as they crossed the Atlantic on a luxury ocean liner.[10]

At the same time Hunt was going for enormous stakes in his recreational gambling, he was taking major risks in oil exploration. He and his now adult sons Bunker and Herbert began looking for oil in completely new areas of the world and undertaking high-risk and expensive technical challenges. Hunt Oil consequently managed to remain competitive with much larger corporations in the search for new fields and new ways of bringing in the oil they discovered. Even in a business where everyone must be a gambler, the Hunts and Hunt Oil Company developed a reputation as risk takers. Often during this period, the risks paid off, and the Hunt fortune continued to grow.[11]

SIX

AFTER his brief stint as a proposer of social policy in the 1930s, H. L. Hunt disappeared from the political scene for almost twenty years. His life as an active public political figure did not begin until several years after he gained national notice as *Life's* "richest man" in 1948. It was in 1950, the year his last child was born, that Hunt, in an interview with the *Dallas Morning News*, described a plan he had developed to reclaim 6,000 acres of worn-out farmland he owned in East Texas.

Hunt visualized the development of a "Farm Facts Foundation" that would serve as the ideal setting for progress both in agricultural technology and in social development.[1] The core of the project, to which he said he was willing to commit $25 million, would consist of having groups of unemployed young men live at the farm sites as students, and training them in soil conservation and agricultural methods. These students and those who visited the farms would also learn about his views as they extended beyond purely agricultural issues, into the area of "public policy." This particular project did not develop past the planning stages, but it did lead Hunt in a direction he would follow for years to come: exposing people to his political beliefs and philosophy.

Hunt believed that if he could bring the correct "facts" to the attention of the American public, their value and truthfulness would be so self-evident that everyone would endorse them and promulgate them. With this objective in mind, he began writing about his principles in 1950 and printing and distributing his writings himself. Within a short period, he decided to broaden his reach by funding a radio program, which he called *Facts Forum*. The program presented

not just Hunt's side of the story; it pointed up its value by juxtapos-
ing it with other points of view. Listeners were encouraged to "acti-
vate themselves," to look at varying aspects of important questions
and make their own judgments.

The guests on *Facts Forum* ranged from Senator Joseph McCarthy
to Louis Budenz, a former editor of the *Daily Worker*. Although
Hunt was able to obtain and maintain a tax-exempt status for the
program, based on its educational objectives, many people saw it as a
one-sided political forum, rather than a balanced presentation of
ideas. Hunt, however, continued to believe that his program was
objective.

> When citizens look at issues from viewpoints of both Right and
> left, the left-siders know that too many citizens will vote against
> the theoretical dreams of Marx and his successors. Therefore,
> *Facts Forum* had to be defamed and slandered in efforts to stop
> citizens from thinking for themselves.[2]

When *Facts Forum* was first going on the air, Hunt also became
involved in two other political activities. The first of these was
supporting passage of the twenty-second amendment.[3] This amendment, which would prevent any president of the United States from
serving more than two terms, had been passed by Congress in 1947.
A number of states had ratified it, but in 1951 twelve additional
ratifications were needed. Hunt wrote letters in support of its passage to specific states, proposing the idea that presidents who served
more than two terms in office became virtual dictators, who could
destroy the country. He began what he called his one-man campaign
on January 10, 1951. Over the next six weeks, the additional states
required to make the amendment part of the Constitution voted in
favor of the amendment, and it became law on March 1. It is not
clear what part, if any, Hunt played in influencing actions in these
twelve states, but, as will be seen later, he believed in retrospect that
his role was significant.

The second area in which Hunt was active around this time was in
supporting General Douglas MacArthur for president.[4] His support reportedly included an investment of $150,000 in the cam-
paign, a huge amount of money by his usual standard of political
giving. When MacArthur did not receive the Republican nomina-

tion at the convention, Hunt, rather than support a third-party bid by the general, switched his allegiance to Dwight Eisenhower. As with passage of the twenty-second amendment, Hunt believed he played a large role in MacArthur's political decisions, but his real influence is uncertain.

Meanwhile, *Facts Forum* began to flourish. In 1953, the program went on television. Audiences reached as high as 5 million viewers and listeners per week. There were spin-off radio shows; related publications were offered, such as *Facts Forum News*; and donations poured in from those who followed the programs.[5]

Eventually, Dan Smoot, the host of the show, began to feel that the format of the program should change, and that only the conservative position should be presented. Hunt insisted that its presentation remain balanced, and Smoot left the show.

Hunt continued to support it until November 1956, when the show folded. By then, the political atmosphere was changing: the extreme rightist, anti-Communist trend personified by Senator McCarthy was ebbing, and support for the kind of ideas that many critics saw as always winning on *Facts Forum* was dwindling.

Hunt's desire to go on fighting for the program's tax-exempt status and value as an educational tool might also have been weakened by the fact that, in May of the previous year, Lyda had suffered a stroke and died suddenly at the age of sixty-six. Even though Hunt had, for many years, carried on serious relationships with women other than Lyda, he had always maintained his own form of loyalty. Many people who knew him agreed that he seemed to lose some of his energy and enthusiasm for life after Lyda's death.

Although Hunt took *Facts Forum* off the air, he never completely gave up on the show's concept, nor did he falter in his belief that the program was a balanced presentation of opposing ideas. His 1973 autobiography—written seventeen years after the last broadcast—shows that the whole matter was apparently still weighing on his mind. His need to set the record straight was evidenced by the fact that he devoted an entire chapter to explaining "The True Facts About *Facts Forum*."[6]

After *Facts Forum* went off the air, Hunt maintained a low political profile for some time. He traveled alone for a while, spending six months in South America. When he returned, he more or less resumed his usual life, though now as a widower.

Of course he still had a large and complex family to contend with. In 1956, his and Lyda's children were grown; they ranged in age from forty-one (Margaret) to twenty-four (Lamar). Most of them were married and had their own children. Hassie, no longer living at home, spent time in various psychiatric hospitals as Hunt continued to look for treatments for him.

In contrast to this grown-up family, Hunt was still deeply involved with the four young children he had had with Ruth Ray, as well as with Ruth herself. By 1957, the oldest child, Ray, was fourteen, and the youngest, Swanee, was only seven.

Late that year, in November, Hunt and Ruth got married. The ceremony was a quiet one; Hunt had not informed his older children of his plans. Newsmen were invited to photograph and interview the happy couple. The new Mrs. Hunt said, "It will be easy to smile [for photographs]. It should be, for the luckiest person in the world."[7] The newspaper accounts of the wedding described Hunt's wealth and said that he was a widower with six children, adding that the bride "was married previously to R. E. Wright of New York City" and had four children. Mrs. Wright's neighbors were quoted as saying that they knew she had been seeing Hunt for some time and that the marriage did not come as a surprise.

H. L. Hunt was now sixty-nine years old; his wife was forty. During the entire time of their relationship, Ruth had lived a strict Christian life, following the precepts of the Bible, attending the Lakewood Baptist Church, located near the house where she and the children lived, and teaching her children her religious beliefs.

When Hunt finally married Ruth, something happened to him. It may have been that the relatively young woman had enough energy to convince him to begin living life her way. Or perhaps Hunt had finally reached a point in his life where he was able to accept the authority of someone other than himself, to step back somewhat and make peace with some of the fears and desires that had driven him for so many years. For the first time in his life, Hunt embraced a religion. Not only did he stop doing things that his wife's church frowned on, like gambling, but also he began to go to church fairly regularly, his attendance culminating in his baptism into the First Baptist Church in Dallas in 1960.[8]

From the political point of view, Hunt's adoption of his wife's religious interests was significant. Within a year of their marriage, he began a new radio program, which incorporated promulgation of his political beliefs and support of his religious beliefs. This program, which he called "LIFE LINE," featured fifteen minutes of "hymns, sermons, and discussion of Christian fundamentalism," followed by fifteen minutes of political commentary.

Although the program was not charged with presenting a balanced perspective on political issues, and in fact was almost rabidly conservative, Hunt maintained a kind of neutrality by keeping his own name—now irreversibly linked with conservative causes—from being used in connection with it. His financial support was also indirect: the program was funded by sponsors, who bought air time, just as any advertiser would. Yet the primary sponsors of all the programs were various products manufactured by HLH Products, a corporate entity wholly owned by H. L. Hunt.

LIFE LINE, like *Facts Forum*, was successful in terms of the number of people it reached, estimated at a high of 5 to 6 million per week. The program also had a long life, beginning in 1958 and running through 1972. Whether it had any political impact is open to question. Some contemporary observers believed that the program was preaching to the converted, and that those who did not already believe in its mixture of fundamentalist religion and conservative politics were unlikely to embrace its message.

While communicating his political views via radio and TV, Hunt was also writing.[9] He began in 1950 with an unsigned broadsheet entitled "A Word to Help the World" and eventually wrote a dozen books of autobiography and political philosophy, and even published his old letters to the editor. His belief that people would see the light once they were advised of the "facts" drove him through much of this production. He published all of his works himself; there is no indication that he ever offered any of them to an established publisher.

The collections of his columns, articles, and letters display the same political philosophy that Hunt promulgated through *Facts Forum* and LIFE LINE: limited government intervention in the day-to-day social and economic lives of citizens; support of the American way of life as H. L. Hunt saw it; opposition to Communism, foreign aid, and the United Nations.

Two of Hunt's books are autobiographical: *H. L. Hunt: Early Days* and *Hunt Heritage*. They present his version of his family and personal history, including how he entered and became rich in the oil business; they also contain defenses and explanations of his political beliefs and actions. The first, for example, has a chapter devoted to his support of MacArthur for president, a chapter on being a "constructive," and another entitled "We Must Be First in Defense."

A third book, Hunt's utopian political novel, *Alpaca*, was intended to be a strictly political tract, though it was written as something of a romance. It describes how a rich, attractive, well-educated young man from an underdeveloped South American country spends a year traveling around the world. His objective is to consult with older and wiser men who can help him develop the ideal constitution for his country. In the course of his travels he meets a young woman who is beginning what promises to be a brilliant career as an opera singer. She gives it up to marry the young man and, just as important, to work for his country's success by means of the new constitution. The constitution, as it finally evolves, is made up of some of Hunt's fondest ideas, among them assigning the number of votes in national elections each person can have, based on the amount of taxes each pays, and limiting the terms of office any individual can hold.

Even in retrospect, Hunt's political activities look impressive—at least at first glance. His radio programs were aired on hundreds of stations across the country and at times attracted millions of listeners. His publications were widely distributed, and many newspapers bought his columns. His name became well known to political conservatives, the religious right, and to those who feared the power of these two groups. However, an objective look at what Hunt was actually accomplishing during the time of his greatest visibility leads to a somewhat different perception of his success.

During this period, when Hunt should have been enjoying power and influence as author, creator of LIFE LINE, and public figure, an assistant to the governor of Texas described seeing him at the Democratic convention in 1960 wandering around "like a lost soul."

> I didn't know what he wanted to do, but he didn't seem to be doing much of anything except trying to find somebody who would talk to him. He wandered into Lyndon [Johnson]'s suite, which was right next to ours. There were a lot of people in there but they were all too busy to talk to Hunt, so he wandered on down the hall and talked with me. I thought, 'What the hell, here's a man with all that money who can't get anybody to talk to him.'[10]

By 1964 and the next convention, Hunt had been politically active for fifteen years. He had spent millions of dollars promulgating his beliefs. At age seventy-five, he was a well-known public figure. Yet his inability to influence the political world was even more pronounced. According to one of his biographers, "Hunt didn't get onto the convention floor at all. The tall, shambling figure was seen by several persons in hotel corridors, slipping LIFE LINE pamphlets under doors."[11]

SEVEN

ALTHOUGH H. L. Hunt's political activities ultimately had little impact on U.S. social policy, he seems to have received a great deal of gratification from them. They led him to people who were willing to take his money and respect him for having it. When he offered funds to General MacArthur for a political campaign, when he offered spots on LIFE LINE to well-known people, whether liberal or conservative, he met with more acceptance. H. L. Hunt was an important man to these people, and he enjoyed certain benefits of their favor, such as political trips and inside information on their plans.

Furthermore, Hunt could, in his political pulpit, speak out in support of a system that could ultimately reinforce his own idea that the self-made man was important and influential. In much of what he wrote and supported, the value of free enterprise, entrepreneurship, and financial success was touted. In Alpaca, the ideal society, Hunt would have been granted more votes than almost anyone else. The occasional liberal aspects of his political beliefs could be explained as the magnanimity of a society enriched by the industry of men like H. L. Hunt.

By the time Hunt wrote his autobiographies, he seems to have concluded, at one level, that he had been vindicated, that he had proved once and for all that he had attained personal and social success. But the way he expressed his accomplishments has a grandiose tone, a tone that belies an underlying note of deep doubt. He writes about his novel, *Alpaca*, for example, in just this tone:

> [T]he Alpaca Constitution was so good and was appreciated so much by those who read it carefully that it was translated from

English into Spanish and later into Arabian [*sic*], November, 1966. The Jesuit Order caused it to be translated into Vietnamese to make it of use to South Vietnam's Assembly. The Vatican caused it to be translated into Russian and into Mandarin, which can be read by almost 700 million Chinese people. It was translated into German and French in March, 1967. No doubt other translations have been made from some of these and the impact of the Alpaca Constitution can never be adequately calculated. Despite every advantage, the communists have had an exceedingly difficult time taking over completely in most of these new nations which have been exposed to the Alpaca Constitution.[1]

In passage after passage, a haunting picture springs to mind: a very old man telling everyone, particularly himself, that he is important, that he is competent, that his ideas are worthwhile, and that his money is good at the bank. The fact that he expresses himself in political terms in a political forum is almost incidental to his need to feel special and valuable.

By the time he was writing his final works, Hunt was in his early eighties. Although he had become somewhat religious and had settled down to maintaining only one family in one home, in some respects he had become more extreme in his old age. It was not so much the content of his beliefs that changed; rather, the change came in the way he expressed them.

Looking at H. L. Hunt in his final years, it is tempting to label him a paranoid. In *H. L. Hunt: Early Days*, for example, he sees enemies everywhere; he portrays them in vivid terms; he attributes the worst possible motives and objectives to them.

> Total destruction of private property, together with enslavement and often liquidation of the owners, is the undeviating policy of the Community Party, until world conquest is effected. . . . So harsh and rigid is their total concept of government, that only a small number of the people they conquer—about 3% to 5%—are exempt from outright slavery. . . . [T]he nearest parallel to modern communism was probably the Fifth-Century descent of savage tribes from northern Europe, who swooped down upon the civilized peoples along the Mediterranean Coast who had fallen into decadency.[2]

During the last decade of his life, Hunt also developed ideas of conspiracy. In particular, he often talked about the "Mistakens." A feature article on him written in 1968 describes his beliefs:

> "The big money" in the United States goes "pink" through a conspiracy that begins with "placing nurses with babies who will inherit wealth, governesses (and) tutors. It can be through Mistaken playmates, classmates, or teachers skillfully working at the job. It can be through conspiracy—planned marriages, and for those not available for marriages, lovers. The Mistaken will not overlook the proper approach to win the senile."[3]

Still, even in his later writings, Hunt continued to maintain a kind of optimism that was in stark opposition to his complaints about what the world was coming to. He described how pursuing the cause of freedom could fill people with feelings of cheerfulness and confidence, even joy. The pursuit could also draw people together, according to Hunt, giving them a sense of unity and cooperation.

Furthermore, he believed in the future, and that everything would turn out all right in the end. He thought that freedom and democracy were assured by the innate ability of young people to seek good. In "Youth, Our Hope," the final chapter of *H. L. Hunt: Early Days*, he states confidently: "Our Republic can safely rely on its young people." He then explained why, in *Alpaca*, he proposed setting the voting age at eighteen, as opposed to twenty-one, which was the law in the United States at the time. He was writing during the era of LSD takers, hippies, and anti-Vietnam demonstrators, but he simply dismissed these people as a five percent minority of young people, who should not distract us from the reliability of the other ninety-five percent. Rarely known for his financial generosity, Hunt even went so far as to invest substantial funds in encouraging young people to speak out about their convictions. In 1966, for example, he funded Youth Freedom Speakers, a group that promoted appearances by young people who delivered "pro-freedom" speeches across the country.

Hunt also belied his fears of conspiracy by refusing to hire bodyguards or to take other steps that might insulate him. Even when he was briefly implicated in John F. Kennedy's assassination and warned by the FBI that he might be in danger, he refused to maintain a low profile, saying that he didn't "get along very well with being scared."[4]

In addition to the elements of paranoia, there is another psychological theme that runs through Hunt's writing, and indeed through his life: his feelings of grandiosity. Hunt seemed to feel the need to let everyone know how important and influential he was. His description of the passage of the twenty-second amendment is an excellent case in point.

In *Hunt Heritage*, he devoted an entire chapter to this accomplishment. He began by magnifying greatly the importance of the amendment to the future of the country, making a long comparison of the United States to Rome during Julius Caesar's time, and talking about the great damage Franklin Roosevelt did during his third and fourth terms in office. He then described how he succeeded, through a "one man campaign," in getting the amendment passed after it had languished in various state legislatures for several years. He opened his campaign on January 10, 1951—and the first state to react to that campaign ratified the amendment the same day! It was, to Hunt, apparently beside the point that the state was Indiana and that his campaign opening consisted of an interview with the *Dallas Morning News*.

He described how eleven more states ratified the amendment in the next seven weeks. His language implied that he was responsible for what happened. He concluded his description of the final push for ratification as follows:

> There have been many proud and happy moments for me through the years, but surely none as important for the future of our Republic as that moment when the 22nd Amendment became the law of the land. To win is pleasant and rewarding for anyone. For an individual, winning is always important, although not always vital. For a nation, as General Douglas MacArthur so wisely and correctly declared: "There is no substitute for victory!"[5]

Clearly, Hunt had identified himself with his political hero, General MacArthur, and he was leaning toward equating his own activity with that of winning the Second World War.

Throughout Hunt's writing there are innumerable examples of his taking credit for things over which he could or did have little influence. Whereas others have described Hunt's drifting aimlessly through the Democratic convention, he claimed to have persuaded Lyndon Johnson to run for vice-president. Even in nonpolitical areas, he could not resist enhancing his actions. He was "the world's greatest writer," owned the largest pecan grove in the world, and so on.

But regardless of how Hunt had lived out the final years of his life, by that time he had already left behind the essential legacies that were to have so much impact on his fourteen living children. Well before his death, the children had received these legacies and were already using them, for better and for worse.

II

The Legacies of
H. L. Hunt

EIGHT

NO experience is ever exactly the same for any two people, and so it was with H. L. Hunt and each of his children. In many respects, each child lived a very different life, even those children who were narrowly separated in age or who shared a mother and a set of family circumstances. How much greater were the differences when one child was born in 1915 and another in 1950, when one grew up in a financially insecure but traditionally structured family and another was monied but of untraditional parentage.

Hunt's children's stories, as seen from their perspectives, begin with the births of the first two.[1] Margaret Hunt was born in 1915, in Lake Village, Arkansas. Her parents were both twenty-six years old and had been married less than a year. When she was a little over two years old, her parents provided her with a brother, H. L., Jr., or Hassie.

Margaret entered the Hunt family during a period of relative economic prosperity for Hunt, who was making a good living as a cotton farmer. There was also emotional stability for the family at this time, since they lived near Lyda's parents and her five siblings. When Hassie arrived, it was into an already more tenuous situation. His mother's younger brother, Floyd, had died the summer before at the age of twenty-two, and his father had lost his most recent cotton crop, plunging the family back into economic uncertainty, which was exacerbated by Hunt's subsequent losses in cotton futures and overextensions in real estate. Sometime after Hassie's birth, Lyda returned to teaching to provide financial stability for the family. The parents managed to remain together for most of this time, but in 1921, when Margaret was six and Hassie four, this situation also

49

changed. It was then that Hunt entered the oil business, and lived much of the next year alone in El Dorado. Margaret and Hassie had no new brothers or sisters for over five years.

In 1922, the children were reunited with their father when they moved with their mother to El Dorado. In January of that year, their grandfather, Lyda's father, had died; in April, their mother became pregnant again. The children's sister, Caroline, was born in January 1923.

Most of the information about the early years of Margaret, Hassie, and Caroline comes through Caroline's eyes. Margaret has largely withdrawn behind the anonymity of being Mrs. Albert Galatyn Hill when talk turns to her Hunt heritage. Hassie, too, never having recovered from the severe schizophrenic breakdown of his young adulthood, has remained silent to the outside world.

Caroline describes the family environment she and her siblings grew up in as almost a model of Edwardian restraint and traditionalism.[2] Neither her father nor her mother ever exhibited a loss of temper in front of the children. Margaret, in a rare interview, noted that her mother never said an unkind word, adding that she never heard any slang or curse words at home either.[3] Nor did the children remember that Hunt ever raised his voice to Lyda. And one thing the parents insisted on was that the children not argue at the table. In Caroline's words, "They didn't allow unpleasantness." This avoidance of "unpleasantness" even extended, to a certain degree, to the parents' guidance of their children. Hunt and Lyda generally taught by example rather than by directive. "They practically never gave any directions," Caroline recalled. Although important guidelines were established and maintained in the home, "we had very few rules."

Still, there were conflicts between the children during this time. Although Lyda's tolerant style gave her family stability, it also left a kind of power gap in their daily life. This gap seems frequently to have been filled by Margaret, who felt called upon to play the role of "mother number two," particularly to Caroline. Her relationship to Hassie was less altruistic, the two oldest children often vying with each other for power and attention in the family. Bickering between the two was common. As time went on, Margaret seems to have come to resent her enforced responsibility for her younger siblings.

In addition, the simple fact of Hunt's frequent absences undoubtedly had an effect on his children. "He wasn't around *that* much," Caroline recalled. When he was home, "it was an event." Hunt could be a charming and enjoyable companion, a man still young whose good humor could affect the whole family. "When I was growing up," Caroline said, "Daddy was sort of the gay one. He'd sing when he was happy." But Caroline added that, in retrospect, she knows that she and her father were not really close; to a certain extent she didn't miss him when he was away. "You have to have a certain intimacy to miss someone," she observed.

While Margaret, Hassie, and Caroline noticed and reacted to Hunt's frequent absences—at first often due to his business pursuits—the three children who followed them had to cope with longer and more frequent absences. The three boys, Bunker (February 1926), Herbert (March 1929), and Lamar (August 1932), were born during an eight-year period during which Hunt was in a kind of frenzy of fathering. Three months before Bunker was born, Hunt had "married" Frania Tye. When Bunker was eight months old, his half-brother Howard was born.

The fast reproductive pace continued. Almost exactly two years later, Hunt and Frania had a daughter, Haroldina. Five months later, Hunt and Lyda had a son, Herbert. Nineteen months later, Frania had another daughter, Helen. Less than two years later, Lyda had her last child, Lamar. Slightly more than two years after that, Frania gave birth to her last child, Hue. The total: seven children in eight and a half years.

In looking at the young lives of these seven children and even of the three children born before this period, one thing is clear. Hunt was forced, by the very nature of his dual family situation, to miss important events in the lives of each family, no matter how equally he divided his time. A Christmas spent with one family was a Christmas absent from the other. Even events usually taken for granted, such as seeing a baby take his first steps or a child go off for her first day of school, were bound to be missed somewhere along the line. The children must also have sensed some puzzling distance or disinterest on the part of their father and some kind of competition for his attention that went beyond normal sibling rivalry.

They may also have seen stress in their mothers' lives, although Lyda's relationship with her children is remembered as being very positive. "Mother had a marvelous value system," Caroline said.

"She was extremely tolerant, very forgiving, undemanding, totally honest—not only in the ordinary sense of honesty, but in what she said. She was genuine, a very genuine person, and gentle. Certainly not perfect . . . but she was always *right there*."[4] But there was a price. "She was a woman who made the best of what she had," Caroline said. "She chose her bed and lay on it."

All in all, Lyda seems to have invested herself deeply in her relationship with her children, even when she could not have an ideal relationship with Hunt. The extent of Lyda's influence on her children, even in their late adult lives, was highlighted by three sketches that ran side by side in a feature section of the *Dallas Morning News* in 1984. Bunker, Herbert, and Lamar were asked questions designed to provide insights that feature-article readers might enjoy: What was their favorite comic strip; what did they consider their worst habit? While their answers to these and most other questions varied substantially, when it came to one question they all said exactly the same thing. The question was, "Who had the most impact on your life?" The uniform answer was, "Mother."[5]

One way in which Lyda's children seem to have coped with their somewhat stressful family situation was by joining together, forming close bonds among themselves. Another was to find special activities to do with their mother. Lyda enjoyed traveling and, as the family became able to afford trips, she embarked on long and adventurous outings, usually without her husband. When Lamar was still a baby, the family took an extended trip to California. Caroline described the trip as so long that, when they left, Lamar was a baby lying on a pillow, and by the time they returned, he had matured to sitting up alone.

Some of the need for the children to stick together and for Lyda to find opportunities to take her family away from home may have originated after the family moved to Tyler, Texas, in 1932. By this time, Hunt was beginning to make money in the East Texas oil field he had bought from Dad Joiner. He recalled the time the family lived in Tyler, a total of six years, as one of the family's happiest periods. Lyda got heavily involved in volunteer work, initially all the children of school age attended schools in the community, and their relative affluence enabled the family to enjoy not only a large house but also household help and such treats as a pony for the boys.

But from the point of view of the older children, at least, there was another side to Tyler. In Caroline's words, Tyler was "a nice little going town before the oil boom, with its own well-to-do people. And then all these oil people moved in." Although the children found friends, the family was not easily integrated into the community. "My father was almost the only person in our social set—the people we associated with—who was in the oil business," Caroline noted. "Everybody else was in something else—bankers, lawyers—and they'd been there forever."

Because they were newcomers, both to the community and to the monied life of Texas, the Hunts never exactly fit in. "I never felt like I belonged in Tyler. My parents didn't associate with all my friends' parents," Caroline continued. "All my friends' parents associated with each other—partied together and did things like that, but my parents didn't." And there was the possibility, by the time the family moved to Tyler, that Hunt's gambling, extramarital affairs, and sometimes controversial business dealings had marked the family.

But although Tyler clearly had its own social circles and pecking order when the Hunts moved there, things were changing. In 1932, Tyler had been the scene of the first annual Tyler Rose Festival, a civic event put together by a group of women who were active in the local garden club and a group of men who decided that the local economy could benefit from the publicity a festival might generate.[6]

While the princesses in the festival were chosen to represent organized groups in town and frequently were from, in the words of a princess chairman, "prominent families in the society history of East Texas," the queen of each festival was chosen by one person alone, the president of the festival. From the beginning, these presidents were men who were both active in the traditional civic life of the community and understood the importance of the economic underpinnings of Tyler, including the increasing importance of oil.

The president of the third festival, held in 1935, chose Margaret as queen. That was the year the festival took its first giant step forward, expanding from two to four days and introducing "big-league" college football as a drawing card, with a game between Texas A & M and Temple. Whereas a few thousand people had watched the first festival parade, in 1935 more than 40,000 people lined the streets.

Margaret returned home from Mary Baldwin College, in Staunton, Virginia, for her coronation. Mary Baldwin, a small women's college, was one of the schools traditionally attended by young women participating in what was then called the "Texas Plan." The students left Texas for two years, to study at a school that could expose them to the world beyond Texas and give them social skills and graces that would later be useful in getting along in Texas's social life. But to make sure the outside influence was not so great that the young women might never feel comfortable in Texas again, the students returned to Texas for their final years of college, usually at the University of Texas. There they could reclaim their cultural heritage. The young ladies might also use the opportunity to find a Texan husband.

Even while Margaret was gaining the increased sophistication available from Mary Baldwin, the Hunts were looking ahead to the social and educational futures of their younger children. The Tyler public schools, which Margaret had attended through high school, were not academically strong and were also seriously overcrowded; Margaret's senior year had been spent in a half-day program. Consequently, Hunt and Lyda sent their other children away to school even before college, with the boys attending prep schools out of state and Caroline going to Hockaday, in Dallas.

Hockaday Academy, a private girls' school established by Miss Hockaday in 1913, was already, by the 1930s, a sort of Texas institution. Miss Hockaday described as her long-range objective having her girls "grow into clear-eyed, forward-looking, magnificent women, sympathetic and helpful mothers and honest, public-spirited citizens."[7] Hockaday clearly offered not only a good education for a young girl from a small town like Tyler. It also offered a kind of introduction to the world that perhaps not even Mary Baldwin could match.

It was undoubtedly important that by the time the Hunts were sending their younger children away to school—Caroline went to Hockaday in 1936—they were able to afford the tuition, the room and board, the trips to Europe and Alaska. Things had not always been this way; in fact, the change had come fairly recently for the family. The first beneficiary was teen-aged Caroline; the child who missed the early advantages was Margaret. "As my sister said to me," Caroline said years later, " 'You're the one who got all the advantages. You got the dancing lessons, you got to go to Hockaday. . . . I had no education; you're the one with the education.' "[8]

Although everyone else considered Caroline privileged to go to

Hockaday, she felt differently about it. She had had friends in Tyler, as well as the emotional support of her mother and her siblings. But Hockaday was a completely new world, in which she had to make her way alone. Although she became close friends with her roommate, a girl from Mexico, when the family moved to Dallas eighteen months after she began boarding, she wanted to go home "the minute my family moved."

This family move took place in 1938, when Hunt decided that it would be easier to run his growing business, which now included overseas activities, from a major metropolitan area. By this time, Dallas was already a banking and commerce center. As Hunt found out when he was turned down by the prestigious Dallas Country Club, it was also, perhaps even more than Tyler, already a closed world socially.

Caroline expected that having a family in Dallas, ensconced in the large and visible house her father had purchased, would make things easier for her at Hockaday. This was not the case. "The bad situation socially then was that the Dallas people always thought of me as a boarder. It wasn't as if I were a new person who moved to town. I had to make an effort to make friends with the Dallas people." Even in her sixties, Caroline still remembered her problems at Hockaday with discomfort. She attributed much of her youthful unhappiness to a lack of self-confidence, a situation that was apparently aggravated by the family's never "fitting in" to the social worlds to which they were increasingly entitled and exposed as they became more affluent and then undisputably wealthy.

By the time Caroline was grappling with being a "Dallas girl" at Hockaday and the continuing conflicts this brought, Margaret had solved her social problems by getting married, an event that took place shortly before the family moved to Dallas. She was twenty-three years old; her husband was an accountant at Hunt Oil. To a certain extent, even before her marriage Margaret had put herself outside some of the ups and downs of Texas social life by becoming involved in business. She acted as a business aide and confidante to her father, who also brought her husband more and more into his business dealings as time went by.[9]

This early training under Hunt's tutelage apparently gave Margaret a grasp of the oil business that continued to stand her in good stead throughout the rest of her life. In fact, stories of the family's dealings during the crises into which Bunker and his younger brothers were later to plunge the family often referred to Margaret as the quiet power behind the family empire, the person who had the final say in how things were decided, the oldest sister who continued to lead the younger family members even after they were in their fifties and sixties.

Margaret's involvement in Hunt Oil was somewhat unusual for a woman at the time; prior to the Second World War most women who could afford to remained outside the work force. Her choice seemed to reflect the fact that one of Lyda's and Hunt's values, which they communicated to their children, was the virtue of hard work.

"In our family we don't consider anything social life," Margaret said in a 1983 article. "Whatever we're doing is all business. We're workaholics—that's the way of our mother and father."[10] Much of the example of hard work came from Hunt himself. "[My father] was a person of great vitality and amazing physical stamina," Caroline recalled in 1982. "And he had an intensity about working, six or seven days a week."

Caroline added that her mother liked to work, too. "Both my parents really believed in the value of honest work. They believed very strongly—well, you don't have to *work* but you have to work *at* something. . . . You can't just sit and do nothing and be worthwhile." Clearly the children absorbed this work ethic and never lost it. "I wouldn't *feel* worthwhile if I didn't do something," Caroline said when she was in her sixties.

Not surprisingly, if work was important for the girls in the family, it was equally important for the boys. Just as he had involved his oldest daughter in the family oil business by the late 1930s, so Hunt had involved his son Hassie. He believed that Hassie had a natural talent for the oil business that extended to a very unusual "gift" for finding oil. Hunt had begun teaching him the business when Hassie was thirteen, and the two had spent a year together, living in the oil fields near Henderson, Texas. When Hassie was nineteen, in 1936, he had dropped out of college, made a psychological break with the family, and started doing oil exploration on his own, quite successfully. Although throughout the next half-decade Hassie and his father apparently had a conflicted and frequently changing relationship, due in large part undoubtedly to Hassie's increasing mental illness, Hassie did work successfully during most of this time.

As the younger group of boys began to mature, they too were brought into the family business, often at ground level. Bunker, for example, spent a summer as a roughneck on one of the Hunt rigs, where he was subjected to the same kind of harassment and regulations that any newcomer would experience.[11]

On the one hand, the children of Hunt and Lyda were growing up in increasing affluence, with a relatively stable home environment assured by their accepting and tolerant mother. They had both the formal and informal educational benefits that more money could buy, but they still were taught the importance of working and earning their own way. On one level, the Hunts looked like the ideal family.

But on the other hand, there were real problems. The family that did not argue at the dinner table often sat down without its father. The mother who involved herself with her children, her community work, and her church was part of a troubled marriage. The children who were receiving the benefits of travel and education were haunted by feelings either of deprivation—as seen, for instance, in Margaret's adult protests that she did not have the advantages the other children enjoyed—or of being misfits—as Caroline remembered. And those who have spoken least about the conflicts of their youth, but who seem to have had the most dramatic problems in adult life, are the three youngest sons. These children were born when their father was frequently away, heavily involved in his other family, and increasingly on call to his burgeoning oil business.

These boys also grew up in the shadow of their troubled brother Hassie. While Hassie's unconventional behavior was accepted and tolerated by his parents, it undoubtedly created problems, or at least confusion, for the younger boys. And when Hassie suffered a total breakdown in 1943, his brothers were still young and impressionable: Bunker was seventeen, Herbert fourteen, and Lamar only eleven. Perhaps they came to wonder, as they grappled with prep school, Texas society, and their first oil-field jobs, if they too might be destined to cross over what Caroline described as the "thin line between genius and insanity."[12]

It was a time when an era in Hunt's first children's lives was coming to an end. The older children were leaving home. Meanwhile, unknown to most of them, Hunt was also breaking off his relationship with Frania Tye. The time was, in fact, ideal for the father, his emotional and physical energy split for so many years, to focus on his three younger sons and their need for his support as they became men in their own right.

But it was not to be. For one thing, as Hassie became more ill, Hunt became more devoted to "curing" him. "The saddest thing in my father's life was my oldest brother's illness," Caroline said many years later. "My father devoted [to it] years of his life—it was a sign of his persistence. . . . He was dedicated to getting him well, which he never could do." Second, though Hunt's businesses were extremely successful, he saw the entry of the United States into the Second World War as a demand that he work harder, now for his country as well as for himself. And, finally, as he ended his relationship with Frania, he found another woman, who would play an even greater role in his life. An era for the first family was ending, but the ways of the father remained the same, and the ultimate effect of Hunt's choices was only beginning to be seen.

NINE

BECAUSE of H. L. Hunt's relationship with Frania Tye, the children of his original family were to mature in an environment that was increasingly rife with hidden conflicts. But this family at least was structured around a reassuring semblance of well-being, as Lyda found her own way of coping with her problems and largely protected the children from an early exposure to things they could neither understand fully nor affect in any way.

This shield was to be largely denied to Frania Tye's children. It was when the first three children were only seven, five, and three, and the last child not yet born, that their mother found out about Hunt's other life. Despite her apparent attempts to protect her children from the impact of the situation, its existence was to create stresses and strains on the four children that made the problems of the original family's children pale in comparison.

The relationship of the children's parents had not begun in conflict. In fact, one of the most striking things about it, at least prior to the time Frania found out about Hunt's other life, was its apparent normalcy. The reader of newspaper accounts of the depositions and testimony during the lawsuit Frania brought against Hunt's estate, fifty years after the two originally met, must remind himself that if what Frania says was really true, the life she describes prior to 1934 was dramatic only in its ordinariness.

Because Frania's claims and recollections were never upheld in a court of law, they are and will remain open to dispute. She is the only living witness to the ceremony of her marriage to Hunt, and the legal documents supporting this union do not present an indisputable picture of such an event's taking place. Furthermore, just when

Frania found out about Hunt's other family has not been determined once and for all. But Frania's emotional responses to Hunt, her analysis of his personality, her experience of their time together have a psychological validity that makes them worth accepting when it comes to understanding her children's legacies from their father. The following look at these inheritances will, therefore, take Frania's perspective, as she presented it in 1978.[1]

The family into which the first three children of Hunt and Frania were born was not unlike others in the late 1920s, particularly when the husband was in the oil business. After the couple's marriage in November 1925 and a honeymoon of three or four days in the Tampa area, Hunt went straight back to his business ventures. Frania, who later said she knew nothing about the oil business at this time, believed that Hunt was an oil-field worker. Later, when Hunt had more money, she assumed that he had been promoted into better positions.

Almost all men in the oil business moved frequently from one job to another during this time, with boom towns springing up around new fields and then quickly petering out. Because these men worked under what could only be called primitive conditions—in seas of mud, in intense heat or cold—and lived in tents or shacks with no sanitary facilities, wives and families were often left behind in some more civilized area. In fact, this was the situation in which Hunt's legal wife found herself during this same period, as Hunt moved to El Dorado, then to Henderson, and the family followed later, finally, to nearby Tyler and Dallas. For Frania, Hunt's frequent traveling probably seemed completely normal. If she had discussed her situation with any other women in Shreveport, even one who knew more about the oil business, she would have learned that Hunt's style of work was accepted as commonplace.

As the couple settled into their "married life," and Frania found she was pregnant, she and Hunt began to sort out roles and responsibilities for themselves. He chose Shreveport as the place where they should live; they both agreed not to rush into buying a house; she found the apartment, had the utilities turned on, and paid the rent. Hunt provided money for her, and later the children, to live on, at first giving her $200 or $300 at a time. It was her responsibility to manage the money and allocate it appropriately. Sometimes she had extra money, and sometimes Hunt told her to make what he gave her last.

During the first few months of their union, Hunt usually spent weekends with Frania, and was almost always absent during the week. The details of his locations and specific jobs were completely unknown to Frania. "He told me he was working in the oil fields," she testified. "It might as well have been Africa." Frania had found she was pregnant around the time they moved to Shreveport, and since Hunt was away so much, he arranged for her sister Jennie to come to Shreveport to be with her when the baby was expected.

Their first child began life with an absent father. Hunt was not at home; he had been talking to Frania almost every day, and sometimes twice a day, on the phone, and when he called on October 25, 1926, Jennie told him the news. The next day, Hunt reappeared in Shreveport from wherever he had been and visited Frania at the hospital. The couple had already agreed on a name for the baby: Frania had always liked the name Howard, and Hunt suggested Lee because it was a Southern name.

When Frania and the baby went home from the hospital, Hunt decided that they should move from their apartment into a house. He bought what Frania described as "a very lovely bungalow, nothing pretentious, just a lovely home." He also signed all the papers relating to the sale. What Frania did not know at the time was that, instead of buying the house in his own or Frania's name, he had put it in the name of Jennie Tye.

Although Howard was born into an apparently traditional family, his early childhood and that of his two sisters was spent in an environment that Frania described as less than idyllic. "I was always either pregnant or we were moving," Frania recalled. Just a little more than a year after Howard was born, Frania found she was again pregnant.

Again Hunt was in frequent phone contact with her, when he was not at home, as the time of the birth drew near. This child too arrived, on October 26, 1928, to an absent father. The baby, a girl, was named by Hunt. He chose a very unusual name—Haroldina—but, as Frania said, "he was a very unusual man."

While Haroldina was still very young, Hunt began suggesting that Frania move to Texas. The couple went so far as to sell the house they were living in; but then they did not relocate. Instead, they leased another house in Shreveport, and it was there that Frania discovered she was pregnant for the third time. Now Hunt did decide that a move was a good idea. During the summer before the next child was born, Hunt bought a house in Dallas, and Frania moved there. It was 1930, and the Depression was underway. But, according to Frania, she and the two children continued to be well provided for, with Hunt sometimes giving her as much as several thousand dollars at a time for expenses. The house in Dallas reflected Hunt's affluence: it was a large two-story house on a corner lot in a nice Dallas neighborhood.

Frania knew, by then, that part of the money Hunt gave her came from his gambling. Despite her frequent pregnancies and the family's two, and then three, young children, Hunt often took Frania on trips with him. On one trip, to New Orleans, Hunt invited her to sit in on a poker game in which he was playing. According to a newspaper account of Frania's testimony regarding this occasion, "She went under orders to 'say nothing' during the course of the game. She said 'tremendous sums' were bet in the game, that Hunt was a winner, and a day or two later he told her he won something like $60 or $70,000."

Although Frania recalled being careful in how she managed the household money, her knowledge of Hunt's gambling plus the way in which he handled his money undoubtedly put her in a position to know that he was far from poor. "One day he came in and just put his hands in his pockets and threw money on the dining room table," she recalled. Hunt almost always gave her the household money in cash, never writing checks. He did not carry his money in a wallet, but preferred to have a large roll of bills in his pocket.

Hunt also, apparently, made all the decisions for the family that had to do with legal affairs and large financial undertakings. At one point, Frania told a lawyer during the 1978 trial that "when Mr. Hunt presented me something to sign, I just signed it. I could have signed my life away." Frania's willingness to accept Hunt's guidance in these areas was to turn out, after their breakup, to be very important.

In Dallas, the couple's third child, Helen, was born, on October 28, 1930. A period of relative calm followed Helen's birth. Frania and the children stayed in their house in Dallas, and Frania did not become pregnant again until early 1934. This was the period during which Hunt was heavily involved with his development of the East Texas oil fields he had bought, just a few months after Helen's birth, from Dad Joiner. This was also the time when Lamar, Hunt's final child with Lyda, was born, on August 2, 1932. Lamar had been born in Tyler, less than 100 miles from Dallas, though around this time Hunt was not living in Tyler himself but in Henderson, with Hassie, separated from both families.

Frania was four months pregnant, and her children were three, five, and seven, when a close friend told her that "Franklin Hunt," her husband, was actually H. L. Hunt, who was married and had another family. Frania, as she had learned more about the oil business, had apparently had her questions about Hunt, especially because she knew that Franklin was working in the East Texas oil fields, where H. L. Hunt had made his big strike. Her husband had first explained that H. L. was his uncle, but when confronted with the friend's statement, he confessed the truth. Frania added, "He was rather shocked, but it didn't take him long to recover. I think he was expecting it."

Perhaps because he had believed that his increasing success in East Texas would ultimately result in his unmasking, Hunt had already suggested to Frania that she and the family might move to New York, nearer her parents. Now that the truth was out, he asked Frania to be patient, to move, and assured her that "we would discuss all our problems after the baby arrived."

Frania was deeply upset by her situation. She called her father to ask for his help and advice, then flew to New York to talk to him. She decided that she should move to New York at once, and Hunt began making arrangements. Frania later described her emotional and physical condition at this time as "not too good."

Although Frania apparently wanted to be closer to her family, for some reason she and Hunt agreed to find a house in the suburbs of New York City, on Long Island, rather than in upstate New York, where her parents still lived. By this time, Hunt had enough money to purchase a very nice house. The one he chose was in Great Neck, in an estate section where all the houses were on half- to one-and-a-half acre lots.

Despite her conflicts about her relationship with Hunt, Frania chose to approach life on Long Island in the most positive way possible. "I became Mrs. Haroldson Lafayette Hunt immediately," she said. But her personal anguish apparently did not abate even though she developed a socially acceptable facade for herself. When it was time for her fourth child to be born, Frania refused to go to a hospital, though her other three children had been delivered in hospitals. Instead, she virtually hid herself in her lovely house, where the child, Hue, was delivered in October 1934.

The period that followed was confused and chaotic. As was to happen so often in Hunt's life, things looked good on the surface. In Great Neck, "Mrs. Hunt" lived in her large house with her four children; Mr. Hunt apparently lived there too, though he was frequently away on business. This may well have been what the young Hunt children themselves continued to believe. It was certainly what the neighbors thought.

But for Frania, the conflicts continued. She was still a Catholic, and did not believe in divorce, so there was no hope that she could marry Hunt on her own terms any time in the immediate future. Hunt was the father of her children, and the children loved and respected him regardless of what his relationship was to their mother. Frania also needed Hunt's financial support. She had a new baby, as well as the other children, and though she had supported herself before she met Hunt, she had never had a career that would enable a family of five to live in comfort. Finally, according to the reports of one of Frania's best friends, she still loved Hunt and was not ready to end their relationship forever.

Hunt, for his part, was apparently unwilling to abandon his relationship with Frania or to alter his relationship with the children. After all, from his point of view nothing had really changed. Consequently, he not only continued to spend time in Great Neck whenever possible and to provide financial support for the family, but he also wrote to Frania when he was away, pouring out his feelings in prose and poetry. He also sent telegrams, including one that said he was en route because "too strong the urging, my engine is surging," and once sent so many flowers that "the place looked like a funeral home."

Life continued to be completely "normal" from an outside perspective. According to Charles Bradley, who was Howard's age and lived across the street at the time, the children had friends in the neighborhood; Frania, who, everyone agreed, was a lovely, sweet person, had friends too, including Bradley's parents; and Hunt was just somebody else's dad, a nice guy who wasn't really part of the group because he was away on business so much. He may have had his quirks—there was a story that made the local papers about his winning something like $100,000 at Belmont Park, the local race track, in one day—but to Great Neck, New York, H. L. Hunt was just another loving father with an unusually demanding job.[2]

For several years the children, though confronted with Frania's unhappiness and perhaps instability, at least had the security of their life in Great Neck. But as Frania's "illness" continued, Hunt decided that the family should move to New Orleans, to see if this would help her. In 1936, when the children were nine, seven, five, and eighteen months, they left their friends and routines behind. When the move to New Orleans did not make a big difference to Frania, however, everyone went back to Great Neck, and remained there for several more years.

As she and Hunt continued to try to sort out their impossible situation and as the initial shock of learning about Hunt's other life dulled, Frania gradually grew less troubled. Hunt came up with some very creative solutions in his attempt to keep the relationship alive. At one point, for example, he phoned Frania and asked her to come to Salt Lake City, Utah, where he was seriously ill. She immediately flew there, only to be met at the airport by Hunt, "well and waving his hat to greet her." He had lured her away from the children under false pretenses: he wanted her to stay in Utah and find out more about the Mormon religion, in which, he told her, "having two or three wives was normal." This was too much for Frania. "I told him I would never accept it," she said. Conversion was out of the question, even if it could resolve her conflicts.

By the time Hue was three and the other children were eleven, nine, and seven, Frania was more or less herself again. She apparently had made peace, at least temporarily, with her relationship with Hunt and was willing to go along with his less extreme plans. Consequently, in late 1939 or early 1940, when Hunt decided that he wanted Frania and the children to move to Houston, she agreed. He "wanted me to be closer to him," she recalled, and added that Hunt said that their "children would get a better education in the South than in the North." Again the children, who now ranged from five to thirteen, were uprooted from Great Neck, this time permanently. They moved to Houston, to a neighborhood comparable to that in which they had lived in New York.

Houston was only 250 miles from Dallas, where Hunt now lived with his other family, and the world of Texas oil barons that encompassed both Houston and Dallas was a small one. But through the years in Great Neck and during the brief time in New Orleans, Hunt had been successful in having his second family known as Mrs. H. L. Hunt and the Hunt children. He and Frania had gone out socially, they had had friends, and the children had used his name. It was even possible that Frania's children, though they had lived with their mother's uncertainty and unhappiness for the last five years or more, still believed that their parents were married and would have been confused to use any name but their father's.

Frania and her family began an active social life in Houston. Renewed fantasies of maintaining a traditional family life were quickly shattered, however, when Frania met a woman named Ruby Matthew, who gave a "very large and elaborate tea party" to introduce Frania to her friends. The affair was written up in the Houston paper, and it was then that the real beginning of the end of the Frania-Hunt romance occurred.

"I got a telephone call from a lady" who did not identify herself, Frania recalled. The caller demanded $5,000 to keep quiet about who Frania really was. When Frania refused, the woman apparently began telling other people that Frania "was not Mrs. H. L. Hunt but a mistress or something to that effect." Frania received at least fifty telephone calls. It was a terrible and embarrassing experience, and she demanded that Hunt come to Houston to help her deal with her crisis. When he did not come, she became despondent as the reality of her situation closed in on her again.

Impetuously, she developed a plan to force Hunt to acknowledge her existence, her situation, their children. She took the children to Dallas, and they checked into the Adolphus Hotel, a large downtown establishment. Then she called Hunt and told him that he had "to take the children off her hands." Telling Howard, age thirteen, to take care of the other children, she simply left them and went back to Houston.

Regardless of how the older children had viewed their situation up to this point—and the three oldest, thirteen, eleven, and nine, were certainly old enough to recognize marital discord when they saw it—now they must have found out definitely that things were very troubled between their parents. When Hunt went to the hotel to see about the children, he took Margaret, his oldest daughter, with him. No one has ever described publicly how Hunt explained Margaret to the other children—perhaps she was introduced as a distant relative. Perhaps, if this was the case, the children even believed their father. But their mother's dramatic behavior, her abandonment of them, their father's appearance out of nowhere must, at the very least, have led the children to question the facts of their everyday world and to feel tremendously uncertain about what would happen next in their lives.

The immediate crisis did abate: Frania returned to get the children after Hunt assured her by phone that they would "make some arrangements." The family went back to Houston briefly, then moved to Los Angeles, where the children again had to adjust to a new house and new schools. It seems that at this point Frania finally began to face the fact that there was no solution to her problem. She would not become a Mormon. Hunt was not going to leave his other family for her. He had even, by now, introduced Frania to Lyda. Although he obviously cared about her and the children in his own way—it was at this time, April 1941, that he set up trusts for each of the four children—Frania was actually and completely on her own.

In January 1942, she went to Dallas with a close friend, Martha Kreeger, and a lawyer, to work out a settlement with Hunt. Again, the scene of the meeting was the Adolphus Hotel; this time the children were left at home. For a week, Frania and her supporters met daily with Hunt. Sometimes Martha was asked to leave the room, and she retired to her own room next door. Once, during the week, she heard Frania scream. Another time, Martha later testified, Hunt came into her room and offered her $10,000 if she could persuade Frania to accept his settlement terms. She refused, telling Hunt that she understood he had bought most of Frania's other friends but that her friendship was not for sale.

It was, according to Martha, a strange week. "We'd fight all day and at night we'd eat. He would kiss Frania on the hand." In private, Hunt assured Martha that he still loved Frania. "You know, I'm always going to take care of Frania," he told her. But with Frania, Hunt was apparently taking a harder line. What he wanted was for her to renounce any marriage claims and to develop an explanation for their relationship and the birth of their children that cleared him of anything worse than adultery. In return, he offered Frania a million dollars.[3]

It was this hard demand and offer of payment that made Frania very angry. "I screamed that I would never sell my children," she said. But "I think he wore me down after three or four days of meetings," she went on. Perhaps part of the wearing down was Frania's realization, which she described later, that Hunt's basic desire in all of their negotiations was not to take care of her or their children but to arrange things "so he would not be revealed as a bigamist."

The document Frania did finally sign gave Hunt almost all that he wanted. It stated that he and Frania had never lived together, that they had met in hotel rooms, that she had gone to El Dorado, where Hunt's legal wife lived, during the early days of their relationship, that she had never been involved in any way in Hunt's business ventures. It ended by stating that any and all claims Frania made for damages or on any other grounds were "not recognized or agreed to by H. L. Hunt, but are by him expressly denied."

In return for signing what could only have been a demeaning description of her relationship with Hunt, Frania received $100,000 in cash, payment of $25,000 in legal fees to her attorneys, and income from certain East Texas oil fields in the amount of $2,000 per month.

Thirty-five years later, Frania said that she agreed to sign the statement, not for economic reasons, though she did use the money "to educate my children—to feed them," but as her contribution to "the man I loved." She did not question the wisdom of making such a blanket renunciation of her claims because "women who are in love are not philosophers—nor are they lawyers." Furthermore, she said that Hunt agreed that he would ultimately acknowledge his relationship to her and to the children—not then, while Lyda was alive and all of the children of both families could be affected, but sometime before the end of his life and certainly in his will.

Frania never revealed what she told her four children about the settlement she reached with Hunt. But the children quickly knew that something had changed, because, only twelve days after their mother signed the settlement papers, she married another man. John Lee was an employee of Hunt Oil whom Frania had met previously, but according to Frania's later statements, she and Lee had not had an ongoing romance prior to her final break with Hunt. Indeed, she said that she came to know John Lee well only about the time of the 1942 negotiations.

So the children suddenly confronted a new man in their mother's life, and this man quickly became their stepfather. Not only did their mother marry a relative stranger, but once again the entire family was uprooted, moving this time to Atlanta. Settling in there was somewhat disrupted by the fact that their stepfather was called up for active duty in the military and did not live with them during the early part of the marriage.

After Frania's marriage, the children were told by her that from now on they would use the name Lee, rather than the name Hunt. They all knew that H. L. Hunt was their father; indeed, they continued to see him occasionally, and he and Frania remained in contact with one another.[4] Frania even told the children that they should continue to love and respect Hunt. Meanwhile, life began anew in a new place, in a new family situation, and without any regular contact with their father.

In Atlanta, the Lee family lived in what was a typical house and neighborhood for them. Their new house, Flowerland, was what was described in Atlanta as "a mansion," located on a very large tract of land in a good section of the city.[5] There John and Frania gave lavish parties to which they invited the socially prominent people they met when they joined one of the most socially desirable clubs in Atlanta, the Capital City Club. A certain amount of gossip developed about the family; primarily, it centered on speculation that the Lees' wealth was Mrs. Lee's and that it derived from a personal relationship she had with H. L. Hunt, who was also the father of her four children.

But the gossip was not confirmed, and the Atlanta community appeared willing to accept the "striking couple" and their children more or less at face value. This was not so surprising. Regardless of Mrs. Lee's past, she had, according to an Atlanta society article, "money and she bought the things money can buy, including fine clothes and the final gloss and polish that hairdressers and beauticians can provide." She also had "unerring good taste" and was a "very warm" person who "not only reaches out to win friends but is generous in giving of herself, her time and her money."

As the four children grew up in Atlanta, they apparently fit into the community and became part of it. But each one also began to find his or her own way of coping with the complex and largely secret family history.

Howard, the oldest child, who was sixteen when the family moved to Atlanta, chose to go to college at Georgia Tech.[6] A tall, big-boned young man with blond hair and a round face, Howard looked startlingly like H. L. Hunt. But he was careful always to use the name Lee and never to allude to his past. He was an open and honest person, rather outgoing. He enjoyed life and did everything on a big scale, whether it was eating, traveling, or spending money. In contrast, though, he had an introverted or closed side, particularly when it came to the details of his life. He was very protective of his own story and did not want to share it with anyone.

After Howard graduated from college, in 1950, he took a job working for Placid Oil in West Texas. There he was joined by Charles Bradley, who had lived across the street from the Hunts in Great Neck. "Howard was in the land department, I believe," Bradley recalled in 1987. "They had given him a job there. He didn't have much in the way of answering to anybody. He came and went pretty much as he wanted." Bradley speculated that H. L. Hunt had gotten Howard the job, and that lots of people in the area knew or thought they knew about the Hunt connection. Howard, however, tried not to give anyone an opportunity to go beyond speculation and wouldn't talk about Hunt or the past with Bradley. Howard was also careful about how much he drank when he was in the oil fields, for example, because he was afraid he might get drunk and accidentally let slip the true facts of his life.

Part of the gossip about Howard may have been based on how he handled his finances. "Howard was not ostentatious about having a lot of money," Bradley recalled. "He had money, but only when he needed it. I never knew where it came from. I remember one night when we were in his car, going out to eat. I said that I didn't have any money for dinner and Howard said he didn't either. Then he said, 'Wait a minute—look in the glove compartment.' I opened it, and there were ten or fifteen uncashed paychecks.

"Howard was always able to do big things even though he appeared to be broke. He'd go into a men's clothing store and buy three or four or five hundred dollars' worth of clothes at once. That was a lot of money in the fifties. Then he'd turn to me and ask me if I wanted the same things."

During this time, Howard remained in contact with Hunt, mentioning to Bradley, now and then, that he was meeting his father somewhere. Once, the two young men were driving through East Texas, and Howard suddenly said that he had to stop in the little town they were passing through. They went to the hotel, and Howard excused himself to go upstairs and visit with his father. He offered to take Bradley up with him, but when he asked his father if his friend could join them, Hunt adamantly refused.

Although Howard had graduated from college and, over the years afterward, had held a number of oil-related jobs, including some outside his father's realm, he was not a particularly brilliant or dynamic businessman. "Howard was never going to make it as a business tycoon—far from it," Bradley observed. "He never would have been a big financial success. He was just a nice guy."

Haroldina, the next child in the family and the oldest daughter, seemed to have the greatest problems in dealing with the complexities of the family's life. "She took it the hardest and had the roughest time," Bradley recalled. She reached young adulthood functioning more or less normally, however, and in the mid 1950s married a doctor, with whom she had a large number of children. However, whatever conflicts she felt apparently took their toll during her early married life, and she suffered bouts of serious mental illness, which were to have repercussions throughout her life.

Many people who knew Haroldina and her husband, Robert Franch, observed that the family had more money than a young doctor who went on to pursue a career in academic medicine would usually make. They lived in a large house on two acres of land in a very upscale part of Atlanta called Buckhead, and the children attended private school. But, perhaps because the family lived unostentatiously except for their large house, few people tended to tie Haroldina to the Hunt name and the Hunt money.

Haroldina's younger sister, Helen, was the child who seemed to emerge most unscathed from the conflicts of her early years. She matured into a very attractive woman—a tall, stately blond who was extremely outgoing and had a "great personality." She was also Hunt's favorite child in this branch of his family. Reportedly, when Helen graduated from high school, Hunt gave her a mink coat.[7] After she graduated from Marymount College, in New York, he encouraged her when she embarked on an acting career and he tried to line up support of her undertaking from some influential friends. Frania also seems to have enjoyed having Helen as her daughter. She gave a debutante party for her that was one of her most elaborate social events.

Like her older sister, Helen got married and settled in Atlanta. She translated her interest in acting into support of community theater activities. She and her husband, William Cartledge, became well known as Atlanta art patrons. The couple had one child, a son they named Ron.

Frania's youngest child, Hue, was only seven when his mother married John Lee and the family moved to Atlanta. But instead of being comfortable with his new identity and family situation, Hue, over time, seems to have had recurrent conflicts in integrating his Hunt heritage into his later life. Like Hunt's sons Bunker, Herbert, and Lamar, Hue attended prep school, then, like his older brother Howard, he went to Georgia Tech. Later he attended Harvard Law School for two years, but never completed his degree.

While he was growing up, Hue began using the last name Hunt, unlike his brother and sisters. But one day, when he was thirteen or fourteen, Howard told him that there was a problem with the relationship between Hunt and their mother that went beyond a simple divorce; consequently, he should be careful never to call himself Hunt. Hue said that he later discussed the matter with his mother, and she explained the facts: that she had married Hunt but later learned that he had already been married and had another family, so they had to separate.

After these revelations, Hue returned to using the name Lee, but when he was older he began calling himself Hunt again. During this time, Hue also changed the spelling of his first name several times, alternating between Hue and Hugh. Reportedly, he once confessed to an interviewer that he suffered from "an identity problem."[8] This may have stemmed from the fact that, although he and the rest of his family lived with John Lee, they continued to be in contact with their biological father, whom Frania told Hue "we were to respect . . . as our father and he would take care of us." Lee and Hunt apparently were on comfortable terms with each other, even if Hue found their relationship confusing. For example, the family often returned to Shreveport in the summer, where John Lee would generally "tend to matters concerning the Reliance Trusts," and Hue and the other children would see Hunt. Like Howard, Hue also appears to have received money directly from his father as he finished school and embarked on his adult life, money that was not part of his trust or of Hunt's settlement with Frania.

In 1957, when her youngest child was thirteen, Frania divorced John Lee. Lee remarried and moved west. Frania did not marry again. She did, however, remain socially active in Atlanta, moving to an "immense and sumptuous" house, where she continued, into the early 1960s, to give outstanding parties, which, in the words of an Atlanta social columnist, "brought almost universal admiration."

TEN

BY the standards and mores of the early 1940s, Hunt's family with Lyda could be divided into two groups, each of which was doing almost exactly what was considered appropriate for children to do during this era. The girls, Margaret and Caroline, were completing their educations and getting married. The boys, Bunker, Herbert, and Lamar, were finishing school and picking up the reins of the family business.

The tone for the two girls was set, as usual, by the older sister, Margaret. Although Margaret had taken the somewhat unconventional step of working for her father for some time, she had nonetheless gotten married when she was twenty-three. And although she took her time about having children, here too she did what was expected. Her first child, Lyda, was born in 1942, when she was twenty-seven.

Caroline, on the other hand, always the cooperative daughter who followed in her respected sister's footsteps, capped an early graduation from college, at age twenty, with an immediate marriage.[1] "In those days, all a girl ever wanted to do was get married," she recalled. She had majored in ancient history and English literature in college, but had never considered a career; none of her friends had either. Besides, she was in love with a handsome man, a Navy pilot stationed in Texas. It was 1943, wartime, and he was going off to fight, perhaps never to return. Clearly, getting married seemed the right thing to do.

Caroline's early married days were not, in some respects, typical of those of the rich and sophisticated young Dallasite. In fact, at this time Caroline apparently did not know that her family was rich; she later said that she found out about her father's wealth at the same time the rest of the world did, when *Life* ran its story about Hunt in 1948.

As a young adult, Caroline was still as shy and unassertive as she remembered having been at Hockaday. Even her physical appearance was that of an innocent young girl. "She had that darling, fresh, round face," recalled one of her college sorority sisters in a 1984 interview. "She was so sweet and easy to get along with."[2]

Caroline conducted her personal financial affairs in an almost childlike way, too. In college, she was known as the person who could always find a bargain, who'd recommend to an extravagant friend, "Wait before you spend your dime; think about it." After she was married, this continued. Caroline later said that she was not interested in buying clothes for herself, and that one Christmas her father gave her a new wardrobe of five dresses. Although they were a gift, she dealt with them frugally. "I put up a little chart of my dresses and made a mark every time I wore one because I wanted to feel sure I was getting my money's worth," she said in a 1983 interview.

Although Caroline was unassertive and continued to be a dutiful daughter after her marriage, she did seem to enjoy the measure of independence marriage brought. She and her husband, Lloyd Sands, moved a number of times during their early days together, as he pursued his Navy career. They lived in thirteen places in two years. "We were assigned to a squadron, so we moved with people we knew," Caroline said. "I loved it. In Maine, we lived in a big, old house in the country. There were five couples, and it was like a big house party."

The lure of this independence may also have been what made clerking at Neiman-Marcus a more memorable job for Caroline than getting a glimpse of the inner workings of Hunt Oil. While her husband was stationed in the South Pacific, she did work in her father's office, but when she recalled her job there, it was as a job in passing rather than the kind of involvement Margaret had had. A more important job, in Caroline's eyes, was her stint at Neiman-Marcus. "I was taken on as temporary help, and I was proud that they offered me a permanent job in the gift department. I learned a lot in that job."

After the war ended, Sands took a job with his father-in-law's company, and the couple moved to Marshall, Texas. But soon it was back to Dallas, in 1946, where Caroline's first son, Stephen, was born. Two years later, Caroline had a second boy, Bunker, followed after another two-year interval by a third boy, David.

Superficially, these were good years for Caroline. She embraced the role of mother, reading every book she could find on child development. At one point, when her sons were very young, her father asked if she would be willing to learn the oil business. "Daddy, I'm happy," she told him. "I feel like I'm doing what I should be doing with my children. I don't want to become involved in the business."

On the other hand, Caroline became very isolated during this time. Her shyness and discomfort with the Dallas social scene, left over from her youth, did not quickly go away. And there were tensions developing in her marriage that contributed to her alone-ness. Her husband did not like to socialize and he did not encourage her to go out; indeed, as time went by, he discouraged her from doing anything except her involvement in her church.

Sands continued to work for Caroline's father and, as Hunt with-drew from day-to-day operations, for his brothers-in-law. This was also something of a problem. As another family member described the situation much later, "They didn't listen to him. They'd discount him. He wasn't one of the boys. He wasn't a brother. And to be the only outsider—there's enough of us here as it is. We don't need anybody else."[3]

During the time that Caroline's husband was grappling with his status as an outsider, however, Margaret's husband was having a somewhat different experience. In fact, the early days of Margaret's married life seem to have been quite different from those of Caroline in most respects.

To begin with, of course, Margaret was Margaret, the oldest child, the responsible daughter, the assertive woman who had had firsthand experience with Hunt Oil before she was married and who was her father's confidante, even in such sensitive areas as his per-sonal life.

Somewhere along the line—perhaps as a result of her knowledge of her father's unconventional and socially undesirable "other" life— Margaret had taken a careful look at the positive side of being the daughter of H. L. and Lyda Bunker Hunt. Around the time she got married, her mother had commissioned a genealogical study of the family.[3] This study—a copy of which Margaret later presented to the New York Public Library—indicated that Lyda could trace her family back to noble Europeans of the 1200s, to William the Conqueror, and to the royal house of Castile. Ancestors came to America in the early seventeenth century, and one gentleman, a citizen of Massachusetts, proved his farsightedness as well as his wealth by donating $10,000 to the founding of Harvard University.

Armed with this knowledge of her family's social integrity, Margaret, beginning in her twenties, became active in civic, cultural, and society organizations in Dallas. These seem to have provided her with an interpersonal outlet and given her a chance to exercise her substantial management skills in a way that was acceptable for a woman in the 1940s and 1950s. Some of the organizations in which Margaret became active were open only to people with the "right" genealogy: the Daughters of the American Revolution, the Mayflower Society, and the Magna Charta Dames. Some, such as the Junior League and the Dallas Women's Club, did not require a certain lineage but were known to accept only the socially desirable. Others, such as the Women's Guild of the Dallas Historical Society, Margaret simply founded herself to reflect her own interests.

As Margaret made her way in Dallas society, at the same time bearing two more children, Alinda and Albert, Jr., she continued her involvement with Hunt Oil, but in a less direct manner. Like Caroline's, Margaret's husband, Al Hill, worked for the family business. But Hill had two advantages over Lloyd Sands. First, Sands was more or less a peer of his three brothers-in-law, entering the firm shortly after the war, just as Bunker did; Hill was ten years older and began working for Hunt Oil during a period when Bunker was just another summer roughneck and when Herbert and Lamar were still in grade school. This meant that Hill was able to weather his father-in-law's initial testing and still have time to establish his own place in the organization.

Second, Hill was flexible when it came to his position in the company. As one member of the third generation put it, "He's a softer person. Some men are just better at [getting along] than others." According to one of Hunt's biographers, what really happened was that Margaret was still Hunt's heir apparent, and her husband was more or less her stand-in.[5] Hunt respected Margaret and her business acumen; she was the power behind the throne, with Al Hill, and everyone involved was willing to go along with this arrangement. Margaret maintained her appropriately ladylike position, Al his dignity, and H. L. his ultimate control.

During this time, the young Hunt boys were coming along well. Bunker joined Hunt Oil after serving in the Navy. Herbert had emerged as the industrious member of the family, at one point in his youth raising chickens and other fowl in the family's backyard and earning his mother's praise as "my little businessman." Like Bunker, he had attended boarding school, but he followed this with a decision to continue his education away from home, at a small Virginia school that was in many ways the men's equivalent of Mary Baldwin. It was from this school, Washington and Lee, that Herbert earned a bachelor's degree in geology in 1950.

This was before Hunt Oil hired its first full-time geologist, and Hunt was still relying on a certain amount of "creekology" (to use his own term) to identify fields. Reportedly, Hunt expressed his skepticism about Herbert's credentials by saying that the degree "was going to cost us," but once Herbert entered Hunt Oil and displayed his ability to pay attention to details and to follow through on projects, Hunt began to view him as a potentially successful oilman.[6]

Although there are stories of Hunt's ups and downs with Bunker and Herbert, of their coming into and falling out of favor, of Bunker being "fired," of the heirs, apparent and otherwise, being played off against one another, there was one overriding factor in the management of Hunt Oil during this period.[7] Beginning shortly after the Second World War, when first Bunker and later Herbert were getting into the oil business full-time, Hunt Oil entered its single greatest growth period. Consequently, there was tremendous opportunity for any employee, old or new, to learn new things and to increase his or her area of responsibility.

Employees were constantly being reassigned and moved from one area to another as wells started producing in previously undeveloped areas and old fields or related businesses were revived or renewed. "When I first came here . . . this company seemed to have so much confidence in its employees, even its newest ones," a woman recalled in *The History of Hunt Oil Company,* a book published to commemorate the company's fiftieth anniversary. "And it loaded them down with responsibility. It impressed me. I think it probably brought out something in people like myself. It made a responsibility surface that might not have otherwise surfaced. . . ."

Employees who remember this period also have emphasized that, as Ray Hunt put it, "you'd come in in the morning and there was no telling what you'd be doing by the afternoon. If Mr. Hunt had a new idea he might call you in and tell you to do something where you had no experience at all. He'd say, 'Go learn how to do it.' "[8] Regardless of what family feuds took place, during the late 1940s Hunt Oil was a place where any ambitious person, even if he *was* Hunt's son, could learn an enormous amount about the oil business in a relatively short period.

Each of the sons and sons-in-law made investment decisions on his own and began to pursue his own projects, but there was a tremendous amount of interaction between projects and employees. Consequently, the Hunt family members often found themselves working together. According to recollections in the company history, "Hunt personnel many times are unsure of which of those hundred or so accounts [Hunt Oil Company maintained] paid for which well, or which Hunt company found which field, or even which Hunt company payroll they were on in specific years. A person who joined the organization as a Hunt Oil Company employee might have ended up on the H. L. Hunt payroll or the Placid payroll or the Panola payroll."

Because of the way the company was structured at this time, Bunker and Herbert had a number of opportunities to work together. These shared activities, shared experiences, during their early years in the family business, were to give the two men a common perspective that was to have a profound impact on the family fortunes.[9]

Although all of the Hunt properties were mixed together from an accounting point of view, one person could spearhead a given project, and it would remain more or less his. The first big success for Bunker was in 1948, when at age twenty-two, he was responsible for bringing in a strike in a new area; it eventually proved to have reserves in the $7-million range.

Part of the opportunity for Bunker and Herbert to develop their own projects stemmed from the fact that, beginning around 1948, before Herbert joined the company, their father was beginning to withdraw from the day-to-day operations of Hunt Oil and to become involved in public affairs. As the anniversary history put it, "Hunt's interest in the oil industry was somewhat diverted. Younger members of the Hunt family were entering the business, and the senior Hunt had confidence in their abilities to 'take hold' and the abilities of his experts who continued to lead Hunt Oil as it changed and grew in the field and the headquarters office." It was during this time that Hunt first conceived of the educational farms he wanted to set up, that he made major new investments in non oil-producing land (for example, buying the 250,000-acre Hoodoo Ranch, near Cody, Wyoming), that he set up *Facts Forum* and campaigned for passage of the twenty-second amendment.

While getting established in the family business, Bunker and Herbert also fulfilled social expectations by getting married, Bunker in 1950 and Herbert in 1951. Both married women who had graduated from Hollins College, another old established Virginia women's college. Bunker and his wife, Caroline Lewis, had two daughters in the first few years of their marriage, followed by a son and another daughter later. Herbert and his wife, Nancy Jane Broaddus, had two daughters and three sons over the next dozen years.

The youngest of Hunt's sons with Lyda was also entering young adulthood during this period. Lamar, six years younger than Bunker and three years younger than Herbert, had not gone away to college, as had his two older brothers. Instead, he had attended Southern Methodist University, which was about a fifteen-minute drive from his parents' home.

SMU was a large university situated in sylvan splendor in the middle of Dallas's two most prestigious residential communities, the "Park Cities," Highland Park and University Park. These cities, which were incorporated independent of Dallas but surrounded by the larger city, were filled with beautiful homes on large lots, blessed with an excellent public-school system, and largely inhabited by Dallas's socially prominent families or families with enough money to aspire to prominence. Academically solid, SMU was known as a school that accepted the kind of young men and women who might have grown up in the Park Cities and whose parents were in a position to contribute to the school's endowment, although the students themselves were not in a position to get into Harvard.

Perhaps Lamar was attracted, at least in part, to SMU because of its football team—one of the university's proudest achievements. When he was six, his older brother Bunker had taken him to his first Cotton Bowl game.[10] Reportedly, Lamar fell in love with football that day and never lost interest. In fact, a 1982 newspaper interview reported that Lamar attended the next forty-three Cotton Bowl games after his first, and, at age fifty, was still going strong.

Football was not the only game in which Lamar was interested as a child. His family nicknamed him "Games" because he was always inventing games and trying to engage the older children in playing them with him. His interest in games and sports went beyond the simple playing, too. Apparently, some of his father's mathematical gifts were passed on to Lamar, in a slightly altered form. As a teenager, he was "a serious student of box scores and probably the only person, other than a team's owner, who memorized the attendance figures." No statistics were too mundane: in college, Lamar kept stats of his fraternity brothers' answers to a Dallas newspaper column called "Test your horse sense."

At SMU, Lamar played football. However, in a world of players that included future professionals such as Don McIlhenney, Lamar, playing third-string end, never attained greatness. By this time, his father had become well known as "the richest man," and Lamar did earn a nickname during his football days: "Poor Boy."

Lamar's ability to fit in to a demanding SMU football environment and to get along with his fraternity brothers stemmed from his easygoing and likable personality. He had a dry sense of humor and an enjoyment of mild practical jokes, such as throwing surprise parties, that showed a rather endearing side. He graduated from SMU with a degree in geology in 1954 and got married the same year. He, too, became somewhat involved in the oil business, though less deeply than his older brothers.

By that time, H. L. Hunt was either more comfortable with geologists or far enough from his company's day-to-day operations no longer to oppose hiring them. About a year before Lamar's graduation, Hunt Oil had created a Geophysical Department and moved into scientific oil exploration once and for all. It was not a completely convincing transition in some ways. One of the newly hired geologists recalled that some of the older employees referred to the members of his department as the "geophysicians" and thought they could have done just fine without "these educated folks."[11]

By the mid-1950s Hunt Oil Company, overall, was in excellent shape. Not only was the company ending a period of dramatic growth, but it also appeared well positioned for the future. Like his business, Hunt's children with Lyda were also growing and well fixed. The sons and sons-in-law were in the business, the daughters were happily married, and the grandchildren were arriving with regularity.

The great pain of Hassie's illness had not gone away, but Hunt remained optimistic that a "cure" would be found sooner or later.[12] During the ten years since Hassie's breakdown, he had investigated a number of solutions to Hassie's problems that had initially seemed promising. Although none of these had provided a final answer, there were always new ideas coming along. Hunt had placed Hassie in a number of different hospitals and residences during the course of his illness. He had also authorized a treatment for Hassie that seemed at the time like an excellent solution to the violent moodiness and unhappiness that plague schizophrenics: in the late 1940s, Hassie had undergone a prefrontal lobotomy.

Despite appearances, there were still underlying and hidden conflicts in the rest of the family too, many of which could be traced back to Hunt's own choices. During this period, when the children of his original marriage were maturing, marrying, going to work, Hunt was beginning the relationship with Ruth Ray that was ultimately to produce four children and another Hunt marriage.

As Hunt entered into this, the third major relationship in his life, the fact that he did not consider it unreasonable to have more than one family at a time was already known to his oldest daughter, Margaret, and to his wife, Lyda. Both of these women had met Frania Tye and knew exactly what role she played in Hunt's life. Although neither Margaret nor Lyda ever discussed what they knew—the fact that they knew about Frania had been revealed by Frania herself—it seems likely that as Hunt began his relationship with Ruth, Margaret might well have had some idea about what was taking place, and Lyda's knowledge was almost certain.

In contrast, the other members of the family—ranging from Caroline through the three younger boys, who were, at the time, involved in working out their own identities and futures—reportedly did not know about either Frania's family or Ruth's during the 1940s and early 1950s. Harry Hurt, the biographer who has looked most exhaustively at Hunt's life, said that in 1954, when Lamar was getting married, he asked a family confidant if his father had a second family, in Oak Cliff, another part of Dallas. He was assured, quite truthfully, that Hunt did not; the fact was that Hunt had a second family in Atlanta and a third family in a part of Dallas miles from Oak Cliff. Supposedly the three boys found out for certain about Hunt's other families only when Herbert discovered some information about the Reliance Trusts, which had been set up for Frania's children; when he asked his father directly about these trusts, his father told him the truth.[13]

Hunt's relationship with Ruth Ray had begun in 1942. During the otherwise halcyon days when Bunker was arguing with geology teachers, Herbert was attending prep school, and Lamar was compiling attendance figures for local ball games, Hunt was again often away from home, spending time with his other family. However, since Ruth moved to Dallas less than two years after she and Hunt began their relationship—Hunt bought a house for her near Mt. Vernon in 1943—his time away from home must have been structured much differently than when he visited Frania Tye, who always lived at least 100 miles from Hunt's other family. All of Ruth's children recalled that they usually spent major holidays with their mother's family in Oklahoma, rather than at home in Dallas, so perhaps Hunt chose to put in his appearance at home with Lyda, while Ruth—who, unlike Frania, was well aware of his marriage to Lyda—made her own plans.

During the time her own children were growing up and leaving home, and while her husband was becoming increasingly involved both with another woman and with new political and societal interests, Lyda continued to live in Mt. Vernon and to lead a life suitable for Mrs. H. L. Hunt. Although she did not become as active in volunteer organizations as she had in Tyler, she did join a number of clubs and took an active role in her church.

As her children married, she continued to be a part of their lives, but in the nondirective and tolerant style that had characterized her mothering of them when they were young. "I always felt my mother's love and support," Caroline said, about this time. "If you were sick, she appeared with boiled custard. . . . She'd show up. Other than that, she stayed out of our lives. She never told me how to run my house."[14]

But there was another side to Lyda's staying out of their lives, a kind of isolation that she seemed to develop for herself. "If I wanted her to keep the children, she would," Caroline explained, "but she didn't let anyone impose on her—at least, I was taught not to try to impose on her." As a result of this distance from her children and her husband's continuing frequent absences, she was alone most of the time—"though she didn't mind," Caroline observed. "A man who worked at the house said, 'Mrs. Hunt, you're alone here so much.' And she said, 'Oh, don't worry about that.' She was a person who kept to herself."

Yet even in the late 1940s and early 1950s, as she moved into middle age and beyond, Lyda still seemed to care about Hunt, to take his companionship when it was available. "Up to the end," Caroline says, "she'd make two reservations. She liked to travel, so she'd always make two reservations and hope that he'd go with her." But the reality did not change. "And then usually," Caroline concluded, "she took a lady friend."

By 1955, Caroline believes, when Lyda was sixty-six, she was ready to give up. It was that year that Lyda suffered an unexpected stroke and died shortly thereafter. "I never grieved about [my mother's early death]," Caroline explained twenty years later. "My mother emotionally was ready to die. Certainly I grieved, but I really felt that God was answering her prayers. It had only been a few months prior to that that she was at my house. She took medicine to keep her blood pressure down. She said, 'Oh, I can always tell when my blood pressure's down because I feel terrible. I don't have any energy.' Of course she was a very energetic person. And she made the comment, 'It's hard to get into this world and it's hard to get out.' So I felt that she was ready to die."

Lyda's stroke had occurred on Monday, May 2, 1955. Hunt had her rushed to the Mayo Clinic, in Rochester, Minnesota, where he believed she would have a better chance of receiving life-continuing medical care. However, according to Caroline, the doctors caring for Lyda decided to do an angiogram to determine the cause and effect of her initial stroke, and this test provoked a final stroke. On Friday, May 6, Lyda died.

With Lyda's death, another era ended, for Lyda's children and for their father. The loving and nurturing mother who had, in Caroline's words, "made the best of what she had," who "chose her bed and lay in it," was no longer present to hold the family together, to maintain the illusion of a close-knit family centered in the Mt. Vernon estate. The children were already going their own ways in some respects, marrying, raising their own children. And yet a certain desire to remain united persisted: all of the children lived in Dallas, all were involved in the family business.

But now the person who had pulled it all together was no longer around to do so. The reality of H. L. Hunt's other lives, other relationships, as well as the reality for each of the children of the effects this behavior had had on them would now emerge and, in some respects, come to dominate what was happening in their individual lives.

ELEVEN

WHILE the children of H. L.'s marriage to Lyda Bunker Hunt were growing, maturing, and finding their way into adulthood, Hunt himself had continued his quest to find his own version of the good life. There were two largely hidden but nonetheless painful issues whose impact Hunt may have hoped to lessen: his final break with Frania Tye, and Hassie's increasingly undeniable problems in functioning in the normal world. But more motivating may have been the vision he still held of what his *own* life could be, a vision that went beyond what would already have satisfied most men: running a successful business, fathering five grown children who were doing what their parents and society expected of them, and maintaining a marriage to a long-faithful though now clearly middle-aged woman. Hunt's vision and its fulfillment would create the world into which his last four children would be born and in which they would find their own ways of dealing with the legacies Hunt would bequeath to them.

In 1942, when Hunt was fifty-three years old, the essence of his quest for fulfillment lay in establishing another romantic liaison and beginning another family. Behind these actions, one of his children suggested in her own adulthood, was "an imagination that was too big"—an ability to visualize a situation in which H. L. Hunt could successfully love, not one, but two women, successfully father, not four or five children, but nine or ten. From Hunt's point of view, he had, in fact, done this very thing over the last fifteen years, during the time he maintained a household with Frania Tye as well as one with Lyda Bunker Hunt. Now he would simply do it again. The possibility that having more than one family might create problems or pain for the members of those families seems not to have occurred to Hunt, who, another daughter once said, had, at least some of the time, "a total self-absorption." If he could conceive of such a utopian life for himself, then, he seemed to believe, it could, and perhaps even should, also be perceived as such by the others involved.

And so Hunt came to meet, court, and—eventually—marry the sweet and loving girl from Oklahoma, Ruth Ray. When he met Ruth, he was already a very successful oilman, an established and respected man. Ruth was a young woman of twenty-five. According to the recollection of one of her daughters, 1942 was a difficult time in Ruth's life.[1] She had left college after one year and gone to work; not only was she supporting herself by this time, but she was also taking care of her sister, who had TB. Although she was living with her sister, she was otherwise alone in what was, relative to the town she'd grown up in, the big city of Shreveport, Louisiana.

Hunt was not only a successful man, but also an imposing person. An employee of Hunt Oil who went to work for Hunt around the time he met Ruth described him as "a large, tall man; he stood over six feet tall . . . his hair was solid white, and he had a habit . . . of running his hand through his hair. Instead of smoothing it down after doing that, he would leave it almost standing straight up. . . . He never walked very fast. He impressed me even then as a man who was always thinking." A few years later, a Dallas writer added to the picture of Hunt, describing him as a dramatic-looking, impressive man with blue-green eyes in a "full, ruddy, sensitive-looking face."[2]

Although Hunt was an important man in the world Ruth Ray entered, and though he was certainly physically imposing, he also maintained a certain humanity that undoubtedly made him appealing. According to his daughter Helen, in many respects Hunt never saw himself as set apart, as special or different, but, rather, as "connected to the flow of humanity."[3] Especially during the 1940s, before his sons and sons-in-law assumed day-to-day responsibility for the operations of Hunt Oil, Hunt was deeply involved in most aspects of the company and was well known and loyally supported by most of his employees. Possibly this connectedness attracted Ruth as much as did Hunt's power and strength.

There was one other, important, side to the man Ruth Ray came to love. Hunt was a sentimental person, even romantic. The romantic letters he had written to Frania Tye during the 1930s, his later love of romantic operas, even an affection he had for a flowery eighteenth-century painting at home entitled "The Engagement"— there was always this side to Hunt, too, another aspect of the fun-loving, lively, singing father that Caroline remembered from an earlier era.[4]

Hunt and Ruth Ray fell in love. The couple had their first child in April 1942, a son whom they named Ray Lee after his grandfather, Walter Lee Ray. A year and a half later, after Ruth had moved to Dallas into the house Hunt bought for her near his own home, their second child was born. This child, a daughter, was given both her parents' names: Ruth, her mother's name, and June, her father's childhood nickname.

Sometime over the next few years, the couple lost a third child, but then, in 1949, they had a second daughter, Helen LaKelley, and finally, in 1950, a third daughter, their last child, whom they named Swanee, after one of Ruth's siblings. These two girls, who were only fifteen months apart, were dubbed "the babies" by the rest of the family and were frequently paired, though as children they had quite different temperaments.[5]

The person who retains the most vivid memories of the growing-up years in the mid-1940s and early 1950s is June Hunt. She recalls times that were both happy and sad. Many of her happy memories— and, in fact, those of the other three children—revolve around the frequent trips Ruth and the children made to Ruth's hometown, where they would visit their grandmother and her family. "It wasn't just Christmas and Thanksgiving and summer," June recalled. "It was every Mother's Day, every Valentine's if it hit on a weekend— any excuse would do."

Grandmother's house was still in Idabel, Oklahoma. Ruth's family had moved there several years before the Oklahoma land run of 1889, when Oklahoma was still Indian Territory. Her father, Walter, established a real-estate and insurance agency in the town, which was the county seat and a commercial center for the area's farmers, lumbermen, and businesses.

Before his death from tuberculosis, at age forty-three, Walter had been active in Idabel in civic areas, serving as county clerk, in his church, in the Masonic Lodge, and as a Boy Scout leader. He and his wife, Grace Sims, whom he had met when both were students, had six children, of whom Ruth was the youngest.

During Walter's lifetime, the family had been comfortable, though never rich. According to Hunt's description, to which he devoted the better part of a chapter in one of his autobiographies, the family lived in "a large, comfortable house, situated on a tract covering several acres near the edge of town. The place had a vegetable garden, an orchard, a vineyard, and beehives. There were milk cows, and there were two carriage horses and a surrey, which the hired man would drive to school for the children when it rained." These were what Hunt characterized, apparently quite accurately, as "the charming agrarian aspects of Southwestern townlife in the early days of the Twentieth Century."[6]

It was to this charming little town that Ruth frequently returned after she began her relationship with Hunt. Although her family was undoubtedly aware of the situation Ruth was in, they welcomed her return home. Ruth was, according to June, "like a precious porcelain flower and yet she was resourceful—she had a strength. No one would want to hurt her in any way." In some ways, it seems, Ruth continued to be the youngest child, the person who needed to be taken care of, even the person around whom the others rallied, just as they had a few years earlier when they pooled their resources and sent Ruth off for a year of college they could ill afford.

All of Ruth's children enjoyed the trips to Idabel. "Ray and I paired off with two boy cousins who were Ray's age and a couple of years older," June recalled when she discussed the frequent trips. "We were kind of a foursome. . . . We played football and baseball and Monopoly. Anything there was to play, there'd be the four of us. It was a positive—a very positive—experience in little Idabel, Oklahoma."

"The important thing was the soul of a gathering," Helen said about the family get-togethers. "We didn't go out on a yacht. We didn't have theater tickets. The important thing was just to talk and to be."

There was also the aspect of being involved with the other people in the community, which the children noticed when they went to Idabel. "At Thanksgiving, we'd take food over to the poor section of town," Swanee recalled. "There was a sort of rootedness in the country values that was very much part of my family—helping other people."

If there were idyllic aspects to the children's and Ruth's involvement in the life of Idabel and to their frequent trips there, there was also an element of escape in these trips. During the entire time the older children were growing up and for a significant part of the younger children's lives, their parents were not legally married; in Idabel, this situation was forgotten or put aside, and the children could simply be themselves. "We never—none of us—ever discussed our family situation, growing up," June said in a 1987 interview, "but we knew how to stick together. I think there was a bonding in the midst of the barrages that we had to face."

To a certain extent the children were protected when they were at home in Dallas by the fact that they attended a private school outside the neighborhood. There, they were known by the name Wright, which Ruth Ray had chosen when she told others that she had married in 1942. But later, after Ruth and Hunt married, the neighbors interviewed by enterprising reporters all said they were not surprised by the match, because the couple had been "seeing each other" for some time. It seems most likely that the couple's relationship was an open secret, and that the children all grew up with some awareness of this and of the neighbors' reactions to their situation.

As Ruth and Hunt's children grew up, they also had to come to grips with the complexity of Hunt's relationship to Ruth and to all of them. "I don't know what he was like [when he was younger]," June mused from her adult vantage point. "I've wondered myself. . . . Did he do typical father things when he was much younger? . . . I had to learn to accept him as living on another plane. He was just— different. . . . I couldn't expect him to play with us or to give us attention, to talk with us about what *we* would want to talk about. It just never occurred." Helen recalled that at the dinner table, "children were supposed to be real quiet and proper. . . . We didn't really talk about our activities so much."[7] Instead, Hunt would turn the radio to a political program, which the entire family then listened to. He'd follow the program with some comments of his own on politics or issues of social change.

Although Helen and June remember their father as being somewhat distant and focused on his own interests, Ray's memories are of warmer interactions. "We had a very unusual relationship," he recalled. "A lot of people were intimidated by Dad, but we just had a very close relationship." To a certain extent, their closeness was based on Ray's acceptance of and even admiration for his father's authority. "I thoroughly enjoyed listening to him and learning from him," he said.[8]

But there was also something else, almost an echo of the kind of relationship Hunt had had earlier with his first first-born son, Hassie. Hunt had always attributed to Hassie an almost mythical ability to find oil, an attribution that seemed to say that Hassie had inherited Hunt's own skills, point of view, even genius—that Hassie was his own true son, spiritually as well as biologically. When Ray talked about his relationship with his father, he described the same kind of unusual closeness. "I could go for months without seeing Dad," Ray said about the years after he graduated from college, "and walk in the room and it would be like plugging in a lamp—and vice versa. He could almost read my mind and I could almost read his."

Although Ray and his father were close, and the younger girls seemed to have a more distant but tolerable relationship with Hunt, June saw a dark cloud over her adolescence. She was deeply troubled by an inherent tension she saw in Hunt's relationship with Ruth.

There was a real basis for June's concern. In a 1987 radio program entitled "How to Live with a Difficult Mate," on which Ruth appeared (invited by June, who hosted the program), Ruth recalled times when she was so angry and hurt by Hunt that she could no longer cope.[9] Sometimes, she left him and went to her mother's house, the idyllic home in Idabel, taking the children with her. There, her own mother, whom she described as "wise and godly," would pray for her and encourage her to return to Hunt. "Mother had a way of helping me to realize that with God nothing is impossible," Ruth recalled, adding that in situations like that in which she found herself with Hunt, "there is no way we could do it alone and keep our sanity."

Some of the greatest conflicts between Hunt and Ruth seem to have taken place after the two were married, in 1957. Up to that time, each had maintained a separate household, and Ruth had raised the children according to her own beliefs. Despite her unconventional relationship with Hunt, Ruth was a deeply religious person, who believed in the teachings of the Bible and who raised her children accordingly. She was also very close to the children, all of whom, as adults, continue to describe her as "approaching sainthood." As long as Ruth and the children had their own household, they were more or less on their own, despite frequent visits by

Hunt. Once Ruth and Hunt married and moved to Mt. Vernon, the balance of power between the parents appears to have changed.

One thing Hunt did that Ruth and the children found extremely difficult was to adopt a "divide-and-conquer" strategy toward his family. For example, at one time he prohibited Ruth from going to tell the children good night. She was not allowed to tuck them in, kiss them, or listen to their prayers. He would go to June's room and say that she and the other children were not to be around Ruth. They were a "bad influence on her" and were not to be with her after dinner. Sometimes, June recalled, Ruth would "pop upstairs, as if going to the bathroom, and she'd race in and hug us and kiss us and she'd race out. It was almost a panic zone—not wanting to be caught."[10]

A continuing area of conflict for June was her knowledge of her father's relationships with women other than her mother. Hunt's two main biographers, among others, have reported that he did not confine himself to the relationships he had with the three women by whom he had children.[11] Rather, he also had affairs that were generally of short duration but that continued to be initiated until quite late in his life. In the 1980s, June talked about her father's infidelity, emphasizing the fact that this caused her mother great anguish and that she, June, believed it was her duty to protect her mother and take care of her in the face of what she saw as mistreatment by her father.[12]

One day not long after her parents were married, June challenged Hunt on his infidelity. "He did not see himself as having to go by the ethics of—anything," she recalled. "In fact, that is how he acted. In any area, I think, though he would not use this phrase, it was as though he was a god unto himself who could make his own rules. And the end justified the means." In this case, Hunt's specific response to June was to tell her, " 'I'm not a Christian. I do not have to go by Christian ethics.' That was it. And then I got severely punished."[13]

Apparently June's punishment was to be sent away from home— specifically, to Hockaday, as a boarder. Ruth disagreed with Hunt's decision, but said later that she thought opposing him directly would only make things worse. She did, however, develop an ulcer, and June had to come back home to help with the family.

Helen and Swanee, still less than ten years old, seem to have been spared knowledge of the intensity of Ruth's and Hunt's problems by their mother's protective behavior. Ray, meanwhile, was involved in his own activities outside the home, first at St. Mark's, then at SMU. But young, idealistic, and protective June decided that someone had to take a stand. "*I* was the one who was bitter and reacting," she recalled. It was almost as if she were taking responsibility for resolving all the conflicts in the family, whether they were her problem directly or not.

At one time, June was so torn by what she perceived that she carefully plotted a means of "doing away with" Hunt as a way of protecting her mother. "It sounds kind of ridiculous now but I was very serious," she recalled. "And I went to my mother and I asked if I could talk to her for a moment. And I said, 'Mother, I've figured out a way to kill Dad. I just want to know if it would be all right.' Instead of making fun of me or anything like that, she said to me with the greatest sensitivity, 'June, I understand what you're trying to do. That really won't be necessary.' "[14]

As soon as Ruth became Mrs. H. L. Hunt, several external changes also took place in the children's lives. First, the children all changed their name from Wright to Hunt. Second, they all began attending different schools. Whereas the children had gone to the private Greenhill Academy, a small school, opened in 1950, which extended from preschool through high school, they now began attending two much older and more prestigious schools in Dallas. Ray transferred to St. Mark's, a boys' school where many sons of the elite of Dallas could be found preparing for college; the girls began attending Hockaday, which had remained, since before the time their half-sister Caroline had gone there, the most outstanding girls' school in Dallas. It was at this time that June was briefly "sent away" to board.

Ray, who was fourteen when his parents married, does not appear to have suffered from these changes. He took on St. Mark's energetically. He was editor of the newspaper, on the yearbook staff, president of the band, and played football and ran track. In his senior year, Ray was elected class president—not because he was the most popular, but because he could get the most done.[15]

The source of Ray's energy and competence may have been the experiences he was having outside school. Two summers before, he had begun to spend time with people in Hunt Oil, "just sort of hang[ing] around." He started in the map room, helping to color in the various lease maps the company used to monitor land position; each company was given a different color, and the map was then used to follow leasing commitments. "I worked each summer following the eighth grade, doing a variety of different things," Ray reported in the Hunt Oil history. "Initially I was assigned to the accounting department and then to either the Land Department or the Geological or Engineering departments." Ray emphasized that his summer jobs were something he wanted to do, and that his father never forced him or any others in the family to become involved with the business. But the pride both he and his father apparently took in his involvement may have made the transition to life at Mt. Vernon much easier for him.[16]

June, on the other hand, did not make adjustments so quickly. When Ruth and Hunt married, June was almost thirteen. The strong personality and character she has today undoubtedly were already there in the emerging woman. Whereas in adulthood June could soften her strength through her social skills, at thirteen she was not yet able to draw on these. She remembers that she was not particularly popular with her peers; though she wanted to be, she couldn't quite figure out how to go about gaining popularity. In school, she said, she was shy and didn't have any really close friends. She may have been uncomfortable in school because of whatever "barrages" she and Ray had weathered together; other people undoubtedly were aware of the unconventional relationship of June's parents, and this may have created problems for her.

June also appears to have had a more black-and-white view of the world, and of how things should be, when she was a young teen-ager than she would develop later. She was very analytical, "loved math and hated English." Because of her youth and inexperience, she may well have been less attuned to the emotional complexities and subtleties of relationships, such as that of her parents and that of herself to her father, than she needed to be to get along easily with Hunt.

Then there was Hunt himself. June described him during this time as domineering, "a dictator. What he said went. It was almost impossible for him to ever change any course of action and his word was law and it wasn't ever a point of negotiation." This was, apparently, exactly the kind of attitude the adolescent June found extremely difficult to deal with.

Furthermore, June, who was shy and considered herself unpopular, found no personal support from Hunt as she faced the trials of adolescence. "He had a way of making you feel very small—about yourself and all . . . it was hard to keep your self-image intact."

The specific incidents that June recalls about her conflicts with her father range from embarrassing to profoundly painful. For example, in a newspaper interview in 1985, she recalled a series of humiliations that arose concerning her singing.[17] As often happened between them, Hunt began by making demands of June; June countered by trying to outsmart or outmaneuver Hunt. "All through my teen-age years," she said, "Dad would have me sing. Oh, I was in such an awkward stage. There was no way I could have sounded melodious. He had me sing in front of company, and it seemed we always had company." Most of these calls to perform were made after dinner, so June countered by leaving the dining room immediately after the meal was over and going to her room. "When he called, I wouldn't answer," she continued. "But he outfoxed me. He started calling on me in the middle of dinner. I would have just taken a bite of mashed potatoes. I would stammer—put on this delay tactic, and he'd yell out, 'Sing, sing something.' . . . While I was singing, he would actually yell out, 'Put some sweeping arm action into it,' and I would feel my face flush."

Although to an outsider the scene has its amusing aspects, at the time it had a powerful effect on June. In recalling these events twenty-five years later, June, according to the reporter interviewing her, cringed and even blushed.

The younger children, Helen and Swanee, were also called on to perform. Helen remembers being asked to sing for guests, just as June was. The two younger girls were also commandeered for a public appearance when Hunt published his book *Alpaca* in 1960. While he waited to autograph copies of the book at Cokesbury's, the major Dallas bookstore at the time, Helen and Swanee drew a crowd by singing Hunt's own version of "Doggy in the Window," which began "How much is that book in the window?" (It was priced to sell at fifty cents a copy.)[18] Helen and Swanee apparently lacked the kind of painful self-consciousness June felt when she was asked to sing, even at home; they escaped, therefore, some of the conflicts their older sister felt so keenly.

For June, the problems of living with Hunt and following his parental guidance extended beyond what happened at home. One set of problems had to do with her new school. Although she felt she received a good education at Hockaday, most of her specific memories of her time there have to do with being an outsider, with different views from many of the other students, of not getting the honors she badly wanted, of being left out of activities in which she wanted to participate.

Hunt had insisted that June attend Hockaday, but he did nothing to help her fit in. In fact, she felt that his attitudes simply made things harder for her. "He did not care what people thought," she recalled. "He wasn't into image . . . he could just steamroll a person and not be sensitive to where they were in their lives." There was, for example, Hunt's car. "He had Gastro-Magic [a patent medicine marketed by Hunt's food company] stickers all over his car. It was a pink-and-white car . . . with orange fluorescent stickers. It's just hard as a teen-ager to be picked up in something that looks like a circus car every day."

At school, as at home, the experience of the younger girls was somewhat different. Swanee found her experience at Hockaday a real asset. "I went there for ten years," she remembered. "There was a real mix [of people]. You had your conservative oil people and you had your successful Jewish retailers and developers, who were much more liberal. It was wonderful. The world was bigger than this small compartment. And in that world, I was continually coming across conflicting philosophies and basically being taught how to think."

In addition to Hunt's relationship with Ruth and his apparent insensitivity to some of his children's more subtle emotional needs, there was one final aspect to the family's life together during the time immediately following the marriage that necessitated a certain amount of adjustment on the part of all four children. In several situations, Hunt—or Ruth on behalf of Hunt—put other things before the needs of the children. For Hunt himself, the children were sometimes simply used to further his interest in politics, an interest that approached obsessive levels at times. "In later years, my father became a philanthropist in his own way," Helen observed. "He wanted to find a way to preserve the specialness of the country, its freedoms, how to protect these. He put his money, his time, even his children into doing that." Thus there was "Book in the Window," listening to patriotic radio programs during dinner, and demands that the children participate in patriotic youth programs and make public appearances, whether these activities were what the children wanted for themselves or not.

The other important area in which the children's needs became secondary to other considerations had to do with the well-being of their half-brother Hassie. Shortly after Ruth and Hunt married, Ruth suggested to Hunt that Hassie return home from the psychiatric institution where he was then living and rejoin the family. "Mom knew how much Dad loved him and she thought if there's any way that a home environment could help him, then we could all try, we could do our best," June said. "It was quite sacrificial, if you think about it. How many mothers would be willing to subject their children to someone with—it's not just that he was incapacitated in certain areas, but—he could get very *upset*." June recalled how the children had to be careful how they walked, and where, and at what speed to avoid upsetting their half-brother. Hassie himself would walk along the sides of rooms, inching his way along and only slowly getting settled at the dinner table or in an armchair.

Although none of the children report in retrospect that Hassie was frightening to them—in Swanee's words, "We got used to him"—his presence might certainly have given them second thoughts about bringing friends home from school or planning meetings or activities at home. On the other hand, Swanee felt, as an adult, that the time Hassie spent with the family when she was young had given her a great deal of empathy for people with mental illness or with other problems that affected their ability to interact with others and get along in the world. Regardless of how the children dealt with Hassie, then or later, he was a real presence while they were growing up and a constant reminder of Hunt's previous life and other family.

About three years after Hunt and Ruth were married, another change took place in the family. This was to prove a more positive change and was to have a major effect on Ruth and her three daughters in particular. As part of his interest in "saving the Republic USA," Hunt decided that the family should join a different church.[19] The denomination to which Ruth belonged had been found, by some extensive survey that Hunt ran across, to be somewhat socialistic, or, in the jargon of the era, "pink," in its beliefs. The church Hunt wanted to join was a Baptist church; the survey had shown Baptists to be the most conservative politically. In particular,

Hunt was interested in the First Baptist Church, in downtown Dallas, a church headed by a man whose conservative Christian beliefs, as well as his charisma in the pulpit, were known throughout the South.

June recalled that she, in the midst of her adolescent crises, was very reluctant to "visit" the Baptist church, because she had grown up thinking of Baptists as "holy rollers." As usual, however, it was June against her father, and her father won out; she was given no choice about her attendance. "Of course," she said, "it wasn't anything like what I expected. The music was magnificent; it was like the Mormon Tabernacle Choir. It was beautiful. It was majestic. And the Bible study during the Sunday School was unlike anything I had experienced. Everyone had their own Bibles, and they'd really teach you right from there. It wasn't 'Be a good citizen.' It wasn't 'We need to appreciate the world and the trees.' It was real teachings. It was so substantive: How does this apply to your life?"

Hunt, too, liked the church, and the family began attending it regularly. It had a particularly profound and immediate effect on June, the lonely, unpopular, and angry young woman, whose life was so different from that of the other girls at Hockaday. At First Baptist, she recalled, she began to see that some of the people her age whom she met there had something special about them that she wanted to share. They seemed to have purpose and integrity in their lives, to hold deeper values. "The interest wasn't in fashion," she recalled. "They wanted to know God in a deeper way. They wanted to memorize the scriptures that would give them the right focus."

Although these teen-agers had a spiritual aspect to their lives, June added, they were not detached from school or normal adolescent achievements. "In fact, many of them were the leaders. They were senate members of their own student councils, for example, and they could be very sharp. You had a mixed bag . . . but it was an entirely different atmosphere."

June looked at these people and decided that what differentiated them was that they had committed their lives to God. "I decided that God knew more about me than I knew," June said, "and He knew what I could be, what I should be, and instead of me dictating my life, I just relinquished control, as best I knew how, and I gave my life to Him, asking Christ to take control of my life. . . . He can enable you to think with a different perspective. And I needed a different perspective because I was just caught up in how wrong, wrong, wrong my father was. I saw my father at that time as the archenemy. I didn't see him as the person with needs, with great needs. I just saw the pain that he inflicted. And I will have to admit my perspective did change dramatically."

Suddenly June had found a way of handling her head-to-head conflicts with her father. At the same time, she became part of a group of young people whose values she respected and who accepted her as she was. It was a powerful experience for her, and one that influenced both her career choices and the way she chose to live her life for many years.

June's embracing of the way of living and learning taught by First Baptist was reinforced by the fact that her mother also became deeply involved with the church and its teachings. June believed that the change in Ruth's life to a more spiritual approach helped her develop a different attitude toward Hunt. Rather than focusing on how he treated her or the children, June said, "she was more concerned about his salvation—about once this life is over, where will he be? So her emphasis was on his need for a personal relationship with God. Her focus was on his need, not on what he inflicted upon her." Ruth's changed focus, her new-found ability to handle Hunt, seems to have helped June feel less responsible for having to protect her mother and more able to look at her own development.

During the time the family was becoming involved in First Baptist, or perhaps as a result of their involvement, life for Ruth and her four children became less stressful, more fulfilling. By this time, Hunt was in his early seventies and, in Swanee's words, "mellowed—sort of with the rough edges smoothed." Even June believed that her father had changed. She attributed this softening to "a steady stream of unconditional love," which Ruth administered. "I think more and more he became dependent on Mother for the strength he needed."

Although there were still to be ups and downs—for instance, each child planned to go away to college, but Hunt insisted that they stay in Dallas and attend SMU—the family was finding its own center, its own pace. But, not surprisingly, even as Ruth and Hunt made peace with one another, even as the children settled down, the rest of Hunt's family in Dallas had their own reactions to these developments and their own feelings about Ruth's role in their relationships with their father. As Hunt's first set of sons and daughters moved out of early adulthood into their maturity, each of them was forced to come to grips with personal and career issues that interacted, sometimes with pain and conflict, with those of Hunt and his family by his second wife.

Below: H. L. Hunt at twenty-two. (*Courtesy the Hunt Family Archives.*)

Inset: A Texas oil field in the 1920s, at the time Hunt entered the oil business. The crews lived in the small houses shown in the foreground. (*Courtesy the Daughters of the Republic of Texas.*)

The photo that put Hunt in
the public eye: *Life*
magazine, 1948. (*Courtesy
the Hunt Family Archives.*)

H. L. Hunt (left) and son
Hassie (second from right)
with two Hunt Oil
employees, the 1940s.
(*Courtesy the Hunt Family
Archives.*)

Hunt in front of Mount Vernon, ca. 1966. (*AP/Wide World, Inc.*)

Inset: Lyda Bunker Hunt in the 1950s. (*Courtesy Caroline Hunt.*)

Right: H. L. Hunt and Ruth Ray Hunt feeding the pet deer at Mount Vernon. (*Courtesy the Hunt Family Archives.*)

At the publication of *Alpaca*. From the right: Swanee, Helen, Ruth, Hunt, Lamar, and a Hunt Oil employee. (*Courtesy the Hunt Family Archives.*)

Helen Hunt in New York City, 1988. (*Photo copyright © J. Boisseau. Courtesy Helen Hunt.*)

Swanee Hunt visiting a Hunt Alternatives–supported project, 1988. (*Photo by Larry Laszlo, CoMedia. Courtesy Swanee Hunt.*)

Troubled legacy: Herbert,
Nelson, and Lamar talk to
reporters during a recess in
their 1975 federal
wiretapping trial. *Below:*
Less than three years later,
the family was back in the
news—and in trouble—
when Frania Tye Lee
(accompanied by son Hugh)
filed a suit in which she
claimed to be the late H. L.
Hunt's wife by bigamous
union. (*Both photos AP/Wide
World, Inc.*)

Caroline Hunt with her pumpkin cookbook, the 1980s. (*Courtesy Caroline Hunt.*)

As Ray's Reunion project had done in the 1970s, Caroline's Crescent Court redefined the boundaries of downtown Dallas in the 1980s. (*Courtesy Rosewood Properties, Inc.*)

Fiddling while Rome burns: Despite the economic problems some of the Hunt children faced, they continued to lead active lives in Dallas society. *Above:* Margaret and her husband, Al Hill, at a Dallas event, 1987. (*Photo by Joe Laird. Reprinted by permission of the* Dallas Morning News.) *Below:* Bunker and Herbert and their wives at a display of their collection of ancient treasures, 1984. (*Photo copyright © Shelly Katz/Black Star.*)

June, the evangelist, at work, 1988. (*Courtesy June Hunt*.)

Two generations of Hunts: Ray in his offices, 1986, before a portrait of his father. (*Photo copyright © C. Thatcher*.)

TWELVE

H. L. HUNT had gradually withdrawn from the day-to-day management of his oil company during the late 1940s and early 1950s. It was a period when the oil industry itself was undergoing some important and far-reaching changes. Whereas the earliest oil wells had been little more than shallow scratchings in areas where oil was already seeping to the surface, and the wells of the teens, twenties, and thirties were usually drilled to modest depths of 3,500 feet or less, this began to change as geologists found new ways of determining where oil could be found.[1]

First, as the science of petroleum geology became more sophisticated, scientists began to identify oil reserves at much deeper levels underground than before. On the basis of geological knowledge, rather than on drilling a few thousand feet, oil explorers began sinking wells up to 10,000, then 20,000, and eventually even 35,000 feet—wells that required substantial technological advances to develop. Second, during this time geologists also determined that there were major oil reserves under parts of the ocean. Even the challenge of deep drilling on land paled against the emerging perspective provided by the consequent development of offshore drilling.

Not surprisingly, as oil exploration moved heavily into these new and difficult areas, the cost of bringing in new wells increased steadily. Many oil explorers—whether major oil companies, independents, or wildcatters—changed the focus of their searches. A field that promised a total output of a few hundred thousand barrels of oil might barely manage to pay back the tremendous expense of finding the area, deep drilling or offshore drilling the wells, and setting up the infrastructure to move the oil from the area, particularly if it was in the middle of the Gulf of Mexico, to refineries and markets.

But a field that would ultimately yield 100 million barrels of oil was another matter altogether. This was a "giant" or an "elephant" field—a huge lumbering creature that could be subdued and domesticated to the enormous profit of the exploring company or individual.

By the middle 1950s, after a decade in the oil business, Hunt's son Bunker began looking around for an "elephant" that he could claim for his own. He had had his successes in bringing in more modest fields. But for the sake of Hunt Oil's future, as well as for his own satisfaction, it was time to look for a bigger find. In 1955, the same year his mother died and left her children to deal with the largely unacknowledged existence of their father's other household, Bunker took definitive action. He began his elephant hunt by hiring a geologist and charging him with finding the most likely major undiscovered oil-field sites in the world.[2]

Bunker's geologist conducted his investigation strictly from a scientific point of view, without considering politics or business-investment implications. He identified three areas where he believed huge fields could be found: Pakistan, the Middle East, and certain parts of Africa. Bunker chose to begin his explorations in Pakistan, simply because it was the first of these areas that became available for new exploration. The Pakistani government was eager to cooperate and even offered to share development costs.

Bunker began drilling there in 1955. When he came up with one dry hole, he drilled another, and another still. This willingness to keep going was a characteristic Bunker shared with his father, and with some other successful (and unsuccessful) independent oil men; the next well, or even the next ten feet of the same well, could always bring a strike. And if that strike was the first well in a field with almost inconceivably vast reserves, any number of dry holes would be only a minor expense in comparison. Unfortunately, Bunker found no oil at all in Pakistan, and although no one agrees on exactly how much Bunker ended up losing before he bailed out—perhaps he never really knew himself—estimates begin at $11 million and range as high as over $30 million, a large sum by any standards.

Around this time, drilling concessions were becoming available in

Libya, and Bunker was able to win two of these in competition with major oil companies, including Esso and Mobil. It was now 1961. Not only was Bunker still under the self-imposed directive to find a mammoth oil field, but he may also have been motivated by some dramatic moves his younger brother Lamar was making into the business world, and by the fact that his half-brother Ray was poised to come in and make his mark on Hunt Oil as well.

Bunker wisely began his Libyan drilling in the tract that was located in an accessible area of the country, on the coast, which would, consequently, be less expensive to develop. There he found oil, but not enough for a commercially viable well. He then decided to explore the second area, an isolated inland tract that was much more difficult to reach and more expensive to explore. By the time he was ready to take this step, however, he had completely run out of capital. He had drained his own trust fund, and it could be years before his holdings elsewhere would throw off enough cash to continue his exploration alone. Although Bunker had a certain amount of access to additional funds, through the loose structure of Hunt Oil, the amount of money he needed to continue exploration of his second site was large enough to require someone else to buy into his pursuit.

In order to raise the money he needed, Bunker first went outside the family business. He sold half his holdings to that traditional opponent of the independent oilman, a "major," in this case, British Petroleum, one of the big oil companies that independents were constantly competing against. Because the majors were publicly held corporations, often with enormous assets, and were run by teams of professional managers, their way of doing business was almost always at odds with that of the independents, who invested their own money and ran their own show. Although many independents over the years ended up selling their holdings to the majors or entering development projects with them, the truce was always an uneasy one, particularly when the independent was someone with strong ideas about what he wanted and how he should go about getting it.

Bunker and his unlikely partner drilled in the new area and produced two dry wells. A third well hit oil. Bunker and BP now had a strike, and Bunker had a commitment to his partner to invest whatever was necessary to make the well commercially viable, whether he had ready money or not. Obtaining commercial viability for this well was no small matter. The well was 320 miles inland, so there would be not only drilling costs, but also the cost of building hundreds of miles of pipelines to transport oil to the nearest port and of constructing loading facilities there. Bunker had to compromise his independence again, but this time it was within the family. He obtained a loan from his father.

Development began. Soon Bunker and BP both concluded that they had made a wise decision. Reserves at the new site were estimated at 8 to 10 billion barrels of oil; fifty percent of these reserves, Bunker's share, would sell for $6 to $8 billion at oil prices current at the time of the find. Whereas for BP the money was potential corporate earnings, for Bunker it would almost all be money in his own pocket. Now, of course, the extremely high risks he had taken in Pakistan and in Libya, and the compromises he was forced to make by bringing BP in on his field and by borrowing money from his father, looked rational and sensible. Bunker had found his elephant, and it was a big one.

While Bunker had been conducting his problematic but ultimately highly successful explorations abroad, Lamar was involved in his own adventure at home. SMU football player and sports enthusiast Lamar had graduated from college, married, and become the father of two children by the time Bunker was determining that Pakistan was not going to make him rich. He had maintained his interest in sports after he finished school and joined Hunt Oil. With the cash generated by his holdings in Hunt Oil, he was in a position to continue that interest by buying a major league sports team. Football was Lamar's first love, and in 1957 he began trying to buy a franchise in the National Football League, at that time the only professional football league in the country.[3]

There was another wealthy young Texan trying, around the same time, to buy a team. This was Clint Murchison, Jr., a Dallasite about Lamar's age. Both men were advised by the NFL commissioner, Bert Bell, to try negotiating with the owners of the Chicago Cardinals; at that time, Chicago had two football teams, and the Wolfners, who owned the Cardinals, were courting people who might want either to add financial support to their team or to move the team to another city.

One day in 1959, after an unsuccessful visit to the Wolfners, as

Lamar later said, "It was like a light bulb came on in my head, like in a cartoon. It's the only time in my life I can remember that happening. I said, 'Hey, how about forming a new league?' I had the [financial] ability at a pretty young age, and I was naïve enough to think this idea might work. . . ."[4] In part, Lamar's idea may have originated in the Wolfners' announcement that *lots* of rich sports enthusiasts were looking at their team. If there were so many interested people, and if the NFL was reluctant, as it had been for several years, to add new teams, then a second league was not such a crazy idea after all. There had been two leagues in professional baseball for sixty years. Why not create a similar structure for football?

Although Lamar had the financing available to start a team, and even a league, and to lose money while he did so, he was relatively inexperienced in what he was later to call the "show business" of sports. A veteran sportswriter, quoted in *The Rich Who Own Sports*, described Lamar's first press conference. "We shuddered on his behalf," he said. "Here was this poor little rich boy, son of one of the world's richest men, standing up there like he was making a speech in catechism class. He spoke almost in a whisper, without any force or authority." The writer went on to say that it was like watching the first act of a Japanese kabuki play: "No matter what else happens, you know the last act's gonna be a beheading."

Part of what contributed to the sense of impending disaster was the fact that after Lamar announced his new league, in which he would be joined by seven other charter franchise holders, the NFL decided that they would expand their league after all. They granted two new franchises, one of which went to Clint Murchison, Jr. Their locations? Houston and Dallas.

Several weeks after the initial announcement of the expansion, the NFL approached Lamar. He was offered an opportunity to start the NFL team in Dallas in the next season, when Minneapolis would also be fielding a new team, and the year after that Houston would get their team. "Obviously, we [Lamar and the Houston franchise holder] were being asked to leave the American Football League in its present embryonic state in return for the NFL franchises we'd originally wanted," Lamar observed later. "We both agreed that we had made a commitment to the other fellows in the AFL and we felt we had to live up to our commitment."[5] Because he chose to stick to his plans, Lamar was now not only taking on the entire professional football establishment, but also starting up a team in a city where another team would be debuting as well.

For the next three years, from 1960 to 1962, as Bunker continued to drill dry holes in Pakistan and then began what was to be a massive investment in Libya, Lamar poured his money into football. In the beginning, despite a modest TV contract with ABC, all the AFL franchisees lost money: a total of $3.5 million in the first year. The situation was particularly acute in Dallas, where the Cowboys and the Texans were going head to head. The extent of Lamar's losses, like those of Bunker in Pakistan, is unknown. But a story began to circulate that implied that Lamar's personal red ink added up roughly to a million dollars a year.

According to this tale, which Lamar later maintained was purely apocryphal, someone asked H. L. Hunt what he thought about the fact that his son Lamar was losing a million dollars a year with his football team. "Well," Hunt supposedly sputtered, "at that rate he's going to go broke—in 250 years."[6]

In fact, Lamar was not unconcerned during these early days. According to a *Dallas Morning News* story, he did everything he could to make a go of his team and of the league, including scouting, recruiting players, and selling tickets.[7] When all these efforts continued to fail to generate a reasonable return, Lamar admitted defeat in Dallas and moved his team to Kansas City for the 1963 season. There the Dallas Texans became the Kansas City Chiefs.

Although the Chiefs continued to lose money for several years, by 1966 they were in the black, and remained there for most of the next twenty years. By that time, too, the AFL had become established, with the help of a more lucrative TV contract, with NBC, in 1964; the signing of a number of big-name, charismatic college athletes; and the financial shoring up of the most fragile teams.

By 1965, the NFL had started to take the AFL seriously. As the two leagues competed for players, often resorting to "body snatching" or hiding an athlete until they could convince him to take an offer that might include "honeymoons, convertibles, cattle and gas stations" as well as close to half a million dollars a year, individual team owners and the league managements began to feel that cooperation might be preferable to, and cheaper than, competition. The details of a merger were worked out, by Lamar and others, and in June 1966 the official amalgamation of the two leagues took place.[8]

Meanwhile, in Libya things were moving ahead for Bunker. But, just as Lamar had to wait a while to see a return on his football investment, Bunker did not find money pouring in right away. It was not until January 1967 that he began to receive any return on his investment. During the long wait, he became disenchanted with British Petroleum. He believed the field could be developed more quickly, that BP was taking its time in order to keep world oil supplies artificially scarce, thus raising profits from production in other fields. When the pipelines to transport the oil from the field to the coastal port were finally opened, Bunker felt that BP was under-using the facilities. Not unexpectedly, the wishes and desires of Bunker Hunt, entrepreneur, frequently differed from those of the huge corporate structure that made up British Petroleum.

After several years of this uneasy but highly profitable alliance, something occurred that led Bunker to overlook his differences with BP. In September 1969, power in Libya changed hands. Aging King Idris was deposed by a military junta led by radical young Colonel Muammar al-Qaddafi.[9]

Qaddafi's ambitions, once he had attained power, went well beyond controlling his small and underdeveloped country. He hoped to expand his leadership by acting as a unifier of the Arab Muslim nations, while also setting an example as a rebel against the economic oppression of the developed nations and their minions, the oil companies, doing business in the Mediterranean area. With these objectives, Qaddafi first ejected "foreign imperialists" from Libya, particularly those who held military bases. Successful at this, he next went after the oil companies.

He began pressuring foreign oil companies individually in June 1970 by proposing an increase in the taxes they paid to Libya, in the form of a percentage increase, and in the demand that they produce more oil on which taxes would be paid. His message was clear: if the companies did not comply, they would be closed down.

At first, there was a complete lack of unity on the part of the threatened oil producers, owing to the infighting that had long been underway between majors and independents. By January 1971, however, the producers, who had been under pressure to raise prices, pay more taxes, and turn over assets, not just in Libya, but in a number of OPEC nations, decided to cooperate with one another. A group of major oil producers in Libya, most of whom were huge corporations, proposed a "safety net" for themselves. They would all stick together in dealing with Qaddafi, and if any one company's holdings were nationalized, the other companies would contribute part of their earnings to compensate the nationalized company. Bunker agreed to participate in this arrangement, but hesitantly. It seemed to him unlikely that in the long run the interests of the majors would correspond to those of the independents, even when the two groups shared a common opponent.

In December, the first nationalization did, in fact, take place. Unfortunately for Bunker, Libya went after the holdings of his partner, British Petroleum. Bunker was expected to chip in part of his profits to compensate BP, and, as BP's partner, the production he previously would have assigned to BP in payment for their capital investment was claimed by Qaddafi instead. He was in the difficult position of trying to serve two masters, who had different ideas about what he should be doing.

The Bunker-BP-Libya disagreements temporarily became minor when Libya, in the fall of 1972, demanded a fifty-one-percent participation in all oil wells in the country. The oil companies stuck together in denying these demands, but, independently, they began trying to make their own arrangements with Qaddafi. Bunker's attempts to negotiate brought mixed results. In December, his wells were shut down; in January, they were reopened.

Throughout his dealings with the Libyans, observers have said, Bunker tended to take what was described as an "arbitrary" position; he decided what was fair and appropriate regarding his holdings and then refused to compromise. Other producers apparently took such politically expedient steps as funding schools and hospitals in Libya; they agreed to assign fifty-one percent of their holdings to Libya; they compromised, soothed, and hung on. Bunker, however, took the position, according to a former oil operator in Libya, "that they weren't going to take him over—either 51% or 100% or even 25%. His position was that he was going to fight them."[10]

His approach was a disaster. As the same observer commented, "It's been proven over the years that fighting the Libyans is a big waste of time." Given Qaddafi's desire for power and OPEC's unified strength at the time, Bunker could not beat Libya at its own game. On May 24, 1973, Bunker's holdings in Libya were completely and permanently nationalized.

Meanwhile, Libya's strategy of breaking up the united front the oil companies had attempted to present was successful: as the oil companies were forced to deal with Libya individually, they dropped the safety-net approach and forged separate agreements designed to protect their own holdings exclusively.

Bunker believed that he, who had so recently provided compensatory funds to BP, was entitled to receive payments from the other oil companies, whether they were still banded together or not. There was supposed to be a safety net, and he expected it to cushion his fall. His position on this, too, was not open to compromise. But his former allies did not see it that way. It was now every man for himself. To them, Bunker Hunt was just out of luck.

This put Bunker in an extremely difficult position. He now had no personal recourse available; he could obtain satisfaction neither from Libya nor from the majors. But because he continued to be convinced that he was right, he sought the intervention of a higher authority. He sued. Qaddafi was out of his reach, but not so the oil companies who had remained in Libya. His suit charged that fourteen oil companies had conspired to prevent him from obtaining his due after his holdings were nationalized. The amount of the suit was appropriately large for a man who had lost a tax-free income of $30 million a year: $13 billion.

Even while Bunker was preparing to have his day in court, BP, whom Bunker had also not gone out of his way to mollify, was doing the same thing. Since BP could not obtain any additional satisfaction from Libya, it went after what it could get: the money Bunker was supposed to repay BP for capital investment, which had been the source of discussions among Libya, Bunker, and BP back in 1971, after the first round of nationalization. BP, in a British court, demanded $76 million from Bunker. Even though Bunker was not a British citizen, if the findings went against him, his assets in England, including a large collection of valuable race horses, could be confiscated.

While Bunker was realizing great success with his elephant field and then suffering great pain in losing his holdings in Libya, Lamar continued to grapple with ups and downs that were—at least from an outsider's perspective—largely of his own creating.

The first up came shortly after he moved his football team to Kansas City, gracefully accepting defeat in Dallas, as Bunker could not in Libya. In January 1964, Lamar, who had been divorced several years before, married for a second time.

Norma Knotel was an American history teacher at a Dallas area high school, where she had worked since graduating from North Texas State University in 1960. She had been president of her sorority, Top Coed on Campus, and Woman of the Year, was in *Who's Who in American Colleges and Universities*, and graduated with honors. After college, she had spent a year in Ireland on a Rotary Foundation Fellowship. Norma was smart, she was pretty, and, best of all, she loved sports. She and Lamar had met during the summer, when she had worked on sales and promotion for the Dallas Texans. Norma and Lamar honeymooned in Austria, where they celebrated by attending the 1964 Winter Olympics.[11]

Even as he was embarking on this new marriage, Lamar began to look for a new sports undertaking. He purchased a half-interest in a minor league baseball team the same month he was married, and he continued to entertain all kinds of crazy proposals, which people were constantly making to him. At age fifty he looked back at this period in his life and said of his open-mindedness to new sports ideas that "years ago, I could not envision myself as a businessman. I didn't like the idea of a coat and tie."[12] Elsewhere, he added: "I wouldn't have an interest in investing in XYZ business, where you invest $1,000 and hope for an 8 1/2% return. That's almost a coupon-clipping situation. I'm not a crusader, but I think sports are good— and a good business."[13] As a result of this attitude, Lamar's next elephant hunt was again in the area of professional sports.

In 1967, Lamar decided that he had found the new challenge he had been looking for. He had identified one sport that attracted international attention, drew avid and even frenzied crowds throughout the world, but was largely neglected and almost unknown in the United States. This sport was soccer.

Professional soccer had debuted in the United States in 1933, with the formation of the American Soccer League.[14] Throughout the thirties, forties, and fifties the league had limped along, surviving only on revenues generated by hosting appearances of well-known foreign teams. The franchise teams were characterized as having "small budgets. . . . [They had] ethnic followings, played in dusty ovals, had part-time players and small crowds." Most club managers had full-time jobs, with soccer as their avocation. The only thing the

ASL did have going for it was exclusive professional-soccer franchise rights in the eastern United States, where most of the few people who followed soccer lived. These rights had been granted by the U.S. Soccer Football Association (USSFA), which governed all soccer in the country, from sandlot games to Olympic efforts.

In 1966, the USSFA suddenly changed its stance with regard to the ASL and removed its exclusive East Coast rights. It was reacting to a sudden siege of applications from businessmen who wanted to set up pro soccer leagues. One thing that had fueled this onslaught of interest was a major increase in the number of large stadiums. They had been built as pro football and baseball expanded. Now their owners had large debts to pay off and were interested in lining up more teams to play in their facilities. The interest spread to people with money to invest directly in teams.

Two things made soccer a particularly attractive sport to bring to these new stadiums. Soccer was obviously capable of attracting huge and hysterically excited crowds. Witness the annual World Cup matches, where the gate for the final one could top $500,000, and the matches leading up to the final could attract 1.5 million spectators who paid $7 million for their tickets. In addition to the dollar and crowd numbers soccer could generate, it was a relatively cheap sport to sponsor. It did not require a great deal of equipment, and, because the mania for high-priced players that characterized a number of U.S. sports had not yet spread abroad, most top soccer players could be signed to modest contracts.

The USSFA finally considered the applications of three groups of sponsors, after informing them of its demands: four percent of gate receipts, ten percent of TV money, and a $25,000 franchise fee from each new club. At this point, two of the three groups dropped out of the competition, leaving a group headed by Lamar Hunt and eight other men to reach an agreement with the USSFA. Lamar's group called itself the North American Soccer League, later renamed the United Soccer Association (USA).

The main risk to be faced was that, although professional and top-quality amateur soccer were a big draw in other parts of the world, soccer was almost unknown in most of the United States in 1967. Most Americans had never heard of the outstanding international players, such as Pele, who were larger-than-life heroes on the international front. The mediocrity of the ASL, after thirty years of existence, seemed to indicate that soccer was a long shot. But Lamar—his equally high-risk football venture now beginning to look like a major success—believed that, with the proper publicity and marketing, soccer could be a hit in the United States, too.

As the fledgling USA began planning its opening season, the first worrisome news the group faced was that the other two groups had merged and were going to field "outlaw" teams, without USSFA approval. These National Professional Soccer League (NPSL) teams were to be put together from scratch for a season opening in April 1967. USA decided to try to differentiate themselves by fielding better and more experienced teams. They would import entire teams to play in their first year, and gradually build new teams later. They would also postpone play until late May to give themselves more time to get organized.

According to the *American Encyclopedia of Soccer*, "It was suspected by some that Ernie Kovacs wrote the script for pro soccer's initial season. There were clowns, jugglers, pratfalls, everything. . . ." Some of the craziest games were played by the NPSL's motley collection of "unproven amateurs, faded stars and journeymen." The USA teams were better, but even so the fans were not impressed. For the year, the NPSL averaged less than 5,000 fans per game; the USA, around 8,000. It was a long way from the World Cup.

In late 1967, after the somewhat disastrous first season, the two leagues merged into the North American Soccer League, with a total of seventeen teams for the 1968 season. Unfortunately for Lamar, his team did not emerge as one of the better ones in the new league. His coach had recruited a team of "untried teenagers, amateurs all," and tried to shape them into a team by taking them on a winter world tour. This approach was not successful: the team was outclassed by every opponent it played in the regular season, suffering losses of 6–0 or 8–2 and failing to win a single one of its first twenty-one games. After the coach was fired, the players coached themselves for a while. Their new coach, when finally hired, was no more experienced than they were; he had never coached before. He did manage to break the Tornado's unchallenged losing streak, however, and the team finished the season at 2–26–4, "setting a standard of failure which has never since been approached."

Even if his team had been better, Lamar's venture would still have been troubled. The crowds for the year averaged only 3,400 per game; every team lost at least $200,000, and one team, St. Louis's, posted a two-year loss of $1.5 million. Only five teams survived to play in the 1969 season. The Tornado, thanks more to Lamar's net worth than the team's skill, was one of them.

While Lamar nursed his soccer team and the NASL, he continued to guide the Kansas City Chiefs, and he participated in the merger of the AFL with the NFL. He also looked at several other ventures that interested him. At this time, Lamar was in his mid thirties and already displaying what his wife called his "hyperactive calm" personality. Although, according to Norma, he was a quiet and easygoing person who did not lose his temper, get too excited about things, or ever get moody, he was also "very productive with his time. He is always engaged in something positive and productive." He was never idle: if he was watching TV, he was also doing paperwork. What his sister Margaret had described as the "workaholic" Hunt personality was displaying itself in Lamar, despite his aversion to spending his life in traditional business ventures, as surely as if he were passing his days looking at geological reports and spot oil prices.[15]

As part of his energetic approach to new areas of interest, Lamar had been looking at a second new sports venture in 1967: professional tennis.

Professional tennis had been functioning in the United States since the 1920s.[16] It had not attained the success of baseball or football for several reasons. Perhaps the most important was that tennis still maintained the identity it had developed in Europe, particularly in England, of being a gentleman's sport. It had been played in England in one form or another since the end of the sixteenth century, and had become very popular during the 1870s. But those who played were primarily from the nobility or the upper classes, people who could afford to support the expensive and spacious grass courts the sport required.

As tennis became more popular in the late 1800s, federations developed, which set consistent rules of play, court dimensions, and other regulations. When the first moves toward turning tennis into a professional sport were made by American entrepreneurs, according to *Tennis: A Professional Guide*, "the club officials and the U.S. Lawn Tennis Association realized that the success of professional tennis would mean loss of their power, so they excluded pros from their grounds," just as the governing body of British tennis had always done.

Another problem with making professional tennis popular was that many Americans had never played it and had not developed an interest in the game. Consequently, when some players decided to turn pro, regardless of repercussions from the federations, they found that the money they could make was, at best, modest. In the early days, two or four players sometimes traveled from town to town with their own portable courts, since most towns had no suitable playing surface. Even into the 1960s, when there were more pros and better places to play, the idea of staging regular professional tournaments or setting up a circuit of tournaments continued to seem somewhat far-fetched.

By 1967, things were starting to look different. Not only were new stadiums being developed, but also there was the probability that TV exposure would interest many more Americans in tennis. Since more economical playing surfaces were leading to more courts being built, and therefore more people playing and appreciating the game, it seemed quite possible that the increasing enthusiasm for all kinds of professional sports might well spill over into tennis, which had a glamorous luster and youthful and attractive players, both male and female.

Once Lamar decided that professional tennis was, indeed, an attractive concept, he moved to put his money behind his belief. He joined with developer Dave Dixon and Margaret's son, Al Hill, Jr., to set up an organization they named World Champion Tennis, or WCT. When Dixon wanted to get out of the organization not long after its inception, Lamar demonstrated what one sports writer described as a "good right hand with a checkbook" and bought Dixon's fifty percent holdings, raising his stake in WCT to seventy-five percent.[17]

One of the first steps the organization took to form tennis into an appropriate game for television coverage was to change the scoring system for professional matches. According to the rules of amateur tennis, ties could go on indefinitely, with the lead in a match theoretically changing hands an infinite number of times. Because the networks needed to be able to plan fairly precisely for match or tournament coverage, the WCT instituted a scoring system that provided for a specific way of breaking ties between players in a limited period of time.

This change pitted Lamar and the WCT directly against the amateur-tennis establishment. The amateur bodies still believed that their most important mission was to preserve tennis unchanged; Lamar's group not only was promoting change, but also wanted change for commercial reasons. The International Lawn Tennis Federation and U.S. Lawn Tennis Association dug in their heels to resist acceptance of WCT as a sanctioned tennis organization.

Some years before, these groups might have succeeded in their opposition, since tennis pros were unlikely to make much money; now their ability to enforce ultimatums was not assured. Lamar and his group signed more and more top amateur players during the first several years of the WCT. If these players were subsequently to be banned from all amateur tournaments, such as Wimbledon in England, Forest Hills in the United States, and Davis Cup matches, soon the prestigious old tournaments would become uninteresting, as they pitted one unknown against another. It was this line of thinking that led the British and then the U.S. organizations to acquiesce and open major tournaments to both professionals and amateurs in 1968.

The truce was an uneasy one, however. Over the next several years, WCT players became more involved with the WCT circuit, which by 1971 had twenty-one tournaments and more than a million dollars in prize money. The quality of play in these tournaments was high, and fans began turning their interest from mixed amateur/ professional events to the WCT games. Lamar's group and the amateur federation continued to trade shots. Wimbledon, for example, specifically excluded WCT players from the 1972 games; Lamar's group countered by scheduling a major tournament on the Wimbledon dates. This power struggle opened the way for the birth of a group that later challenged the authority and privileges of both the amateur federations and the WCT. It was a players' union, the Association of Tennis Professionals, which was established in 1972.

Another offshoot of the jockeying for power had been the establishment in 1968 of the Grand Prix. Originally it was conceived of as a way of solving the uncertainties created by open tennis, in which pros and amateurs played one another. How should players be seeded when they were playing in different kinds of events in different countries against opponents with different standings in the tennis world? By folding all major tournaments and championships into the Grand Prix circuit, it was thought, a system of keeping consistent track of all players could be developed. The Grand Prix concept was developed by the amateur federations under the leadership of Jack Kramer, a former champion tennis player and pre-Lamar pro tennis promoter. Once the players formed their union, and hired Kramer to be executive director, they were included in structuring and managing the Grand Prix. By 1972, the relationship of the WCT to the Grand Prix was still neutral; but problems were to come and take many years to resolve.

As tennis moved, during this period, "kicking and screaming into the twentieth century," in Lamar's words, Lamar himself gradually came to see his role in the evolution of the game as that of an upholder of tennis democracy. The International Lawn Tennis Federation, Lamar said later, looking back, "ran gentleman's clubs and wouldn't let professionals in. If you were a pro, you were poison. But we helped make them accepted."[18] Elsewhere, he described tennis prior to the WCT as "basically controlled by lily-white European federations. They had the mentality of the 1920s that it wasn't proper for anyone to profit from tennis. Players were being paid under the table. Then we came along. . . . The powers that be in tennis threw up their hands and said, 'We've got to stop these infidels, these revolutionaries.' "[19]

To a certain extent, Lamar's perspective was understandable: he was the man who had been called by one British writer "the all-time enemy of England," and some competing tennis promoters who were former players accused him of "saying 'screw it' and go[ing] off on his own" when he didn't get his way.[20] On the other hand, Lamar and the WCT were basically focused on making money. It was money that Lamar and his partner and nephew saw as just as central to the game as status and power. Something Al Hill, Jr., said when the WCT players were shut out of Wimbledon seemed to sum up what he and Lamar thought was the essence of all the conflicts. "Let's face it," he said to a newspaper reporter. "What are our fellows supposed to do, sit around two weeks during Wimbledon and not make any money?"[21]

Whatever Lamar Hunt's role really was in the history of tennis, the indisputable fact of his early days in the WCT was that he personally was not making any profit from the venture. One report said that the WCT lost $300,000 in its first year; much later, in 1983, a newspaper article about Lamar said the WCT had yet to break even and had, so far, cost him $40 million.[22]

In 1968, well before the ultimate outcome of either his soccer or his tennis ventures could be known, and while each was demanding a great deal of his personal time and money, Lamar conceived a new project, one that would take him somewhat outside the world of professional sports. His plan was to turn Alcatraz Island into a huge commercial development and major entertainment center. He had a number of ideas for Alcatraz, an island in the middle of San Francisco Bay that had long served as the site of a high-security federal prison. He would build a Space Age Museum, restore the island's old buildings, plant trees and provide landscaping, and build a shopping area that replicated those of San Francisco's 1890s heyday. Throughout 1968 and into 1969, Lamar pursued this idea enthusiastically. It was only in late 1969, after the San Francisco City Council received 10,000 letters opposing him as a private developer of the island, that he finally gave up. By then, Lamar was looking at the possibility of doing a similar kind of development in Kansas City, including an amusement or theme park.[23]

Over the next few years, while Bunker was fighting for his economic rights and well-being in Libya, Lamar fought to balance his more or less traditional businesses, such as the Kansas City development and a continuing involvement in the family oil company, with his sports ventures. Soccer threatened to meet an early and unprofitable demise in its third season, when only five of the previous year's seventeen teams continued in the league, and attendance throughout the league fell to an average of fewer than 3,000 fans per game. The Dallas franchise remained steadily unprofitable. Lamar continued to pour money into WCT, and while tournaments and players came along, profits did not. Even the Kansas City Chiefs had their problems; during the 1973 season, a no-blackout rule on television coverage cut attendance at their home games.

Throughout this period, Lamar continued to emphasize the fact that for him, regardless of temporary losses, sports investment was a money-making proposition, though it might take time for his teams or organizations to move into the black.[24] Although he admitted that certain aspects of his experiences were disillusioning, he remained committed to making his investments work. At least one observer suggested that Lamar worked hard even when things looked bad because he wanted to legitimize his interests in the eyes of his older brothers, who viewed his investments as a frivolous hobby.[25] Regardless of Lamar's motivation, the fact remains that during this period he was unable to make anything but the Chiefs permanently profitable.

Though Lamar lost money on these sports ventures, he did not appear, during the late sixties and early seventies, to be suffering insolvency as a result. He made headlines in 1970 by buying an enormous Dallas mansion on ten expensive acres well within the city limits. The house, a French provincial building surrounded by tennis courts, a pool, and numerous accompanying small buildings, had belonged to Jimmy Ling, a Dallas entrepreneur who had attracted attention when his company surged into the 1960s acquisition mainstream by taking over several corporations much bigger than itself. In Dallas, stories said that part of Ling's subsequent economic demise came about because he had plowed so much money into his house. "Everyone was surprised to hear that Lamar bought it," a business associate of Hunt's was quoted as saying, "because Lamar is unpretentious, to say the least. But he probably bought it because of his wife. Norma works at being a regular person, but sometimes it shows that she's working at it. To Lamar, being a regular person comes naturally."[26]

In fact, aside from Lamar's dramatic new home, throughout most of his and Bunker's elephant searches, their huge investments, their ups and downs, their lawsuits, the two brothers, as well as Herbert, Caroline, and Margaret, were continuing to live their everyday lives as "regular people." But just as the observations of their father's attempts to lead a normal life had fascinated people for years as they read about his old cars, his cheap suits, and his homemade lunches, Bunker and Lamar were now attracting attention whether they wanted to or not. Steadfastly avoiding anything that could be construed as jet-setting, both nonetheless began to assume their own legendary status. Lamar, who often appeared in public in a blue blazer and gray pants, was asked if he had more than one suit. When he replied, "You can only wear one suit at a time," people said he was just as uninterested in appearances as his father had been.[27] Bunker began to buy race horses, sometimes for large sums of money. But when he flew off to horse auctions or to watch his investments run, via commercial flights—sometimes choosing to fly stand-by—

observers said that he obviously was just as frugal as H. L. Hunt had been. Never mind that Lamar was later to say his suit comment was a joke, that Bunker was to explain that he flew stand-by, not to save money, but because it was the only way he could get on a flight at the last moment. The Hunts were going the way everyone expected them to go, and Bunker and Lamar proved it. They were eccentric, they were unknowable, and probably, underneath it all, they were just as wild and ruthless as everyone was already convinced their father had always been.

THIRTEEN

WHILE Bunker and Lamar Hunt were making major moves in the business world, a great deal was going on behind the scenes in the extended Hunt family. These two sons, as well as their sisters and brother, Herbert, were all working out their changing relationships with their father as the elder Hunt found new interests, reached old age, and, along the way, gave them a stepmother who was two years younger than his oldest daughter. At the same time, Hunt's second wife and her four children, now acknowledged to be his legitimate son and daughters, were grappling with how they could mesh into Hunt's original family. The children also had to make adjustments to their changing personal circumstances at the very time they were embarking, one by one, on young adulthood.

Since Lyda Hunt's death in late 1955, there had been no one to run the Mt. Vernon house and take care of Hunt's day-to-day needs. Because he continued to be so involved in business, his focus outside the home, things there were left to continue as best they could. Into this gap in Hunt's personal life stepped Ruth Ray.

Although Hunt's biographer Harry Hurt reports that the children of the original family were critical and resentful of Ruth, their responses appear to have been rather varied.[1] Margaret, the most proper and traditional of all of Hunt's children, seems to have offered the most resistance to Ruth's entry into the official and legal Hunt family. Margaret's three children ranged in age from nine to fifteen at the time Hunt married Ruth, so they would have been well aware of the loss of their grandmother and the entry of another woman in her role.

Margaret was very active then in Dallas society, eventually becoming president of the prestigious, conservative Dallas Women's Club. Her daughters, too, were active on the social scene, both becoming debutantes, the first in the Hunt family. Margaret and her family, therefore, had, in some respects, the most to lose by their father's affirmation of his somewhat scandalous life-style, and this may have been the source of Margaret's coolness to Ruth and her children. Ruth's daughter, June, for example, later indicated that Margaret had been instrumental in seeing that she was denied membership in any of the better sororities when she began college. At the time, sororities were a girl's entrée into the whole world of college life, not just into a few social activities. Twenty years after the incident, June remained hurt and puzzled by what she saw as Margaret's anger toward Hunt's other children.[2]

In almost complete contrast, Caroline seems to have made every effort to accept Ruth and her children into the family. She continued to visit Mt. Vernon frequently, as did her youngest brother, Lamar.

Caroline's and Lamar's continuation of their old relationship with Hunt was helped by the youth of their children. Laurie, Caroline's fourth child, who was born within a year of Lyda's death, recalled that the children enjoyed going to swim in their grandfather's pool. Unlike Margaret's children, almost all of Bunker's, Herbert's, and Lamar's children, as well as Caroline's two youngest, were born either after Lyda's death or so shortly before that they would not have remembered her at all. For these children, Ruth would have been simply the woman their grandfather was married to, and they grew up taking her presence for granted.

Ruth tried to make the transition to her new role as painless for Hunt's original family as possible. Laurie recalled that because she, her uncle Bunker, and her grandfather all had birthdays in the same month, "Ruth used to have little birthday parties for us. I've always thought very highly of Ruth. She couldn't have been nicer to me." Ruth also invited all of Hunt's children to join them at Mt. Vernon for Christmas, and this continued to be a major family gathering for many years.

Ruth's efforts, whatever their cost to her, were worth it for her own children. They generally grew up feeling that they "got along" with their half-brothers and half-sisters. One of Ruth's daughters went so far as to say, in discussing her half-siblings, "I've never had a harsh word with any of my brothers or sisters."

During these years, as they sorted out the new sets of relationships that Hunt's loss of Lyda and gain of Ruth created, the children of both women were also, of course, developing their individual lives outside the family.

Margaret continued her behind-the-scenes involvement in managing the investments her husband spearheaded officially. Al Hill was an important figure in many Hunt Oil deals during this time.[3] He and Margaret also began investing in what one member of the next generation described as "maverick" deals. One of their most visible ventures was the establishment of a private resort facility in Colorado called "Garden of the Gods."

Caroline remained out of the public eye, too. She was largely uninvolved in any aspect of the Hunt businesses, though her husband continued his involvement. She was living a very quiet life, in part because of her young children—her last son was born in 1963—and in part because of her husband's desires. According to her daughter's assessment of this period, Caroline's marriage was not going well. But whatever her problems with her husband, she, like her mother before her, never considered divorce. Instead, Laurie recalled in 1987, "she spent a lot of time at the church. . . . She became very involved and started the youth program there. I've even seen pictures from the paper, a long time ago, and there's my little mother. There's a picture of one of the richest women in the world and there she is, in the church, with a little hat on, sitting [primly] like this."

Hunt's three younger sons from his original family were all working hard during this period, each following his own interests: Bunker in Libya, Herbert in real estate, and Lamar in professional sports. In addition to work, the sons were developing other interests. Bunker's were the most newsworthy: by the mid-1960s, he was a major contributor, and later a member of the governing board, of the John Birch Society. He was also buying, managing, and racing horses in a big way, with the first of his champions developing on the European race circuit in 1967.[4]

Ray, June, Helen, and Swanee, Ruth's children, were taking their first steps into the world, as one after another they entered college or marriage.

In 1961, Ray entered Southern Methodist University. Less than a decade before, his half-brother Lamar had graduated from there.

Now their father apparently believed that SMU was absolutely the best school for all of the rest of his children. "There was only one thing my father ever told me to do that I really didn't want to do, and it was a very good decision [on his part]," Ray recalled in 1987. "I decided I would go away to college, and I came in and told him I'd visited four colleges and I thought I'd go to Stanford. I think by the next day I was enrolled in SMU." Once there, Ray became just as involved and active as he had been at St. Mark's. "In retrospect that was a wonderful decision," he observed. "A lot of people really look back on their college years with disappointment, but I was terribly lucky. The closest friends I made in my life I made in those years."

During the summers, Ray continued to work at Hunt Oil. One area he became involved in was obtaining leases, so the company could drill in new areas. "I typically would carry a typewriter, sit back with my ears open and my mouth shut while the person I was with would negotiate, and then I would sometimes help type up the lease forms or things of that nature," he said in *The History of Hunt Oil*. "After a couple of years, Roy [Taylor] let me go in and buy some leases on my own. At first, they would want to stay in the room with me, but whoever I was with wouldn't say much. Then I was paid the highest compliment when Ralph [Bollinger] or Roy would stay in the car and let me go in by myself to negotiate for the lease." After graduating from SMU, Ray married a woman he had met there and went to work for his father's company full time.

Not long after Ray began his successful career at SMU, the time came for his sister June to choose a college. Although by then June had found a certain amount of peace in her relationship with her father as she became more involved in the Baptist church, her equilibrium was severely challenged over this decision.[5] June wanted very much to go to Baylor University, a school less than 100 miles from Dallas, which had a marked religious orientation. Hunt insisted that she go to SMU.

June tried to outwit her father. She did well on the standardized college admissions test Baylor required, but did not try to do her best on SMU's test. She also filled out the SMU application very briefly, saying that she did not want to attend SMU, that she wanted to go elsewhere, and that she was applying only at her father's insistence. To her surprise, she was turned down by Baylor but accepted by SMU.

June also became active on campus, though her interests were different from Ray's. She was a music major, but, in her words, "really majored in extracurricular activities." These led to her inclusion in *Who's Who in American Colleges and Universities*, as well as a school award for outstanding contributions. The one thing June did not obtain at college, despite her self-described expectations, was what was known at the time as the "M.R.S." degree—marriage. In an almost relentlessly upbeat book June later wrote, called *Above All Else*, she commented, "Yes, I was still a bachelor but I prefer to call myself an unclaimed blessing!"

As soon as June graduated from SMU, she again fell into strong conflict with her father, and again he won. Hunt insisted that June go to Chicago to work on one of his pet projects, a patriotic youth program. June wanted to do something else; one option she was considering was graduate school. She finally acquiesced in her father's wishes, however, and left Dallas.

Shortly after her arrival in Chicago, a newspaper reporter was interviewing the daughter of the famous oilman about what she planned to do there. At the beginning of the interview, he asked her to tell him, just as a piece of background information, how much she, the wealthy young heiress, had just tipped the cabdriver who had brought her to the interview. June explained honestly that she was almost completely out of cash and so had tipped the man all the money she had left: a nickel and two pennies. Not a man to miss a headline, the reporter took this story back to his paper, which ran June's profile under the heading "Daughter of Millionaire Gives Cabbie Seven-Cent Tip." Apparently this article was too much even for the usually thick-skinned Hunt. June received a telegram: COME HOME. She returned to Dallas, and from that point on made her own career decisions. Her first was to spend the next year in graduate school at SMU.

As June was establishing her agenda for the next year, her younger sister Helen was getting ready to go to college. Although Helen had never had the kinds of conflicts with her father that June experienced, she had felt for quite a while that she needed to spend some time away from Dallas, away from the rest of her family. "Each person needs a certain kind of cultivation," she observed in 1987. "I'm one of the quieter Hunts and I knew from my sophomore year in high school that I needed to be away."[6]

Seeing college as the ideal time to get out on her own, Helen researched colleges and decided that she would like to attend either Vanderbilt or Duke, both good Southern universities but both some distance from Texas. When she discussed her proposal with her father, however, she encountered the same attitude that Ray and June had grappled with: SMU was the school where H. L. Hunt believed his children should go, and Helen was going to SMU.

Helen enrolled at SMU, where she quickly became involved in campus organizations, including a good sorority and the freshman council. She was followed a year later by her younger sister, Swanee. Swanee, too, had wanted to go away to school, though her choice was more dramatic than her sisters' or her brother's. Her first choice of colleges was Radcliffe. But by this time, in Swanee's words, "SMU was the *family* school. There wasn't any choice given."[7]

Although it was now the late 1960s, a time of tremendous social change and upheaval, SMU was far from a hotbed of student activism. Marriage rather than a career was still very much the objective of nice Texas girls, just as it had been for Caroline almost thirty years earlier. At SMU, Helen met a law-school student who was a few years older than she was. His name was Randy Kreiling, and his family was from Peoria, Illinois. The relationship quickly blossomed, and in August 1969, when Helen was twenty, she and Randy were married at First Baptist Church.

By this time the Hunts were important members of the church, and the Reverend Dr. W. A. Criswell, a prominent pastor who had been active in conservative political causes, performed the wedding ceremony. The young couple honeymooned in Hawaii and then settled in Dallas, where both could complete school.[8]

Less than a year later, it was Swanee's turn. Although her choice of early marriage echoed Helen's, she approached marriage differently. In contrast to Helen's lavish affair, Swanee's marriage to Mark Meeks, in May 1970, was a small family gathering in a chapel of First Baptist Church. The Reverend Criswell was joined in officiating by the brother of the bridegroom. There was a large reception following the ceremony, but it was held at the church.[9]

Swanee followed her wedding with a move to Fort Worth, Texas, thirty miles from Dallas. There she completed her bachelor's degree at Texas Christian University, a school similar in style and tone to

SMU. She majored in philosophy. Mark Meeks, her husband, entered a theological seminary.

"I married someone with a tremendous social conscience—a wonderful, wonderful man," Swanee said in 1987. "Mark was certainly the most progressive person I'd ever been close to. And he still is an inner-city minister who believes very strongly and works very hard on behalf of mental health issues, peace issues, social justice, Central American issues. So he and I then made a team that really moved."

Despite Swanee's burgeoning interest in areas that were well outside her father's rather narrow sphere of interest and endorsement, she continued, during the time prior to and immediately following her marriage, to get along reasonably well with Hunt. "I really didn't know him in his strength," Swanee said later, noting that by the time she was setting out on her own, in her late teens, her father was almost eighty. By that point in his life, Hunt had become a lot more pleasant to be with. "He'd become very sentimental, teary. . . . I actually felt close to him as he grew into that stage. He was someone I could nurture a little bit."

On the other hand, once she had made the break with home, Swanee was not eager to return to Dallas or to settle there. When Mark decided to go to Lexington, Kentucky, to continue his studies, she happily went with him. She enrolled in the same school that Mark attended, studying ethics and pastoral care. When Mark graduated, the couple moved to Germany, where Mark was pastor of a church with an English-speaking but extremely mixed congregation. "[Germany] was one of the best times in my life," Swanee recalled. "There were a lot of personal things that weren't so wonderful but somehow the environment carried me—it was so powerful."

Swanee was delighted to be away from the United States. Not only had she always wanted to broaden her perspective on life by living in another country, but she also "wanted to get away from the fishbowl parts of the family. There was a lot I couldn't identify with very well." She had changed her name when she married Mark, and as Mrs. Mark Meeks she spent four years traveling around Europe, learning German, and working on a master's degree in counseling psychology.

Ironically, Helen, the sister who had long known that she wanted to live away from the Hunt fishbowl, remained in Dallas. After her husband, Randy Kreiling, finished school, he went to work for

Hunt Oil. Helen graduated and took a teaching job in an economically deprived section of Dallas. In a 1985 *Dallas Morning News* interview, she recalled her work there. "It was a phenomenal experience. I didn't know how profoundly I'd be affected by it. It dispelled the myth that life is just."[10] The school did not have enough textbooks and materials, and the neighborhood did not receive city services. It was her first exposure to the hidden side of Dallas, to people who were different from herself.

Near the end of the school year, Helen became pregnant with her first child. She shared her news with her students, and they were very excited. "After class was over, about a third of them came up, and they told me what having a baby was like, what to expect from my pregnancy. I had been with these kids six or seven months, and I didn't even know they had children. I learned about a whole different culture."[11] It was this revelation of what went on in the lives of her students outside of school that would lead Helen to begin looking more carefully at her own life, her own affluence, and her own control over what happened to her.

During the time that Swanee and Helen were beginning their early married lives, June was building a meaningful single life for herself. After a year of graduate school, she was offered a job at the First Baptist Church as the junior-high-school director. In her book, *Above All Else*, June recalled her response. "Never having *considered* attending a seminary or being a youth director, I was astonished! After all, this wasn't like teaching a beginner Sunday-school class. [Dr. Criswell] was asking me to head a division of 650 students in the world's largest southern Baptist church."[12] June found herself overwhelmed and even somewhat depressed by the request. However, by this time she was very much a believer in following God's will. She accepted the position, and "ten weeks later I wouldn't have traded jobs with anyone."

June stayed at First Baptist as junior-high director for four years, then spent one year as director of the college and career division. "I really *felt* for the unspoken needs and hurts of teen-agers," she said. "It was invaluable experience so I would not take for granted the pains and struggles and challenges that youth had as well as parents. . . . My sensitivity was stretched a great deal."[13]

In 1971, June, realizing that she was "among the vast majority who had never stopped to do any goal setting," decided that it was important that she find a way of becoming involved in the Vietnam situation. Rather than protest the war, she believed the right thing to do was offer support for the men fighting there. She began trying to make arrangements to participate in a USO tour, on which she would perform "message music"—music that would "communicate a message that will increase awareness in the lives of individuals," particularly regarding "what the reality of God can do in one's life."[14] June had an excellent and well-trained voice, and could also play the guitar. The USO decided that she would be an asset on a "handshake tour," in which performers give small shows and spend a lot of time in one-to-one contact, especially in hospitals.

June's tour was memorable for her. She not only perfected her performances of message music, but also had an opportunity to share her religious beliefs with many individuals who were hungry for a spiritual perspective on the confusion and pain of their combat experiences. Afterward, she began increasingly to focus on traveling and speaking around the country, using much the same format she had developed in Vietnam.

When June was not traveling, she remained deeply involved with her parents. Although she no longer felt that she needed to protect her mother from Hunt, and although she believed that her father had softened due to the influence of her mother's unconditional love and acceptance of him, June's own relationship with Hunt was still painful. There were times when it seemed almost as if Ruth were taking care of June, protecting her the way June had once tried to protect Ruth. Furthermore, as June set up housekeeping, in a very unworldly and spiritual fashion, Ruth took her shopping for furniture and other necessities and kept her grounded in the temporal realities of life.

Ruth also remained close to her son Ray, who continued to live in Dallas with his wife and, eventually, five children. Like his sisters, during his early adult life Ray had to sort out who he was and how he fit into the family. He also had to contend with the issue of where he stood in the family business. For him, however, things fell into place more easily. Perhaps because he felt a basic closeness with his father, Ray was comfortable going into Hunt Oil and establishing himself there, despite the fact that his three half-brothers and two brothers-in-law had been involved in the company for some time.

"I made the decision a long, long time ago," he said from the 1987 perspective, "that I wasn't going to compete with anybody—with Dad, with my half-brothers or anyone else. I was going to do what I thought was right and appropriate. . . . One of the biggest traps that I feel most people fall into is they start allowing their actions and their decisions to be influenced by the expectations of others. Now, no one can live in a vacuum but the minute that starts, once you fall into that trap, that's a whirlpool."

After becoming a full-time Hunt Oil employee in 1965, Ray continued to be a "sponge and learn as much as [he] could while creating as little interference as possible."[15] By this time Hunt was seventy-six years old. Although he continued to work hard, Ray must have been well aware that sooner or later his father would no longer be part of the business. Ray continued and even stepped up his efforts to understand his father, his success, and the environment in which he had built the business. "Sitting there and listening to him visit with somebody who was retired from Exxon and somebody who was an old wildcatter, listening to them just kind of talking about things, was living history that has now been lost with the passage of time," Ray explained.[16]

To a certain extent, Ray was fortunate that he had begun learning the oil business when he was still a teen-ager and while Hunt Oil was a strong and leading independent oil business. By 1965, things were changing, and what had been the company's greatest strength— H. L. Hunt himself—was becoming something of an Achilles heel to the company.

Hunt's approach to his organization had always been simple. "We used to joke before Dad passed away about how if you had to draw an organization chart of the company, you'd have one box with a line to another box," Ray recalled in 1987. "The top box would be Dad and the other box would be everybody else. . . . Dad's basic principle was that you should delegate authority to the maximum extent you can, which implies that you keep the levels of management— i.e., bureaucracy—to a *bare* minimum because your response time is absolutely critical. If you have the right people and if they can make fast decisions (and if you're willing to be accepting of some mistakes), the benefits of the opportunity you realize by doing things that way will far outweigh the costs."[17]

By 1965, Hunt had largely divorced himself from the day-to-day operations of the company. But rather than change the organization's structure and hierarchy to reflect this, he had tried to keep power and authority even as he relinquished responsibility. Consequently, the two-box chart still represented the way H. L. Hunt was running his company. A 1966 *Playboy* interview with Hunt described his "empire" as a "one-man show": "He has no stockholders and no board of directors—extraordinary, considering that the Hunt assets are equal to those of such corporate complexes as General Electric."[18]

What was even more extraordinary was that as a result of Hunt's unwillingness to change things, his empire was running almost by default. His lack of involvement could be traced to the large and ever-increasing variety of interests into which he threw himself; the price was his lack of availability for the decision-making that had to be done at Hunt Oil.

Since the early 1950s, Hunt had focused a great deal of his energy on politics. "By the time I was a teenager, he never spoke of his work," Swanee recalled. "It was almost all about politics—saving the Republic USA from the Mistakens." One major manifestation of Hunt's interest during the 1960s was the writing he did: newspaper columns, letters to the editor, radio scripts, and more books, including a sequel to *Alpaca* called *Alpaca Revisited*. He also went to Washington for several weeks for a reexamination of the structure of the electoral college, and eventually set up a Washington office complete with staff to keep an eye on what was going on in the federal government.[19]

By the 1960s, Hunt was also becoming increasingly involved with HLH Products, his food business, adding farms and processing facilities to the large holdings of land he had begun acquiring in the forties. In 1960, he purchased chicken and tomato canning plants. So many other purchases followed that "the [Hunt Oil] Legal Department developed a 'standard plant purchase form' to use in closing deals," the company history reported.

There were other things that caught Hunt's attention. At one point, for example, according to *The History of Hunt Oil Company*, he "had decided he wanted to be a record-setting rose-grower, and 120,000 rose bushes were planted on new ground at the Smith County ranch. . . . In 1961, roses were cultivated and packaged for sale under the Penrod brand name, to be sold through the network of LIFE LINE radio stations." At another time, the *History* noted, he bought some land in a remote area of West Texas where there were several natural springs and a decaying hotel. There he tried to rebuild a resort, but was hampered by rather large obstacles, such as a total lack of electric power and the area's almost complete inaccessibility.

Hunt was spreading himself so thin by this time that he sometimes seemed to be confused about his own activities. One of the Hunt Oil Company switchboard operators described how "Mr. Hunt would ring us, and I'd answer, 'Yes, Mr. Hunt.' He'd say, 'Well now, who should I talk to today?' 'What about, Mr. Hunt?' 'Well, this project I'm working on.' 'Is it politics, Mr. Hunt? Oil? The food business? The World's Fair?' 'Yes, that's it; let me talk to. . . .' "

Hunt's wide-ranging interests as well as his declining powers presented, of course, the ideal opportunity for him to groom his successor or successors at Hunt Oil. But rather than step aside and allow Bunker or Herbert or Al Hill or Ray to focus the company's direction, Hunt created a difficult situation for his heirs by continuing to hang on to the control himself. H. L. Hunt was, in his own eyes and in the eyes of his employees, still the boss. One employee recalled that the operation where he worked changed ownership among the Hunt companies a number of times during the first years he was there. But "it didn't matter much to many employees, who still viewed the various Hunt companies as one and the same—a unified operation with H. L. Hunt still at the helm."

And Hunt was not content to oversee things from a distance. Though not willing to be a consistent and available chief executive officer, he wanted to maintain the illusion of hands-on management, to continue to be consulted on every aspect of its operation, always on his terms and his schedule. As his long-time secretary recalled, Hunt wanted to be part of everything, almost compulsively so. "He was uncommunicative and often critical of the secretary assigned to him," she said, "seemingly fearful that her presence isolated him from the rest of the office. He abhorred solitude and isolation." Hunt liked to know who all his employees were and what was going on. He continued to make most of their job assignments, in addition to "scribbling messages on a small piece of paper and leaving them on desks for people he knew would 'take hold' and accomplish."

Part of Hunt's need to maintain ultimate power in the organization he had founded may have stemmed from a basic lack of trust in

anyone's ability to succeed him. He apparently continued to view his
sons and sons-in-law as inexperienced and unreliable. He maintained a paternalistic attitude toward the development of family
members in the business. For example, when his son Lamar was
starting the AFL, Hunt told one of the Hunt Oil attorneys to "go out
and help Lamar and get him out of it if you can, but if not, keep him
out of trouble." Even when one of his sons initiated his own project,
as Bunker did in Libya, the fact that all projects were ultimately
under the umbrella of Hunt Oil meant that Hunt himself remained
in a position to oversee and judge almost everything that went on
whenever he chose to do so.

Perhaps under certain circumstances, Hunt's sons or employees
could have wrested control from the aging man. But Hunt's style of
decision-making on the big deals in which Hunt Oil became
involved—and his ongoing success in choosing how to respond to
such deals—created a situation which those around him found difficult to understand fully or to replicate. This mysterious power that
Hunt continued to exercise may have made his sons reluctant to try
to leave him out of the business completely.

Hunt's approach to big deals is summed up perfectly in an incident described in the company history. The time was 1967. Hunt
Oil traditionally had had limited involvement in offshore drilling.
As exploration heated up in the Gulf of Mexico, however, the company joined ten other independents to develop seismic data that
would form the basis for bids for drilling rights to be auctioned off
by the federal government sometime during the late 1960s. The moment of the auction came, and Hunt Oil had to decide what they
would bid for which parcel.

George Cunyas, a long-time employee of Hunt Oil, describes it
this way: "Senior management of the participating companies gathered for the bid meeting in a large locked room in the Houston
LOSCO [the exploration consortium] offices. The Hunt Oil Company group consisted of H. L. Hunt, Hassie Hunt, myself, Dr.
Dahm, Frank Totzke, Tom Hunt [a first cousin of Hunt's children],
Herbert Hunt, and Warren Gray. Over 100 prospects were detailed
by maps displayed around the room.

"The prospects chosen for bid and the bid amounts were determined at that meeting. H. L. Hunt had neither participated in
the prior evaluation meetings nor reviewed any of the seismic inter-

pretations. H. L. Hunt walked into the meeting room, took about five minutes looking around at all of the various mapped interpretations displayed, and then pointed at one map saying, 'I want that one.' "

"That one" was Ship Shoal block 207, for which the group subsequently made the winning bid of $32.5 million. Another Hunt Oil employee reported that the president of one of the major oil companies gloated after the bid's acceptance, sure that Hunt had made a bad investment and that LOSCO would never get its money back. But Ship Shoal 207, which Hunt had selected after his brief walk around the conference room, turned out to be a giant field: it produced more than 100 million barrels of oil and made an enormous amount of money for its lessees.

Ship Shoal 207 was not an isolated fluke. "Hunt Oil Company was planning to bid in the big lease sale up in Alaska," Ray recalled.[20] "Something like two days before the sale [Dad] insisted that Hunt Oil Company pull out of the bidding. And to do it that late is really not according to Hoyle. Companies get together and form groups in order to have purchasing power. If someone pulls out at the last minute it creates a real problem.

"When asked [why he wanted to pull out], he said, 'Well, it's just too near Russia.' Now that, to me, is not the right reason to pull out."

But, Ray continued, "subsequently Herbert and Bunker substituted other accounts. They spent a lot of money on the sale but it turned out that a mistake had been made in the interpretation of the scientific data and the combine of companies that ended up bidding on the leases lost a ton of money."

Ray also described a similar situation, in which Hunt pulled out of bidding for a parcel of offshore land near Santa Barbara, California, saying vaguely that he remembered the San Francisco earthquake and he was concerned about the area. The block on which Hunt Oil had been prepared to make a bid was acquired by another oil company, whose well blew out, creating a huge oil slick, which was one of the worst environmental disasters ever to have happened. "Can you imagine if we had drilled the well that blew out? We might have engineered it differently but we might not have," Ray observed. "[The developer] is awful good and I presume they have awful good engineers. And they were much more familiar with California than we were, but still, if the well that blew out had been ours we would still be fighting lawsuits today."

How did Hunt continue to find the elephants and avoid the graveyards, often on the basis of so little information? Equally important, how could anyone replace him, the man with the mysterious "Hunt luck"? "My father felt he had a strong, well-developed sixth sense. I think that he was very comfortable in putting great confidence in his sixth sense," Ray speculated in retrospect. "He might make decisions and when somebody would ask him, 'Why did you do that?' he'd give some of the most unusual responses and explanations why the decisions were made. The only way I can explain it is that he made a lot of decisions based upon his sixth sense and when asked to supply a logical reason he did his best but the demonstrable logic of the decision was lacking."

What Ray describes as Hunt's "sixth sense" could also be understood as a highly developed intuition, which even Hunt could not describe in conventional words. Like a painter who creates masterpieces without being able to explain his philosophy of art or a great scientist whose discoveries stemmed from following his "hunches," Hunt put together pieces in a way he could not explain and followed rules he could not teach to anyone else.

It was Hunt's intuitive ability that gave him a certain amount of insulation from the wishes of others, especially his family, that he step out of the oil business. Bunker might have his geologists, and Ray his lease agreements, but without H. L. Hunt's magic, no one could help but ask himself, would the company remain the same?

As the sixties progressed, therefore, Hunt kept his position in Hunt Oil, at least when it came to the big deals. But other Hunt undertakings slowly ceased to be off-limits for challenge. HLH Products was one part of the Hunt Oil empire that fell outside the sacrosanct oil-exploration area. When HLH developed increasingly serious problems during this time, Hunt's sons were quite willing to take matters into their own hands.

HLH Products had begun with Hunt's interest in marketing the foods produced on farms he held, and in bringing to other people some of the products he thought were helpful and worthwhile.[21] Hunt, the intuitive decision-maker, did not develop a plan for building a consumer-products company, but, rather, had taken advantage of opportunities as they came along—opportunities to buy a canning facility, to add a new product to his line, to promote his merchandise wherever he wanted, whether it was at the state fair of Texas, the World's Fair in New York, or simply via fluorescent bumper stickers on his pink car. For a man with an enormous positive cash flow dating back more than twenty years, when and how his new investments would pay back was relatively unimportant. By the end of the sixties, HLH Products had fifteen production facilities, 5,000 employees, and sold an enormous range of canned goods, home remedies, natural cosmetics, and other odds and ends.

But by this time, Hunt's approach of buying what he wanted when he wanted was beginning to create problems. Hunt Oil was put into something of a cash squeeze by a new legal limitation on oil production from Texas wells, compounded by the need to continue to upgrade old production facilities, to make them more efficient, and to meet changing federal guidelines for pollution control. The company also had to keep investing some money in looking for new fields as production in old fields declined; and with the increase in offshore and deep-well drilling, each new strike was more expensive to bring in.

In this tightening environment, the food businesses not only did not begin to pay back Hunt's investments, but also ran up large and ever-increasing losses. From the outset, HLH Products reportedly lost $1 million a year. From Hunt's point of view, initially these losses were only a kind of investment in other parts of the empire. One million dollars a year was what HLH Products spent on advertising to consumers, advertising conducted almost exclusively on Hunt's LIFE LINE radio program.

But by 1969, HLH Products' losses were a lot bigger and a lot more puzzling. They reportedly totaled $5 million a year, and could not be seen as benefiting any other part of the Hunt organization. One after another, trusted employees and family members tried to talk to Hunt about what was going wrong with HLH Products. Perhaps, some people were concluding, the problems extended beyond too many products, unsophisticated marketing, poorly coordinated production runs, or other classic business inefficiencies. Perhaps the extremely loose structure of Hunt Oil and HLH Products had created a situation in which someone was taking advantage of Hunt and somehow defrauding the company of the money that should have enabled it to break even on these goods.

After months of talking, Hunt finally agreed that Herbert, Lamar, nephew Tom Hunt, and Bill Beeman, secretary-treasurer of the corporation, could conduct an investigation of their own into what was happening at HLH Products. This investigation turned up evidence of gross mismanagement of assets and operations, perhaps even of fraud. But before any action could be taken against the three employees who appeared to be responsible for the problems, they resigned, within a few days of one another, taking with them a number of potentially incriminating files.

Although the probable culprits were now out of the Hunt businesses altogether, Bunker, in particular, felt frustrated. Not only were they out of reach of legal action, but also his father still did not completely believe that the three, all of whom he had been close to, were guilty. There might also be, he thought, people still in HLH who had been involved. Bunker decided that there was a way of proving to himself, his father, and everyone else exactly what had gone on. He would do what one of his friends in Houston had done very successfully: hire a private detective agency, which could record relevant phone conversations between the three men, conversations that might establish their guilt. In the autumn of 1969, Bunker hired his agency, and thus unknowingly let himself and his brother Herbert in for two decades of intense and often negative public scrutiny.

FOURTEEN

IN November 1969, at the request of Bunker Hunt, several employees of Clyde Wilson Associates, a Houston firm of private investigators, went to Dallas to tap the phones of six individuals living there. All six were or had been employees of Hunt Oil Company. The objective of the taps was to gather evidence that could prove to H. L. Hunt that some of his trusted employees were not to be trusted after all. Once Bunker and his brother Herbert, who was the only other person involved in the undertaking, could convince Hunt of what had been going on, Hunt Oil and HLH Products could take legal steps to recover some of the millions of dollars HLH Products had lost over the past few years.[1]

Unfortunately for the future of this undertaking, what the Clyde Wilson employees were to do was now a federal offense. The Omnibus Crime Act of 1968 had gone into effect on January 1, 1969 banning any and all "bugging" unless court-ordered. Such activity was now punishable by a fine of up to $10,000 and/or four years in prison. Whereas the Clyde Wilson employees and their superiors were aware of this law, many private citizens were not. It was, after all, still three years before Watergate brought the details of wiretapping illegality to the attention of most Americans.

In January 1970, Jon Kelly, one of the investigative agency's operatives, was stopped by police for a minor traffic violation during the time he was monitoring the wiretaps. When he was questioned about the recording equipment in his car, he admitted he was a private detective, though he declined to say for which clients or on what kind of case he was working. Through the Clyde Wilson hierarchy, Bunker and Herbert quickly learned of the arrest, and also—according to their recollection—for the first time learned that the wiretaps they had authorized were illegal. They recommended an attorney for Kelly and offered to pay his legal bills. The traffic case against Kelly was dismissed in March, but whether he would be indicted on federal charges was still uncertain.

Meanwhile, the two brothers decided to have another agency, the Dale Simpson agency, continue to investigate the HLH Products situation. Perhaps some other information could be assembled that would ultimately enable them to collect against their losses, either through their bonding company or by suing the three men they believed had defrauded the company. The new detectives were able to amass what they considered a substantial amount of evidence against the former employees, and in November 1970 Hunt Oil sued the three for close to $1 million.

By this time, Bunker, Herbert, and others in the company had also convinced Hunt that HLH Products was a lost cause. In fact, they had concluded, in part through the information gathered by the Dale Simpson group, that this division of the corporation had lost $30 million already. Subsequently, most of the assets of HLH were auctioned or sold off, until only one manufacturing facility, in Dallas, remained at the end of 1970.

During that year, as the closing down of HLH created a changed organizational structure at Hunt Oil, Hunt either decided himself or at least agreed to expand the board of the parent company. It was then that Ray Hunt became a board member, joining his father, George Cunyus, senior vice-president, and Bill Beeman. A few months later, a representative of Hunt's original family, Margaret's husband, Al Hill, joined the board as well.[2]

Although Bunker and Herbert, as well as some other Hunt Oil employees, had been successful in braking the Hunt Oil losses and indirectly in restructuring the company, they were not in a position to enjoy their achievements. Shortly after their investigation led to the suit against the three former employees, Bunker and Herbert were sued by the wife of one of the employees for $1.5 million; she charged them with invasion of her individual and professional privacy. They also found that they, as well as the entire Hunt family and organization, were the subject of a number of rumors and innuendos, apparently originating with the three former employees.

For the next six months, charges and countercharges, suits and countersuits were traded back and forth. Eventually, in May 1971, having reached a stalemate, Bunker, Herbert, and the former employees decided to drop both their legal proceedings and their rumor war.

This uneasy truce between the two parties did not conclude the wiretap situation, however. Because a federal law had been violated, matters were outside the hands of the Hunts or their former employees. Although a great many other things were to happen to Bunker and Herbert during the extremely long period it took to resolve the subsequent legal actions, it is worth looking at what one Hunt biographer termed the "wiretap caper" in its entirety.

During all of 1970 and for most of 1971, as Bunker and Herbert pursued their investigation and then took steps on the basis of their new evidence, nothing further happened in the wiretap case. Then, on May 12, 1971, Jon Kelly and Patrick McCann, with whom Kelly had been working at the time of his traffic violation, were indicted for the wiretap violations, which had taken place almost eighteen months before. They were convicted on August 19, and on September 9 were each sentenced to three years in prison. Throughout this time, the Hunts continued to pay for the legal defense of the two Clyde Wilson employees; during the same time, neither of the defendants named the employer for whom their company had been working at the time they committed the crimes for which they were soon to be incarcerated.

In the fall of 1971, perhaps in an attempt to have his sentence reduced, Kelly decided to tell his probation officer that the Hunts had hired his company for the wiretaps. Kelly was ordered to testify against Bunker and Herbert before a federal grand jury. But then he changed his stance; he refused to implicate the Hunts or to testify, and, consequently, was cited for contempt.

At this point, Kelly decided he needed a new attorney. He chose Percy Foreman, an outstanding Texas trial lawyer with an excellent record. Unfortunately, he was also very expensive. When Kelly could not meet his fee requirements, Foreman resigned from the case. Apparently deciding he wanted Foreman regardless of who paid the bills, Kelly turned back to Bunker and Herbert; they reportedly agreed to put up a $50,000 retainer, and Foreman was again Kelly's attorney. By this time it was January 1972, two years after Kelly's original arrest.

While Kelly was preparing his appeal, the net of the federal investigators snagged another Clyde Wilson employee. On January 14, 1972, W. J. Everett, a more senior employee of the private investigating agency, was indicted for his involvement in what was now identified as the Hunt case. A few days later, perhaps believing that the government was becoming more interested in the "master-minds" of the case rather than in the operatives, Patrick McCann, who had been found guilty and sentenced along with Kelly, apparently decided to make a deal similar to the one Kelly had considered. McCann offered to provide information regarding the Hunts' involvement in the case in return for immunity from additional charges. His offer was accepted, and he did not change his mind at the last minute: he gave a grand jury the original tape recording of the conversation in which Bunker first made contact with the agency.

During this period, though they were being implicated by the Clyde Wilson employees, Bunker and Herbert were still paying the legal bills for the continuing participation of the expensive Percy Foreman. Despite Foreman's skills, however, in June 1972, the convictions of Kelly and McCann, which had been appealed, were upheld. In July, both men agreed to testify before a federal grand jury about the case, again perhaps in an attempt to have their sentences reduced.

In the midst of this legal maneuvering, Kelly, who was out of jail pending appeal, was working as a night security guard for E. J. Hudson, a friend of the Hunts who had been a kind of go-between for them, the defendants, and the various lawyers. According to Harry Hurt's description, one night in June 1972, after his conviction in the Hunt case had been upheld, Kelly commandeered a notebook he found in Hudson's office in which the Hunts' friend had made notes regarding the cases.

After reading the notes, Kelly became convinced of something he had long suspected: the Hunts had been paying his and his codefendant's legal fees, not so the men could be well represented, but so they could be "controlled," so the damage they could do to the Hunts would be minimized while Kelly and his coworkers would be left to serve prison sentences.

Kelly later said that he had always believed that this was the Hunts' intent, and that at one point their plan was even more blatant:

they had offered Kelly money if he would serve his time and keep them out of the case. Now Kelly, who almost certainly was destined to spend some time in a federal prison, believed he had evidence that Bunker and Herbert had colluded to obstruct justice in the case, to protect themselves even though they knew they were guilty. If he was going to jail, he may well have concluded, he might as well see that the two brothers went with him.

When Kelly made his evidence available to the federal investigators and described to them his "payoff" experience, it became more and more likely that Bunker and Herbert would become directly involved in the wiretap cases. In March 1973, the die was cast. The two Hunts were indicted, along with two of the other private investigators, and were charged with illegal wiretapping. In April, the Hunts pleaded not guilty; the two other men pleaded guilty.

A few months later, the original defendants, Kelly and McCann, went to jail to begin serving their terms. In October 1973, feeling he had nothing to lose, including the Hunts' financial support, Kelly sued the brothers, as well as his former employer E. J. Hudson and the attorney Percy Foreman, alleging they had conspired to protect Herbert and Bunker at Kelly's expense.

As soon as the Hunts were indicted on the first charges against them, they hired a lawyer to handle their own defense. Rather than a criminal lawyer, however, they chose a noted civil rights lawyer, Philip J. Hirschkop. Hirschkop, an Easterner, was known for his defense of controversial figures, including H. Rap Brown and members of the Scientology Church. As part of his plan to have the Hunts found not guilty, Hirschkop began granting interviews in which he questioned the various allegations and charges, pointing out the advantages to other people of making the Hunts look bad.

Hirschkop also encouraged Bunker and Herbert to talk to the press themselves and to give the kind of people who would be likely to serve on a jury judging them an opportunity to see them, not as two rich, spoiled, vindictive brothers, but as two thoughtful and caring sons who had been trying to protect their aging and easily hoodwinked father. In July 1974, Hirschkop's presentation was aided when two of the three men Bunker and Herbert had originally suspected of defrauding HLH Products were indicted for mail fraud related to their dealings at Hunt Oil; in March 1975, they were convicted.

Throughout 1974 and into 1975, preparations for the now apparently inevitable trial of Bunker and Herbert continued. In July 1975, there was more bad news for the Hunts. They were indicted for obstruction of justice, the indictment stemming in large part from evidence provided by Kelly. In this indictment, too, the Hunts were not alone. Their friend E. J. Hudson was indicted, as were various attorneys the Hunts had hired for the Clyde Wilson employees: Percy Foreman, Ralph Shank, Charles Tessmer, and B. H. Timmins. These charges were later dismissed.[3]

Finally, in September 1975, almost six years after Bunker had made the first phone call to the Houston private investigators, he and Herbert were brought to trial on the original charges of illegal wiretapping. The trial was held in Lubbock, a town in North Texas some distance from Dallas. Although the Hunts were certainly known there, the case had received less press coverage than in Dallas, where a fair and objective trial might have been impossible.

Testimony lasted for a week. Hirschkop's defense centered on two things. The first was that both men were originally unaware that what they were asking the detective agency to do was illegal. The second was that they had not acted with "evil intent," but had been trying to protect their aging and ill-used father. Apparently Hirschkop's defense was convincing: after three hours of deliberation, the jury found the brothers not guilty.

"If we'd been just ordinary folks, Herbert and I would have been in real trouble," Bunker said to a reporter afterward.[4] The two men had paid over a million dollars in legal fees to defend themselves, all in a situation that grew out of a wrong they believed had been done them. Bunker told the reporter that if he had not had the money to hire topnotch legal minds, he and Herbert would have landed in jail along with McCann, Kelly, and Everett.

After the not-guilty verdict in the wiretap case, Herbert and Bunker faced one more legal hurdle: the charges of obstruction of justice. This case was resolved by their attorney, Philip Hirschkop, seven months later. In April 1976, the charges were dropped against Herbert. Bunker pleaded nolo contendere (meaning he neither admitted guilt nor contested the accusation) to a charge that he "did knowingly misbehave" when he offered to pay the private investigators if they would not involve Herbert and him in the case. Bunker paid a fine of $1,000, and the case was closed. Eventually, the only other pending legal matter, Jon Kelly's civil suit, was settled out of court. It was all over.

During the seven years it took to resolve the wiretap caper, Bunker and Herbert were involved in a great many other undertakings, including some with legal implications. Although they emerged relatively unscathed from this particular set of problems, there were two significant long-term effects of the wiretapping situation. One was that the two men received a great deal of adverse publicity as the case dragged on and reappeared in the press year after year. And although the press was more sympathetic during the Lubbock trial, the two men were not only well known by the time it was over, but also somewhat marked by the close call they had had with federal marshals.

The second effect was much more subtle, and can, indeed, only be inferred. As the wheels of federal justice ground on and on in the wiretap case, Bunker and Herbert both came to feel beleaguered, as if the world, and particularly Washington, D.C., "had it in for them." The insecurity they may well have felt as they considered the possibility of prison sentences and the implied lack of power and control over their own destinies may have played a significant role in some of the decisions they made to protect themselves and their fortunes during the time they were facing indictment and trial.[5]

Around the time of their indictment on illegal wiretapping charges, Bunker and Herbert first become seriously interested in a set of investments they made to insulate themselves against a changing and perhaps crashing world economy. These investments were in silver.

The year was 1973. It was not a smooth year for either Bunker or Herbert. Besides the wiretap indictment, there was the increasing pressure on Bunker's holdings in Libya, leading to their nationalization in June. There was also the successful formation by their half-brother Ray of a new Hunt Oil subsidiary, Woodbine Development Corporation, which Ray planned to use as the basis of a major new direction for the company, a direction he would determine, to the benefit of himself and his part of the family.

These things, which affected Bunker's and Herbert's personal and economic well-being, took place against the larger backdrop of a complex and unstable world economic situation. Inflation was threatening to erode the value of the kinds of investments Bunker and Herbert had made in the past. True, rising oil prices as a result of the pressures of the OPEC consortium would benefit them. But they, and other members of the family, had enormous amounts of money invested in other holdings—farms, ranches, commercial real estate, and cattle—which might well lose value and even become highly illiquid in the event of a worldwide economic decline ignited by rampant inflation. And if things got bad enough, it would not be long before the OPEC nations began undercutting one another, leading to a decrease in energy prices that would further erode the Hunts' position.

There were several approaches open to Herbert and Bunker as they considered how they could protect themselves and their fortunes. One was to make short-term investments that could keep pace with inflation, thus protecting the basic value of their assets and maybe bettering them. Another, oriented toward the long haul, was to identify investments that were inflation- or even crash-resistant, things that would keep their inherent value in a rapidly changing world and that might serve as the basis for a new economy in the event of total disaster.

The brothers ran across a book, popular at the time, called *Silver Profits in the Seventies*. The author, Jerome S. Smith, was an investment adviser who had a very skeptical view of the future of the U.S. economy. His premise was that in an unstable world, the wise investor needs a stable investment, such as precious metals. If the worst were to happen—if all paper money became completely worthless, and the current economy broke down irreversibly—what would be more likely to become the currency of choice than precious metals, particularly those that had been used for exchange for thousands of years: silver and gold.[6]

The most common way to invest in silver is through the commodity futures market. Futures, the right to purchase a commodity such as grain, pork bellies, copper, or silver sometime in the future, formed a market of their own. Speculators, who usually have no intention of ever taking possession of the products they trade in, take positions in the commodities futures markets that assume the value of a given commodity will go up or down. They could, at one time, even "straddle" the market, buying (for example) in December for an up market in March and a down market in June. Futures trading is quick, easy, and extremely sensitive to changes in the real world, whether the result of strikes, weather, Soviet politics, or U.S. inflation rates.

Besides buying silver futures, it was also possible for Bunker and Herbert to buy the actual silver. One way to do this easily was to buy futures and then let that future "expire." They would then be obligated to purchase the silver and take possession of it. Since the brothers wanted a certain amount of silver anyway, this was an acceptable way of buying it sometime in the immediate future but at a price that was guaranteed from the date of purchase. An alternative was simply to buy silver outright at the current price and take possession of it immediately.

According to what Herbert said later, in explaining the Hunts' decision to invest in silver, *Silver Profits in the Seventies* and other books with similar perspectives had a significant influence on them. As they looked into precious metals, they found that consumption of silver exceeded refining capacity by more than 200 million ounces annually. This imbalance, they reasoned, caused silver to be undervalued, both in absolute terms and relative to other precious metals, particularly gold.

They hypothesized that the true ratio of gold to silver, based on the laws of supply and demand, was five to one. That is, if gold was priced at $100 per ounce, silver should be selling for $20 an ounce. Apparently this idea came from Smith's book, though he had predicted that the ratio would be a more modest sixteen to one, this being the traditional ratio between the two metals.

By 1974, the brothers had begun buying both silver bullion and futures contracts that entitled them to buy more silver in the future at a fixed price. In April, Bunker reportedly already owned around 20 million ounces, and he had become a figure of interest to the commodities market. When he visited the commodity exchange, he was interviewed by a reporter from *Barron's*. "Just about anything you buy, rather than paper, is better," Bunker said, explaining his investment strategy. "You're bound to come out ahead, in the long pull. If you don't like gold, use silver, or diamonds or copper, but something. Any damn fool can run a printing press." He then pointed out that even Switzerland was suffering from inflation, in large part due to the oil situation. He ended by saying that his was a layman's view, but he added, laughing, that "the economists haven't done too well. It's the screwballs and the goldbugs who've been right."[7]

As 1974 progressed, Bunker and Herbert continued to buy silver—not just silver futures, but actual bullion. Reportedly, they took delivery of somewhere between 35 and 50 million ounces of silver during the year. Silver was not their only investment, however. One of the other major deals in which they were involved came out of investment contacts they made in the silver market, but it was in a different commodity area altogether.

In October 1974, Herbert, Bunker, and the husband of their half-sister Helen, Randy Kreiling, heard about an investment opportunity that indirectly involved the commodities market and that looked like it could return short-term profits with relatively low risk. The man promoting this investment was an institutional broker who had previously sold gold stocks to the Hunts. He described to the three men an undervalued stock he was touting in a company called Great Western United. The company's commodity involvement was in sugar; it was one of the largest refiners of beet sugar in the nation, and consequently was active in the sugar futures market.[8]

Based on the information they obtained in a long meeting on October 9 with the broker recommending the stock—and apparently only on this information—the Hunts decided to buy $3 million worth of the company's stock, planning, it would appear, to sell it when the price rose. Around the end of October, an attorney who worked for the Hunts met with financial analysts in New York to find out more about the stock, which by then had already been purchased. What he discovered came as an unpleasant surprise: the stock was not truly undervalued; its low price reflected serious management problems. The bottom line was that it was unlikely to return a profit to the Hunts in the foreseeable future.

Not ready to write off their investment or to wait indefinitely for it to make a decent return, Herbert met with the company's management and offered to buy a controlling interest and then help get the company back on track. This first offer was refused, but within a month, the Hunts were able to take control of the company for a total investment of about $30 million, which they raised themselves, relying in part on a loan from Hassie's trust. Bunker and Herbert appointed themselves chairman and president of Great Western United respectively.

The Hunts' action was not without precedent for them. According to a *Business Week* article that appeared a few months later, Herbert, in 1973, had successfully masterminded a heavy involvement in a company that supplied Penrod Drilling, one of the Hunt

Oil subsidiaries. The company, Marathon Manufacturing, was supposed to supply some offshore drilling rigs to Penrod, but it was running way over on costs and was behind on delivery dates. Bunker and Herbert, joined by Lamar, bought fourteen percent of the company plus a $6-million note, canceled part of their rig order to reduce manufacturing pressure on the company, and saved it from declaring bankruptcy. The article recounted how the deal was struck: when the lawyer Herbert had brought along started working on an elaborate agreement, Herbert and the chairman said they'd just work out something on one piece of paper "and get it over with." Within an hour, they had signed a binding agreement. This shoot-from-the-hip approach was apparently one Bunker and Herbert tried to emulate as they got involved in Great Western.

But as the Great Western venture increased in complexity, Herbert and Bunker were distracted from both it and their silver purchases by a major change in the lives of Hunt family members. About a month before the brothers first heard about Great Western, their father fell ill and was hospitalized. *The History of Hunt Oil Company* says Hunt's health had been declining for several months. By September 13, 1974, he looked unwell, had no appetite, and was becoming weak. That day, he agreed finally to see a doctor.

Hunt's doctor suggested that he be hospitalized. He entered Baylor Hospital, in Dallas, where he became increasingly weak. Ruth was with him constantly, and the family gathered to offer support. Even Swanee, who was living in Germany, made a number of trips across the Atlantic to see her father and help her mother deal with her impending loss.

On November 29, 1974, Hunt died. His funeral was held on December 2 at the First Baptist Church. The Reverend Criswell conducted the service, and June Hunt sang one of her father's favorite hymns. Almost every employee of Hunt Oil attended the service. By then innumerable obituaries of Hunt had appeared, most of which focused on the eccentricities of his later years as well as his great wealth. His children from his first marriage were named, as was his second legal wife, but the children Hunt had with Ruth were generally described as "the children by a previous marriage." Hunt's relationship with Frania Tye Lee was not mentioned.[9]

Almost immediately after Hunt's death, on December 4, news of his will became public, after it was filed with the Dallas County clerk's office. The will was dated February 24, 1971.[10] At the time the will was written, Hunt's children had seemed to be making their own way successfully, with the exception of Hassie, who was still unable to manage his own affairs. Bunker was taking great quantities of oil out of Libya, Herbert was overseeing large real estate deals for the family business, and Lamar was involved in the AFL as well as soccer and tennis. Both Caroline and Margaret were married, and their husbands were working for the company. Helen and Swanee were also married, and June was launching her career as a performer. Ray had recently been named to the board of Hunt Oil and was most involved in the energy operations of the company. Of Hunt's and Frania's children, Haroldina, though not without problems, was also married. Helen had been killed in a plane crash twelve years before, and the two sons, Howard and Hugh, were carrying on their lives independent of Hunt, apparently able to provide for themselves and their families by using the funds Hunt had settled on Frania plus money they had obtained from him over the years. In short, none of Hunt's children was in financial need, and there was no pressing reason for Hunt to provide for them in any way other than through the trusts he had set up long ago.

It was not surprising, then, that Hunt had left the bulk of his estate to his wife, Ruth. The estate consisted primarily of his shares in Hunt Oil and the Mt. Vernon house. What also could have been expected was that he appointed as executor of his will his youngest son, Ray. As Ruth's son, Ray would be in a good position to work out the will's provisions for his mother. As a director of Hunt Oil, he would have, perhaps, the best grasp of the company's position and how it would be affected by probate.

Although Hunt's will indicated that he had made his decisions after careful analysis of his own wishes, he also seemed to have anticipated that there might be some question among his other children as to the wisdom of his choices. Naming Ray as executor and not mentioning by name any of Frania's children clearly created opportunities for infighting and disagreement. Perhaps because of this, Hunt had put a "challenge clause" into his will, which stated that anyone who challenged or aided a challenge of the will shall "lose and forfeit all right to any benefit and all right and title to any property" the challenger would otherwise have received.

Hunt seemed not to have informed any of his children of the specific provisions of his will. Ray said, apparently sincerely, that the appointment came to him "totally out of the blue."[11] None of the other children commented publicly on Hunt's choice, but Hunt's biographer Harry Hurt describes a certain amount of bitterness and frustration on the part of the children who might have expected, due to their age, experience, or position in the family, to have been named executor in addition to or instead of Ray. Bunker and Herbert, in particular, went out of their way to thwart Ray as he attempted to begin his duties, refusing for months to return his phone calls or meet with him face to face.[12]

For Ray, the appointment was not an unmixed blessing. Since his creation of Woodbine Development in 1973, he had been heavily involved in a major project in downtown Dallas, which had demanded a great deal of his time and energy until only a few months before his father's death. The so-called Reunion project consisted of development of a large parcel of land, more than nineteen acres, on the western edge of the central business district. Some of the adjoining land belonged to the city of Dallas; it was the site of the old Dallas railroad station, then in disuse. "Ownership lines between the private (Hunt Oil) and the public (City of Dallas) sectors were so disarranged, it was impossible for either party to develop the land properly," one top Hunt employee said in the company history.[13]

Rather than work alone on a development plan, Ray had spent a year meeting informally with the Dallas city manager to discuss how his company and the city could develop the land to their mutual advantage. He commissioned a $250,000 land-use study to help in the planning. The final proposal was that "Hunt would spend $75 million on land improvement and a hotel / restaurant complex, and perhaps another $180 million in office and convention buildings; the city would renovate the train station, lease open land, and put up a public building," according to *Forbes* in 1981. By the time H. L. Hunt died, Ray had formally presented his plan to the Dallas City Council. It had been approved, and, in the fall, development had begun. At this point, Ray had "decreased significantly" his own time on the project, but its scope and complexity—there would ultimately be a Hyatt Hotel; Reunion Tower, a dramatic multiuse building; a renovated Union Station; and an 18,500-seat sports and entertainment facility—guaranteed that it would continue to demand his careful supervision for years to come.

Another business problem facing Ray when he began to take on his duties as executor of his father's will was that Hunt Oil had been something of a rudderless ship for over a decade. Within the energy business, Hunt himself had focused only on big oil deals, but he had nonetheless limited the opportunities for Ray or any other family member to step into the consequent management gap his absences left. Not only had Hunt Oil been drained by the financial losses of HLH Products and thus limited in the amount of cash it had available to start new projects, but the company had not kept up with trends in energy exploration as well as it should have, nor had it been restructured so these trends could be identified and followed. In the words of the *Forbes* reporter, "the company had been creeping for years toward a slow death."[14]

At first it appeared that, despite the company's problems and Ray's position as executor, business would continue in its highly decentralized way. At least, this was the hope of some family members. Lamar, for example, was quoted in a February 1975 *Business Week* article as saying that Ray's appointment "was a natural thing" but "it does not mean that Ray will run the business. . . . He will have the responsibility of making decisions in relationship to Dad's property, but Dad's operation was much simpler." He continued, "Hunt Oil . . . will be run basically by employees of the company. We all will continue to operate out of the Hunt Oil office."[15]

Ray seemed to have a different plan. Because of his position on the Hunt Oil board of directors, he knew what the problems of the company were and that it was important for someone to "take hold" and get the organization back on its feet. Building on his role as executor and aided by the fact that his mother was now a major shareholder in the company, Ray was officially elected president of Hunt Oil on March 11, 1975, three and a half months after his father's death.

Even before this formal step, Ray had begun planning for the future of Hunt Oil. It was at this point that all the years he had listened to his father talk to old wildcatters and former Exxon drillers or simply reminisce bore fruit. Ray had truly come to believe that his father had done something very, very right as he developed Hunt Oil. "For a man with limited formal education, to start with absolutely nothing and end up creating the kind of organization he created, he obviously did a number of things very well and correctly," Ray was quoted as saying in the company history. "Ray saw in his father a successful entrepreneur and was willing to sit at his feet and learn something, where the other brothers weren't," Jack Evans, former Dallas mayor, was quoted as saying in a 1986 article about Ray. [16]

As a result of his belief in the integrity of his father's approach, Ray tried to capture the essence of this approach before it was too late. "One of the things that I did, a very conscious decision that I made, was I realized that peoples' memories either become dull or distorted over time," Ray explained in a 1987 interview. "In the immediate aftermath of my father's death, in the course of the next twelve months, I wanted to try to identify as many of the principles as I could that were responsible, that my father personified, that allowed a person like him, with a sixth-grade education, to start with absolutely nothing in his pocket, and with a lot of hard work and some challenging decision-making end up as one of the world's great success stories." [17]

Yet, because of his firsthand knowledge of the problems confronting Hunt Oil, Ray decided that he would have to adapt the principles he identified to the world of the mid-1970s. "My basic philosophy is that times and conditions may change but principles very seldom change. The principles that made my father successful, while they might be manifest in a very different manner in today's society and today's economy, nevertheless are probably the same as they were when Dad was a young man."

Ray gradually began formulating his "principles" and acting on them. The principles he identified were relatively simple: attract the most capable people possible, give them a great deal of autonomy, let them have new responsibilities as fast as they can handle them, keep the organization lean, and let the employees know how much you value them, not necessarily through paying top dollar, but by taking care of them as a kind of extended family.

Ray also began restructuring the organization to enable it to meet the challenges of the seventies. He expanded the 1976 board of directors to include Ruth, Bunker, and Herbert, as well as three other Hunt Oil employees. He revitalized and expanded the exploration offices the company operated throughout the country. He began splitting up corporate responsibilities more clearly by appointing a vice-president for marketing, refining, and transportation; a vice-president for land; a vice-president for administration;

and a vice-president for real estate. He started looking for more opportunities for Hunt Oil to invest in offshore drilling projects and international oil-exploration ventures.

It did not take long for the new power structure of Hunt Oil to become as clear as the company's new direction was becoming. Ray and his part of the family clearly held the cards at Hunt Oil in terms of control of assets, and Ray was able to develop the organization in such a way that the employees would support his position. This, in turn, led to the final problem he faced as executor of his father's will and president of Hunt Oil: he now had a completely different kind of relationship with his half-siblings. Although he seemed to be comfortable developing Hunt Oil, his increasing power there created a situation that members of Hunt's original family apparently found both uncomfortable and constricting.

As *The History of Hunt Oil Company* tactfully put it, "In 1975, a decision was made to realign the company's ownership interests, and as an outgrowth of that decision, a long and difficult process of splitting up personnel relationships and properties began." The outcome was that Bunker and Herbert incorporated Hunt Energy Corporation, to embrace their businesses as well as those of the other members of Hunt's original family, and Hunt Oil Company served as the organizing agent for Ruth and her children's interests.

This final arrangement to split up the empire was called the "Prosper Deal." Certain assets of Hunt Oil were split off into a new entity, Prosper Energy Corporation. The eighteen percent interest the original family owned in Hunt Oil was traded for one hundred percent of Prosper Energy. Prosper Energy's holdings were then folded into Hunt Energy Corporation, which was by then the center of the other original family holdings, including those provided to the children in their original trusts, such as ownership of the large and valuable Placid Oil and Penrod Drilling companies. Although this exchange was not made final until December 1977, the formulation of the plan to split up holdings and actions began within a year of Hunt's death.

By July 1975, then, when Bunker and Herbert finally were able to have the wiretapping threat removed from their lives by the jury's not-guilty verdict, when the two brothers were grappling with the management of their investment in Great Western, when they were continuing to buy silver as if there were no tomorrow, they were on their own from a business point of view. Or, if not completely on their own relative to Lamar, Caroline, and Margaret, at least they were making their choices without the influence of their younger half-brother Ray. Whether they continued to be influenced by Ray and the directions in which he took their father's original company can only be inferred. But the fact that they were still influenced by certain aspects of their father's approach to business was to become clear. Bunker and Herbert were embarking on some high-risk ventures, just as H. L. Hunt had, and they were going to follow their sixth sense, wherever it led them, as they aimed to leverage these risks to new economic heights.

FIFTEEN

THE two branches of the Hunt family who shared in the assets of Hunt Oil Company managed to separate their holdings, their offices, and their fates once and for all in 1977. While the final disengagement of the two groups had been taking place, however, the key players in the groups had not been inactive. Ray Hunt was primarily focusing on regenerating Hunt Oil, both through new oil exploration and through enhancing its real estate operations. Bunker and Herbert Hunt were beginning their major investment in silver, grappling with their majority ownership of Great Western United, and continuing to invest in less dramatic but highly varied opportunities throughout the world.

The variety of investments Bunker and Herbert chose to make did not so much bely their tendency to believe in Armageddon—characterized by their stockpiling of silver—as indicate that they were not men to pass up a chance to make money right up to the end. One opportunity they became interested in would allow them to hold on to their silver and realize quick cash returns at the same time.

The silver the two brothers were gradually stockpiling was increasing in value. But during the late 1970s Bunker and Herbert were not in a position to sell the silver and pocket their profits. If they did so, they would be reducing their basic asset base; if the end came tomorrow, they'd be sorry not to have all that bullion stashed away somewhere. Additionally, if they sold the now substantially appreciated silver, they would have, as Bunker put it, "a tax problem"—they would have to pay hefty capital gains taxes on their profits.

Fortunately, there appeared to be a way for them to have their silver and make money from it, too. The plan was to borrow against their silver bullion and invest the cash in new areas of commodity futures. When the futures went up in value, the brothers would sell their holdings, and thus not only recoup their original investment (the money borrowed against silver), but also realize quick returns large enough to pay off the interest they owed on the borrowed money and to give them an attractive profit.

As with silver, the choice of investments began with a simple idea. Dr. Iben Browning, a climatologist from Albuquerque, New Mexico, was a man who believed he could explain the past and predict certain elements of the future by looking at long-term weather patterns. Dr. Browning was a highly acclaimed expert who reportedly was consulted by the CIA. He predicted, in the summer of 1976, that the world would soon experience a soybean shortage that would cross international boundaries.

Bunker was exposed to this prediction at a lunch he attended; he later recalled that it sounded very convincing to him, especially when he learned some other facts about soybeans: U.S. stocks were declining sharply; the Department of Agriculture was encouraging price increases; Brazil was taxing soybeans in order to keep them in their own country. The soybean situation looked volatile and ripe for speculation.[1]

At the time, anybody who wished and who had the capital available could speculate in soybeans as in other commodity futures. Contracts for future production of soybeans were what was bought and sold speculatively. Generally, only those who finally used the commodity, such as manufacturers of animal feeds, would want to take actual possession of the soybeans. But before the beans were physically available, anybody could speculate on their ultimate price.

There was, however, a limit on the amount of futures contracts any individual or group could hold. The 1976 soybean futures contract limit was 3 million bushels per individual or group. Bunker and Herbert each bought up to the limit during 1976 and into 1977, for a total of 6 million bushels. In addition, other members of their families, specifically six of their children (then ages nine to twenty-five) bought futures for another 18 million bushels. These purchases were made with interest-free loans from their fathers.

The fact that members of a single family were holding futures contracts for what was estimated to be one-third of the total annual U.S. supply of soybeans came to the attention of the Commodity Futures Trading Commission. The CFTC requested privately that the Hunts reduce their holdings; the family did so, but only by a token amount.

The CFTC then instituted public hearings, which resulted in an indictment and a request that a U.S. district court order the Hunts to liquidate their holdings. This request was denied, but it damaged the Hunts' trading nonetheless. As part of its request, the CFTC had taken the highly unusual step of publicly revealing exactly what holdings the Hunts had, at what price, and at what expiration or delivery date. Consequently, all the other players in the futures market had in effect seen the hand of the biggest single group of players and could predict the Hunts' future behavior and adjust their own strategies accordingly.

Among the information that came out of the CFTC hearings was exactly what had been going on behind the scenes as the family amassed its holdings. It was revealed that all the family members who were trading had their accounts with the same two brokers; that none of the children had ever traded in commodities futures before; that an accountant at Hunt Oil (which Bunker, Herbert, and their families used as a clearinghouse prior to the breakup of family interests later in 1977) regularly compiled holdings statements that listed those of all family members together. These facts certainly made it appear that the family was trading as a "group." In the hearings, Bunker staunchly denied that this was true, claiming to be unable to recall many of the details about who had opened which accounts and so on.

It is worth noting that apparently a year or so before the Hunts began investing in soybeans, Bunker and Herbert had sought legal counsel regarding their right to trade in commodities in tandem, as well as to trade privately at the same time their corporate entities were trading. They needed the information in part because the authority and power of the CFTC were not clear; the commission had been set up only in April 1975.

A legal opinion apparently provided to them explained that the Commodity Exchange Act prohibited individuals or groups from creating price distortions in commodities by their trading, and that a provision of the Sherman Antitrust Act made conspiring to "corner" or control a commodities market illegal. However, the memo also concluded that "the lines are quite ethereal and indistinct. I [the author of the memo] am unable to say with exactitude 'this may be done and that may not.' "[2]

After the CFTC's first request for court action was refused, it managed to have the case heard, in Chicago, on September 28, 1977. The court found that the Hunts had violated the regulations, but it did not impose any penalties, because the CFTC had not brought the proper kinds of charges against them. The point of the legal prohibitions was to prevent squeezing or cornering the market; the commission had not proved that the Hunts had done this—only that they had large holdings. Indeed, the CFTC legal counsel is reported to have believed they could not have proved that the Hunts violated the intent of the regulations because, just as the Hunts' legal counsel had said the previous year, the rules and regulations were so unclear it was almost impossible to prove anything. The CFTC appealed, and legal proceedings continued.

Meanwhile, because the Hunts' soybean futures contracts were all related to the 1977 crop, despite what happened in a court of law the commodities transactions were coming to a close. The Hunts ended up taking physical possession of the soybeans they had agreed to purchase at a given price; they then resold the beans. Bunker and Herbert claimed that the revelation of their positions earlier in the year had cost them substantial profits, and this may well have been the case. At that point the profits were purely on paper; the gain or loss was not actual until the final transaction had taken place—in this case, until the beans had been sold and changed hands one last time.

Late in 1977, the Hunts were able to make their sales above their initial purchase prices; therefore they did not have an actual net loss in the proceedings. In fact, the CFTC believed that they had realized final profits in the range of $40 million. Although the entire soybean incident was to cost the Hunts something further—the CFTC succeeded in having them fined $500,000 in an out-of-court settlement in 1981, and the Hunts paid legal fees that reportedly amounted to $1 million—they probably came out ahead financially.

But just as in the wiretap case a short time before, Herbert and Bunker had received substantially bad press. Around this time, it began to be said that they had a "bulletproof mentality"—an attitude that they weren't bound by the same rules and regulations that others had to obey. They had now acquired a bad reputation with the Commodity Futures Trading Commission, an organization that, as overseer of all commodities futures activities, could also influence their silver dealings.

Furthermore, as in the wiretapping situation, Bunker and Herbert saw themselves as victims in the soybean affair. Harry Hurt quoted Bunker as saying, in reference to the experience, "I think the reason, frankly, they jumped on us is that we're sort of a favorite whipping boy, you know. We're conservatives, and the world is largely socialist and liberal. And as long as they want to jump on somebody, they want a name and they want somebody that's on the other side."[3] Again, this attitude was one that may have been important in the steps the two brothers later took to build and protect their own empire, steps that were to have their own high cost.

Before these long-term implications became obvious, the brothers' idea of impending economic disaster continued to shape their behavior. Even while they invested in soybeans, they continued to buy silver futures and silver bullion. They had taken the additional step of buying a significant interest in a silver mine, a purchase that would give them direct access to silver bullion, and that also— though they did not think of it at the time—put them in a different position regarding regulators of silver futures purchases. For as mine owners, the Hunts would legally be considered not just speculators but actual members of the commercial silver market.

The purchase of the silver mine took the form of an acquisition of twenty-eight percent of the stock in Sunshine Mining, a publicly traded company located in Idaho, whose principal asset was the largest silver mine in the country. Bunker and Herbert also obtained the right to buy the rest of the stock in the company later at an attractive price.[4]

The Sunshine deal was carried out through the Hunts' other publicly held company, Great Western United. After their initial purchase of a controlling interest in Great Western, in 1974, they found out that the company had just as many problems as had originally been found by their attorney. In fact, during the first year of significant Hunt ownership, the company lost a great deal of money. It had perhaps been in an attempt to recoup this loss that Bunker and Herbert first directed Great Western into buying and selling silver futures. In 1977, Great Western reportedly made a great deal of money in silver, though overall the company still had losses. These speculations in silver had, in turn, led to Great Western's and the Hunts' acquisition of the interest in Sunshine.

While Bunker and Herbert forged ahead with their increasing commitment to silver, Libya once again came to Bunker's attention, in 1978. After incurring over a million dollars' worth of legal fees, he found that his suit against the big oil companies, for conspiring against him in Libya, had been dismissed. The judge ruled that disputes resulting from the action of another nation could not be resolved in U.S. courts. Shortly thereafter, however, a British court, where Bunker was a defendant against BP, returned a different finding. It ordered Bunker to pay BP for its capital investments on his behalf in Libya, ruling that the subsequent events there did not excuse him from this debt. In Great Britain, Bunker owed $32 million. He appealed both decisions, continuing to hope for a favorable outcome. These legal findings probably did not reassure him, however, as he considered where best to make further investments in a rapidly changing and unpredictable world.[5]

For most of the time that the Hunts had been investing in silver, it had remained relatively stable in price. But gradually the silver market itself became a volatile part of the investment scene. A September 1979 *Business Week* article reported that silver had jumped an unprecedented thirty-eight percent in recent weeks, with futures contracts selling for $12.64 an ounce. Gold, meanwhile, was up to $341 an ounce, or almost twenty-seven times the price of silver. The article gave the opinions of a number of experts that these commodities were due for a downward price correction. But, as one observer was quoted as saying, "Who would sell gold or silver short at this point [that is, buy on the assumption that the price would fall]? It would be like playing Russian roulette with five bullets in the gun."[6]

Part of the upturn in prices had to do with the fact that others, in addition to the Hunts, were apparently not only buying futures in silver, but also taking physical possession of the commodity and holding it somewhere. Over time, this meant a reduction in the supply of silver that could be traded—at least until some new sources appeared. These had been known to open up during the preceding decade, for example, when the Mexican government liquidated large silver holdings. But if this did not happen again, and more silver did not come on the market—if the available supply of silver was reduced—the same amount of money the "silver bugs" were eager to invest would be chasing less silver, driving the price up.

At the same time that silver was increasing in price volatility the whole country was in the grips of tremendous economic uncertainty. Inflation was continuing at high levels, interest rates were soaring astronomically, and the federal government appeared unable to handle the financial problems that seemed to grow daily. And there was bad news on the international front, too. In November 1979, Americans were taken hostage in Iran. In December, the USSR invaded Afghanistan. The resulting uncertainty could not have made the Hunts feel any more secure about the future of paper economies; amassing silver bullion still looked like security. Besides, the ratio of gold to silver was twenty-seven to one and Bunker and Herbert had long ago committed themselves to the belief that the free-market value of silver would be reached when the ratio was five to one.

Exactly what silver the Hunts were buying during 1979 and into 1980 and exactly what part they played in the runup in silver prices have been the subject of endless speculation. Many articles have been written about the silver scene during this period and about the Hunts' role in it. One book, *Beyond Greed*, by Stephen Fay, has covered the topic in depth. It asserts that the Hunts were engaged, almost from the time they bought their first ounce of silver, in a plan to drive the price up, to corner (or control) the market by the extent of their holdings, and then to force everyone who needed silver to pay any price they held out for. Fay also describes plans he believed he had uncovered for the Hunts to plot with other wealthy oilmen, primarily from the Middle East, in order to have still more money to put into controlling silver.[7]

On the other hand, there have been a number of arguments made by other reporters and observers that the Hunts were primarily following their original strategy of trying to buy up silver and hold on to it for the long haul. An article that appeared in *The Atlantic* in September 1980 pointed out that the Hunts had been highly visible in making their purchases; those attempting a corner would have operated in secret. And Bunker and Herbert in everything they ever said about their silver purchases—including extensive testimony under oath—asserted that buying and holding was always their one and only plan.[8]

Regardless of their motivation, by the end of 1979, when silver futures were going up quickly, the Hunts both owned a great deal of silver and had committed themselves to buying a great deal more. In order to understand their situation, it is useful to look at the structure of the commodities market in more detail.

When an investor buys futures—the right to purchase a commodity at a given price sometime in the future—he is entering into a relatively unusual sort of a business deal. Using silver as an example, first of all, he is not buying silver, but a right to buy silver later. Second, he has a choice of how he structures his deal. If he thinks the price of silver is going up, he may commit himself to buy that silver at a higher price in the future. Thus, if he thinks silver is going to go up twenty-five percent, he may contract to buy it at a price ten percent higher than it is currently, gambling that he will be able to turn a profit by buying at 110 percent of the current price and selling at 125 percent. This is going "long." If he thinks the price is going to fall, he goes "short"—contracts to sell the silver for a lower price than it is currently worth. He is gambling that the price will go much lower. Thus, if he thinks the price will fall twenty-five percent, he may contract to sell the silver for a price ten percent lower than it is currently. If he guesses correctly, and contracts to buy the silver in the future for seventy-five percent of the current price, he will be able to sell it for ninety percent of the current price, because, of course, somebody else was gambling the other way and went long.

Why don't people actually buy and sell silver itself rather than silver futures if they think the price is going to move? This is the third thing that makes the commodity business unusual. In buying or selling futures, the investor, dubbed "the client," works with a broker, who does the actual purchasing or selling for him. The broker requires from the client only a kind of down payment for the business he does. Rather than having to put up $1,000 to buy a futures contract valued at $1,000, the client puts up only the "margin," a percentage, often relatively low, of the total amount of the purchase. In 1979, for silver this was only four percent of the total value of the contract, so a $1,000 contract could be bought for $40, whereas $1,000 worth of silver could be bought only for $1,000. When a client buys on margin, in effect the rest of the money is loaned to him by the broker, who has the ultimate legal responsibility to settle all futures contracts—buying and selling—for all his clients.

This loan is subject to interest, just as any loan is, and the client is also required by the broker to have some assets that can be held as collateral for the rest of the money the client owes. This collateral can be in various forms. The client can, for example, give his broker a block of stock which the broker then holds. The client can then get money to invest by borrowing against the stock's current value, rather than having to sell the stock and pay commissions and taxes on it. If things go well, the broker never has to cash in this collateral. It is simply his security.

There is one hitch in the margin arrangement, however. At the end of each day, when the client's account is updated, his futures contracts may have changed in value. This was frequently the case during the volatile period of late 1979. If the changes went against the client—for example, if he held a long position in silver and the price fell that day—he lost money. The amount of this loss, if it exceeded the amount of his down payment, had to be made up by the client. If he came out ahead, the amount of his gain would be carried forward and he could use it as the additional margin.

Usually, commodities go up for a while, then down again for a while. Often, too, investors hold positions in more than one commodity, as the Hunts did when they were trading soybeans and silver, and Great Western did when it was trading silver and sugar. Sometimes an investor places all or at least most of his eggs in one basket; the Hunts did this when they invested more and more in silver relative to other commodities they might have held. Sometimes, as in late 1979, prices of a certain commodity just keep going in one particular direction, never faltering for what the market calls "an adjustment." If the prices keep going up, those who bet they would fall—the shorts—will be in trouble; if they keep going down, the longs will have to come up daily with additional money.

By late 1979 and early 1980, the Hunts had taken physical possession of a great deal of silver bullion.[9] Their holdings were scattered across the United States and Europe. They owned silver personally, through their various corporate entities, including their trusts, and in partnership with other individuals and corporations. In the fall of 1979, for instance, in partnership with a group of Saudi Arabians, they took possession of 40 million ounces of silver. In February 1980, the partnership acquired an additional 26 million ounces.

The Hunts, alone and with their partners, also had a substantially long position in the silver futures market as they kept betting that prices would go up more and more. When contracts came due—that

is, when the dates for which they had been drawn up came around—
the Hunts had been rolling them forward—trading a contract that
expired in December 1979, for example, for one that expired in
March 1980. They also kept adding new futures contracts to those
they held, buying contracts for another 32 million ounces as late as
January 1980.

There appear to have been several reasons why Bunker and Herbert kept rolling contracts forward. First, they still expected prices
to go up; they still were shooting for the five-to-one ratio. Second,
there were tax considerations. At the time, investments cashed in for
a profit by individuals in less than one year were taxed at a higher
rate than those held longer. The Hunts happened to have a lot of
futures contracts that they needed to hold at least until March 1980 if
they were going to avoid paying extra taxes on their gains.

Third, there was the cash situation. When a contract came due, if
it was not rolled forward, a physical transaction had to take place. If
Bunker, for example, was committed to buying 1,000 ounces of
silver on March 21, 1980, and he did not roll the contract forward, he
had to come up with the additional money required to buy that
silver, pay it to a seller, take the silver, and close out that contract.
Obviously, if he did not have the cash available to settle the contract,
he had to either roll it over or get the cash, from selling other investments. This became an important consideration later.

During late 1979 and early 1980, coming up with cash did not yet
appear to have been a major problem for the Hunts. Not only were
they finding enough money to take delivery of some silver, but also
their companies were investing cash in assets besides silver. Placid
Oil, for example, was generating $200 million a year from its North
Sea holdings alone, and was making investments in new oil-field
rights and in other energy-related corporations. The Hunts were
also making cash investments in holdings that were related to silver;
they bought their stake in Sunshine Mining and a substantial holding in the Bache Group, the brokerage house with which they did
most of their silver trading.

There was still good reason through mid-January 1980 to be
optimistic about silver. The price upswing of fall 1979 continued;
the price was $34.45 an ounce at the end of December 1979 and rose
steadily to a high of $50.00 on January 17. But, though this was good
news for the Hunts, whose total silver holdings on January 17 were

estimated to be worth $4.5 billion, other people were getting nervous about the price escalation, especially those who needed to buy silver to keep their businesses going and the shorts, who had been forced to come up with more and more money as silver prices kept rising.

The general skittishness led the bodies that regulated commodities trading to look at the Hunts and their activities, in an attempt to determine if they were doing anything illegal. After all, the Hunts had been involved in what appeared to the Commodity Futures Trading Commission to be an attempt to corner the soybean market only a few years before. In October 1979, Bunker and Herbert had a number of meetings with officials of the CFTC. They assured the commission that they were only trying to make reasonable investments for themselves. Whereas their arguments apparently were somewhat convincing, the brothers politely refused to sell any of the silver they had, and this may have weakened the strength of their other arguments.

About that time, one of the other bodies that controlled commodities futures trading, the Chicago Board of Trade, decided to take action; it raised margin requirements and limited the amount of silver futures any single speculator could hold to 3 million ounces. Traders had until mid-February 1980 to liquidate their extra holdings. This deadline could, of course, force prices of silver down, because sooner or later the people holding the futures would have to sell some of them, whether they got their target price or not.

In January, before silver hit its all-time high, the Commodity Exchange Corporation in New York took a stand similar to that of the CBOT. Futures holdings in silver there were restricted to 10 million ounces per trader, and the holders of extra contracts had until February 18 to sell them. COMEX followed this decision with one that put more pressure on traders like the Hunts: on January 21, they declared that no more regular silver trading would take place on that exchange. Nobody was allowed to buy more futures contracts; everybody had to sell what they had.

Although silver was traded on several exchanges in the United States and throughout the world, this stance had a major impact on the market, as did the fact that silver had "come out of the woodwork" when prices rose so high; people were melting down coins and the family tea set in an unprecedented frenzy of silver selling. On

January 22, the price of silver dropped to $34 an ounce and remained below $40 for the next few weeks before gradually declining further. By March 14, 1980, silver, which had hit a temporary high of $50 only two months before, was down to $21 an ounce.

Of course, as the price of silver declined, the longs were faced with the problems the shorts had been grappling with for months, and even years. They had to find additional cash to maintain their margin positions. If they could not, they had to sell investments to generate it. If the worst happened, and they could not meet their obligations, their brokers had the right to liquidate the collateral they held for the clients at whatever price they could obtain for it. In other words, an insolvent client became largely powerless over those of his holdings he had assigned to the brokerage house as collateral.

The largest long holdings were those of Bunker and Herbert. Whereas in November, December, even February, the brothers still had cash to use in buying silver, silver futures, and stock in other companies, now this cash was disappearing more and more quickly. When prices dipped in March, they needed $10 million a day just to keep their accounts current. Suddenly the vast cash flow of Placid Oil—$200 million a year—did not seem so endless. All of Placid's profits would be spent, at this rate, in less than a month.

By March 25, 1980, the Hunts were in real trouble.[10] They were still rich on paper, and their companies were still valuable. They could generate a certain amount of money from these sources, but it was running out. And, because many of their investments were related, directly or indirectly, to silver, if they began liquidating them to meet other silver obligations, they could drive the price of silver down farther, effectively raising their own margin calls and thus putting themselves deeper and deeper in the hole.

That afternoon, after the commodities brokers tallied accounts for the day, Bache called the Hunts to tell them that, by the opening next morning, they had to come up with $135 million. Bunker had already mortgaged hundreds of race horses that day, but had not generated enough money. Herbert, faced with inarguable reality, did not mince words with Bache. He said that he and his brother simply could not make their margin call.

The next morning, Bache, as was its right, began selling off the collateral they held against loans to the Hunts. Unfortunately, this collateral was silver. Whereas a few weeks before, the Bache holdings would have been more than enough to pay off the Hunts' debts, as prices fell the value of the collateral had, too. Bache estimated that the collateral they held against what were, in effect, their loans to the Hunts would be used up in the next day or so. Then, not only the Hunts, but also Bache would be in a precarious position. The company informed the Commodities Futures Trading Commission of their situation and requested that silver trading be temporarily suspended to give them a chance to regroup. This proposal was refused.

The same day, the Hunts, with their Arab partners, made one last attempt to raise cash, this time on a much more massive scale than mortgaging horses. They offered silver certificates to any interested buyers, the certificates to be backed by unnamed banks. In effect, the Hunts were offering to take cash from investors in return for paper certificates guaranteeing the investors a certain number of ounces of silver from the Hunts' holdings, which they described as 200 million ounces. This is more or less what the U.S. government does, for example, in issuing dollar bills. Takers of this offer did not step forward, however, at least not in adequate numbers to save the Hunts.

News of what was facing the Hunts and Bache spread quickly through the commodities and stock markets the next day, March 27. Silver had been continuing its decline, and opened at $15.80 that day as traders anticipated that the Hunts would dump silver, depressing prices, and tried to get in ahead of them, before the market really dropped. The price of silver quickly declined by one-third, down to $10.80, on the strength of the anticipated bad news. At the same time, the stock market started heading down as rumors predicted the fall of Bache and perhaps other Hunt creditors and massive sell-offs of Hunt positions in the stock market itself. The market dropped to its lowest level in five years, temporarily declining more than twenty-five points—a very substantial decline for that time. Trading in Bache stock was halted by the Securities and Exchange Commission, in light of that company's exposure. The stock market regained most of that day's loss, but silver did not recover, and Bache stock remained frozen for a week.

As the dust settled around "Silver Thursday," it was clear that Bunker and Herbert Hunt were enormously in debt. Much of the collateral for their investments was in silver. Their debts were complex. For example, they effectively owed $665 million to a single corporation, Engelhard Minerals, because they had promised to buy more silver from Engelhard. They also appeared to owe close to a billion dollars to other creditors. It took days to get even a rough estimate of their total commitments.

Obviously, what was needed if the Hunts were to meet their obligations in an orderly way, and thus prevent their creditors from suffering great losses, or even declaring bankruptcy themselves, was a loan. Several days of negotiations followed Silver Thursday, involving officers of major international banks operating under the watchful gaze of Federal Reserve head Paul Volcker. The Federal Reserve at the time was urging banks to manage lending closely, due to the limited availability of money for loans; for a loan of the magnitude the Hunts required, the Federal Reserve would clearly need to give tacit approval.

By Monday, the Hunts had the outline of a deal. A consortium of banks would lend to a partnership consisting of Bunker's and Herbert's trusts and Placid Oil, the family oil and gas exploration and production arm, a total of $1.1 billion, which the Hunts could use to pay their immediate debts. As collateral for this loan, the Hunts would put up 63 million ounces of silver, which would gradually be sold for cash to repay the loan, and coal properties worth an estimated $480 million. Placid put up oil and gas properties in Louisiana, the Gulf of Mexico, and the North Sea. Herbert estimated that the value of the collateral, at the time the loan was made, was $8 or $9 billion. It turned out later that the loan made to the Hunts constituted nine percent of all new loans made by U.S. banks during February and March of 1980.

Before the Hunts' arrangements were complete, the silver market crash was being investigated right and left.[11] The CFTC, which had already been unhappy with the Hunts, began an investigation that could lead to disciplinary actions or barring of some traders from the silver market. The SEC started looking into possible violations of federal security laws. A House of Representatives subcommittee began probing the situation, which included looking at whether the CFTC had done its job and which ultimately led to testimony by the Hunts themselves. The Senate also launched an investigation, which involved talking to the same regulators, experts, and, again, to the Hunts.

As information came to light, two things were clear. One was that Bunker and Herbert truly did not know exactly what they held when and where. They certainly had a good idea, but the complexity of their arrangements, their partnerships, their holdings all over the world made it impossible for them—two independent men trained to drill for oil, produce it, and sell it—to know exactly how complex their involvements were. Bunker managed to grab headlines by saying that when someone knew exactly what he was worth, he probably wasn't worth much; his attitude was viewed as cynical by many, as crafty by others. But it was certainly possible that he was simply telling the truth of the matter as he lived with it every day.

The second thing that the investigations showed was that the Hunts still believed silver was a good investment and that in their opinion the chaos of Silver Thursday had more to do with the manipulations of the commodities markets by the CFTC, COMEX, and the CBOT than with the intrinsic value of silver itself. Indeed, there was a lot of support for this belief. Even before the crash, a number of articles in responsible publications like the *Wall Street Journal* had pointed out that the changes in margin requirements were forcing so many people out of the silver market that trading was becoming "thin," and this in turn insured increased market volatility.

There was one other point that Bunker and Herbert attempted—unsuccessfully—to make in their appearances. They both said repeatedly that they had acted independently in their tradings in silver, that they had not colluded or plotted to control the market. Herbert did say, "We know each other. We office in the same building. We do eat meals together, lunch I am talking about." But that was all the togetherness Herbert would admit to. Bunker added, "I think the problem is that we talk too much to each other and not enough to others."[12] But their having lunch and sharing a world view did not a conspiracy make in their eyes. The congressional committee had its doubts. It asked the Justice Department to look into whether or not the two men had perjured themselves in their testimony.

Over the next few months, as they were investigated and as the details of the loans made to the partnership established immediately after the crash were worked out, Bunker and Herbert were subjected to intensive scrutiny by journalists across the nation. An article in a Dallas paper in late May, for example, listed all the Hunts' assets put up to secure the loan, highlighting those that made good copy—a race horse named Goofed, a 2,500-year-old Greek statue, bags of gold coins, a Sears, Roebuck air conditioner. The cost of their loans was revealed elsewhere: $500,000 a day in interest alone.[13]

Bunker and Herbert countered the generally adverse press treatment by granting interviews to a *Fortune* reporter for an article that appeared in August.[14] The brothers "told their side of the scary silver drama" in between phone calls from Bunker to Europe to check on his race horses and health-conscious breakfasts for Herbert. In the article, the Hunts seemed to be ordinary human beings who had had some hard times. It was only the scope of their problem—a billion dollars of debt—that set them apart from everybody else.

SIXTEEN

THERE was a third man involved in the debacle of Silver Thursday and the subsequent negotiation of over a billion dollars in loans. This man did not readily lend himself to dramatic depiction as a shrewd Texas villain hiding behind a slow drawl and a plate of chicken fried steak. The third man's photograph rarely appeared in the papers, in contrast to repeatedly run pictures of the jowly, grinning Bunker and the highly controlled, almost frighteningly serious Herbert. This missing player was, after all, a kind of American sports hero, a member of the Professional Football Hall of Fame. How bad could a guy like that be? The third man was, of course, Bunker's and Herbert's little brother, Lamar.

Lamar had waded into the silver market while his brothers plunged, in the words of one newspaper article. Although he had never made a commitment even close in magnitude to that of his brothers, still he was implicated when the silver market crashed. In part, his involvement was inevitable: along with his sisters Caroline and Margaret and his brother Hassie, his assets were intermingled with those of Bunker and Herbert. Their jointly held corporation, Placid Oil, was both a cosigner of the massive borrowing agreement Bunker and Herbert had negotiated, and a provider of substantial collateral for the loan.

But whereas Caroline and Margaret quickly began distancing themselves from their brothers' dealings, as well as moving to protect the holdings of Hassie, Lamar stayed deeply involved with his brothers as they began to restructure and rethink their battered investments. When it came time to enumerate personal assets that would provide additional collateral, Lamar turned in his list right along with Bunker and Herbert.

What that list revealed was very interesting. Lamar, father of the Super Bowl, mastermind of big-scale professional tennis, staunch pioneer in professional soccer, sportsman *par excellence*, and glamorous role model for those with big-league capital but amateur athletic skills, was not doing particularly well.

A *Dallas Times Herald* article that described how the "Hunts bare financial souls in statements" listed Lamar's assets in his teams not in the form of capital holdings or even secured debt. Rather, he had promissory notes—basically, promises to pay money lent—due from most of his major sports investments. These included the World Championship Tennis Academy: $621,853; the WCT tour: $4,872,860; the Dallas Tornado soccer team: $1,781,900; and the Chicago Bulls professional basketball team: $63,000. So all of these sports entities owed Lamar money. While the total was modest compared to what his brothers owed in silver, at over $7 million it was nonetheless substantial.[1]

Lamar's public declaration of his rather precarious investments in sports was a foreshadowing of the innumerable sports-related problems that were to plague him over the next seven years. While he continued to be peripherally involved in the working out of the drama that had begun on Silver Thursday, Lamar's true tests were to come on the playing fields and in the back offices of league headquarters, where he would have to make one hard decision after another.

Even before the 1980 silver loan, Lamar was beginning to have second thoughts about some of his sports ventures. In a July 1979 *Dallas Times Herald* article, he had talked about how the Kansas City Chiefs had been in the black for fourteen years in a row. But he was citing the success of the Chiefs as a kind of justification for the losses of his soccer team. "The money we've made on the Chiefs has been much more substantial than any Tornado loss," he said almost apologetically. "If you had told me twelve years ago we'd still be losing money," he continued honestly, "I probably would have said I don't want to do that. . . . The facts are, we just have got to do a better job. . . ."[2]

At this point it was still unclear whether the best job the Dallas Tornado did would ever be quite enough to save professional soccer. Initially, the North American Soccer League had steadily improved its performance in terms of attendance, and the number of teams participating in the league had also stabilized. From the lows of 3,000 or 4,000 fans per game in the early days, the league was seeing an average of 14,000 in 1979. Whereas in the 1970 season there had been only six teams, in 1979 there were twenty-four.[3]

But although the number of people attending soccer games had increased, crowds were still small compared with those for major-league football and baseball. Television coverage did not seem to be able to boost the numbers. In 1979, when ABC broadcast nine games live, the ratings were "so low they were almost invisible." The next year saw the last of network soccer coverage in the United States.

At the same time, the additional fans were not plentiful enough to pay for the additional costs the teams were incurring. The big boost in attendance in the mid-1970s was traceable primarily to the league's strategy of signing international heroes who were past their prime on the international circuit but still able to play well enough for the less established U.S. teams. These players significantly increased the quality of the games, but their contracts were expensive. So were the professional coaches, the promotional costs for the teams, and even the rental of large stadiums, which the teams' fans were not able to fill. One of the reasons professional soccer had looked so promising at the beginning was that its costs were low; by now costs had gone up, and income generated by ticket sales had not kept pace.

Lamar's team was hampered by its own problems. At one point the team had a twenty-two game losing streak, not the kind of record that built spectator loyalty. Then there were the facilities where the Tornado played.[4] For some years they used Texas Stadium, home of the Cowboys. Although the stadium was a major sports facility, during the summer months, when professional soccer was being played, the facility was overwhelmingly hot, due to the combination of a partial roof, which blocked air flow, and a lack of air conditioning. People who might be willing to sit through one pre-season Cowboys game in August were not eager to sit through one losing Tornado game after another in June and July.

Even after the Tornado moved from Texas Stadium, there were location problems. The team played for some time at 16,000-seat Ownby Stadium at SMU. It had, in Lamar's words, "sort of a minor league image." At first the field did not even have an automatic sprinkler system, and its lovely natural grass turf became a drawback when the worn-down grass gave way to a packed-dirt surface.

Despite his team's uncertainties, Lamar continued to believe in soccer through the initial days of the burgeoning silver problems. As time went by, however, and he also had to face the demands of World Champion Tennis, even Lamar, whom some called the father of professional soccer in the U.S., faltered.

The end came in 1981. Although Lamar has never gone on record to discuss why he finally lost the desire to keep his team going, others have speculated as to what happened. One soccer associate believed that the problem had to do with Lamar's relationship to the "soccer establishment."[5] Lamar had made many proposals over the years to "Americanize" soccer, with an eye to a return of TV coverage and increased attendance for the whole league. This was the approach he had taken successfully with professional tennis: modifying the scoring system, building in opportunities for time-outs, so spectators could stretch their legs and TV stations could run commercials. When Lamar's suggestions were rejected yet again, he may have decided that professional soccer could never be a truly marketable sport.

Or perhaps it was simply that he got "worn down," as another observer suggested.[6] Whatever the reason, the outcome was that at the end of the 1981 season, Lamar and his co-owner, Bill McKnutt, decided to take the Tornado out of business by merging it with the Tampa Bay Rowdies. They could be minority partners for a year or two, not giving up on soccer altogether but no longer having the major responsibility for a team.

The withdrawal of Lamar from heavy involvement in the NASL signaled, some believe, the beginning of the end for the league. Once he stepped out, the whole tone of ownership changed; one by one other owners became demoralized and dropped out, too. By 1985, there were only two teams left. The season was canceled, and that was the end, at least for the time being, of the NASL.[7]

Regarding the extent of his losses in professional soccer, Lamar remained quiet. A 1984 *Sports Illustrated* article put the losses of other teams, in existence for shorter times than the Tornado, at large amounts. The San Diego Sockers reportedly lost $10 million between 1978 and 1984. The Tulsa Roughnecks lost $8 million over four years. While Lamar's losses might have been less per year during the modest start-up years of his team, it seems safe to assume that he lost at least $10 million during the fifteen seasons he fielded a team.

Although Lamar was able to step gradually out of soccer, his other sports venture of the 1970s, professional tennis, provided enough anguish and headaches to more than replace the relatively painless demise of the NASL.

Lamar had sown the seeds of disharmony in tennis simply by starting World Championship Tennis in 1968, meeting strong opposition from the traditional guardians of tennis rules and regulations, who were also generally strong proponents of amateurism. But even the opposition had seen that professionalism was the wave of the future, and thus various establishment groups had gotten together to mount the Grand Prix, a series of tennis tournaments and events designed to rival the WCT circuit.

The two circuits fought it out during most of the 1970s, each attempting to control or create crowd-pleasing and lucrative events. This competition had clearly succeeded by 1978 in doing one thing: just as the AFL had created bidding wars for top players in the world of professional football a dozen years earlier, the WCT was now doing the same with professional tennis. "WCT was paying out astronomical sums to Jimmy Connors, Ilie Nastase and others in the form of fat contracts to guarantee their appearance at [its] events," *World Tennis* magazine noted.[8] The names were essential for drawing spectators, and the names were costing more and more every year.

It was in 1978 that Lamar reassessed his strategy of having the WCT operate alone. He agreed that year to fold it and its schedule of events into the Grand Prix. The WCT would have eight tournaments of its own, as a kind of "circuit within a circuit." It was "one of the biggest mistakes I've ever made," he said later. After the merger, "I saw that the game was growing, but WCT wasn't. The Men's Pro [Circuit], which rules the sport, didn't want us to contact sponsors, or solicit players, or expand the number of events, or pursue more TV."[9] Once again it appeared to Lamar that he was being hampered by the conservatism of the tennis establishment, even though that establishment had now embraced its own brand of professionalism. The Grand Prix governing body also came to see the alliance as a mistake, and probably did try to cool the Grand Prix–WCT relationship because of growing belief that the hybrid system was totally confusing to most fans and even the media experts.

In May 1981, Lamar withdraw WCT from the Grand Prix. Just as when he began the WCT, he attracted immense and bitter criticism. The most vocal critics charged him with being a profit-oriented businessman who couldn't function in a cooperative venture, with being a spoiler, with throwing his money around as a way of building a power base. Perhaps a fair assessment was that made by Rex Bellamy, tennis correspondent of the London *Times*. He described the WCT as a private business and the International Tennis Federation as an amateur organization responsible for the development of the game. "It was a bad mix," was the way he summed things up.[10]

By now, the Grand Prix circuit had so many events that Lamar had almost no choice but to schedule WCT tournaments at the same time. "There have been only eight top tenners [players ranked as the ten best in the world by the joint ranking system] in Hunt's first seven events," *World Tennis* reported in June 1982. "Attendance has been dismal, totaling only 124,000. This averages out to 17,800 bodies per event." Because someone had to put up substantial prize money to attract any players to these events at all, the losses Lamar was sustaining during this period had to be substantial. *World Tennis* stated that the 1982 tour cost him more than $11 million in prize money alone.[11]

When the WCT encountered serious difficulty in getting players for its events, it sued the Grand Prix, claiming that the players' union and the Grand Prix had conspired to keep WCT out of the major tournament scene. This further alienated the two groups and cut into the number of events WCT could field.

In 1983, Lamar and the Grand Prix reached a new compromise. They signed a five-year agreement, to begin in 1985, for WCT events gradually to be folded into the Grand Prix again. There would be five in 1985, six in 1986, and seven in each of the following three years. Three of the events, including one in Dallas, were granted "championship status" by the Men's International Professional Tennis Circuit, key element in the Grand Prix. The price: the WCT circuit would cease to exist as an independent entity.[12] For all practical purposes, it was the end of the WCT as Lamar had originally conceived it.

Although Lamar's creation lost its identity, many people continued to view him as the father of professional tennis, the mastermind of the game as a popular spectator sport, the man who legitimized professionalism in tennis to such an extent that the game would be forever different. The tennis establishment still saw him as an interloper, however, and once he had made his 1983 agreement, he would probably never be in a position to bring that establishment to its knees and make it do things his way.

Not only was Lamar never to reach the Tennis Hall of Fame, true establishment stronghold, but also he was never to make money from pro tennis. One 1983 article pegged his losses to that point at $40 million, but went on to mention that Lamar believed the game was just about to move into the black once and for all.[13] Another article said that tennis had broken even for him only three of the then fourteen years the circuit had been in existence.[14]

Despite his losses in soccer and tennis, Lamar believed he had a natural talent in the area of "the show-business aspects of sports" and said repeatedly that it was important to him to work in these businesses. "In the oil business, you frequently have to drill a few dry holes to come up with one that produces oil. Sometimes you get a dry hole in the sports-entertainment business, too," he said in explanation of his loss tolerance.[15]

On the other hand, Lamar, who was by all reports always a self-effacing and even modest man, was critical of the actual steps he had taken in developing professional sports. "I think I've done some things okay, and I've done some things wrong. I'm not exactly setting the world on fire with my ventures," he said in a 1982 interview. "I think, 'How could anybody be so dumb? How did I get into that venture?' I'm not a good 'businessman' in the ordinary sense. I procrastinate sometimes. I wish I was more of a specialist."[16] The note of regret was clearly there. "If I have any abilities in the world—I *can* trim bushes—I do have some creative concepts," he went on.

In early 1987, when a Texas recession and low oil prices put ever-increasing pressure on Lamar and his brothers as they continued to attempt to clear up their silver debts once and for all, Lamar put his French provincial mansion—complete with innumerable shrubs trimmed and trained by Lamar himself into fanciful and challenging shapes—on the market. The asking price was $14.5 million.[17] The house was sold, and Lamar, Norma, and their youngest son moved to a house in Highland Park, the same prestigious but conservative neighborhood in which Caroline, Bunker, Herbert, and many members of the third generation of Hunts were already established.

Meanwhile, Caroline, who had been living in Highland Park for thirty years, had just leased her house to a friend for a year and moved, alone, into a luxury hotel on the edge of downtown Dallas.[18] Her decision originated in events that had taken place even before her father's death.

In 1973, Caroline had been married to Lloyd Sands for thirty years. She had three grown children, a seventeen-year-old daughter, and a ten-year-old son. Then the couple divorced. A relatively short time afterward, Caroline remarried. Her new husband, Hugo Schoellkopf, Jr., known as Buddy, was the son of an old and well-to-do Texas family. Buddy, retired from his family business, was a person who seemed to know how to enjoy himself and frequently acted on that knowledge.

According to Caroline, he had "charisma." After their marriage, the two began going on jaunts to Alaska to hunt and fish, two of Buddy's favorite activities. "Buddy is a frontiersman, very self-sufficient, a real individual," Caroline's son Stephen said.[19] But he also liked to socialize and party, and Caroline began to enjoy socializing, too. "At 5 P.M. Buddy will invite 10, 20 or 30 people for dinner," said one of the couple's friends. "Caroline will walk in, and there's a party in the making. She puts her purse down and ties her apron on and goes to work. She's never flustered."[20]

As much as anything, Buddy and Caroline seemed to enjoy each other. "They're very much in love," Caroline's daughter Laurie reported a decade after the marriage. "They write notes to each other, and they still hold hands."[21]

They began doing some business investing together, particularly in a charter air service, which built on Buddy's interest in aviation. They named it Pumpkin Air in reference to Caroline's hobby of collecting recipes using pumpkin and of favoring the color in decorating schemes. As she got involved in many of Buddy's interests, Caroline gradually became more outgoing herself, more confident.

One area in which she became active without Buddy was the management of her own fortune. Like her brothers, Caroline had large holdings, nominally sheltered in a trust fund, which dated back to the heyday of the original Hunt Oil organization. Throughout the years of her first marriage, these holdings, though officially overseen by trustees, were managed by Sands. After the two were divorced, her older sons became actively involved in setting investment strategies and long-term objectives for the trust.

One direction these investments took was quickly to throw Caroline and her holdings into the public spotlight. She had become interested in a piece of real estate in Dallas that she frequently passed as she drove around town. It was the Sheppard King house, a large eccentric mansion located right off Turtle Creek Drive, one of the most prestigious streets in Dallas, which was also conveniently near downtown. The house, built in the 1920s, had a Moorish design and included many wonderful architectural and decorative details, such as elaborate tilework, imaginative rooflines, and oddly shaped spaces. The building had served as an office space for some time, but had slowly fallen on hard times.

Caroline and her children, including Laurie, who was also becoming involved in the family business management, began thinking about the possibility of building a restaurant or a restaurant/hotel combination based in the old house. Caroline's trust acquired the building, and in 1980 they opened their restaurant, "The Mansion on Turtle Creek."[22]

The Mansion on Turtle Creek was an immediate success. The setting was convenient, yet off the beaten path; the interior decoration was lush and comfortable; the chef was a star, and the menu was a creative tour de force. Within a year, the restaurant was framed by a new nine-story building with 129 guest rooms and fourteen suites.

The hotel measured up instantly to the restaurant. The decor was described as lush and luxurious, the atmosphere as exclusive. "Handcrafted marble floors, oak-paneled walls, Iranian travertine baths, dhurrie carpets, Chinese antiques, original art, Limoges china, Texas limestone fireplaces, exotic fresh flowers, gourmet foods and emphasis on service," gushed *Parade* magazine.[23] "Life today is very impersonal. I want my hotels to recreate a different time—when there were servants," Caroline was quoted as saying. "Elegant but not ostentatious," she described her goal elsewhere. Each room was as "individual as possible" and "distinct and reflect[s] the community in which it is located."[24] Almost immediately the Mansion began to set new standards for hotel luxury, to give the people Caroline described as American royalty—the successful business travelers—a new challenge for their expense accounts, and the restaurant continued to offer the ever restless high-society Dallasites a great place to see and be seen.

Throughout the initial excitement of opening the restaurant and the hotel and of being recognized as a kind of first lady of luxury, Caroline's personal values did not appear to change. She continued to live as she always had, using little help in her own house, though her hotel had 290 employees for 150 guests, driving a car that appeared frumpish in her hotel's parking lot, never appearing in *haute couture* gowns even when the Mansion opened with a $1,000-a-couple gala. Caroline just kept tying on her apron and cooking for the thirty people Buddy brought home for dinner.

But in 1981, something happened that brought a change to Caroline's life. By then, Rosewood, which was the name Caroline and her children had chosen for their hotel business, was considering expansion. A reporter for *Fortune*, Roy Rowan, had gone to Dallas to interview Stephen Sands, Caroline's oldest son, for an article about the highly visible Rosewood investments. While he was at it, he asked Stephen if he thought his mother would be willing to be interviewed also. Stephen asked Caroline, and she consented— though reluctantly—thinking that any additional publicity she could generate for the hotel would be a plus.

The interview went extremely well. Afterward, Caroline overheard the reporter telling his editor over the phone that "Mrs. Schoellkopf is wonderful" and proposing that he change the entire focus of his article to highlight her. The result was "Bunker Hunt's Savvy Sister," which appeared in October 1981. One Time Inc. publication had catapulted H. L. Hunt into the public eye in 1948; now Caroline suddenly became public property, and hot property at that, through another.

"It wasn't that I really wanted personal notoriety," she said in retrospect, "because I didn't." But, like her father, who first became actively involved in politics on the basis of the fame *Life* brought, Caroline saw an opportunity to take advantage of her publicity and accomplish something that was important to her. She became willing to continue as a public figure because "I saw that it really helped the hotels, to have a personality behind them."

The support that her personality lent to the Mansion became more important immediately after the *Fortune* article appeared, as

Rosewood first took over management of The Mansion on Turtle Creek (the hotel and restaurant had originally been managed by the 21 Club) and then went on to design and build a hotel in Houston and acquire and renovate the Bel Air in Los Angeles.

Numerous requests for interviews came to Caroline. Her story quickly attracted society writers and observers of the social scene: after all, she was a fabulously rich woman. *Town and Country, Interview,* even *Parade* ran stories about her. Most of these stories and interviews portrayed a woman who was nice, sweet, and not terribly dynamic, and in some respects they were accurate. The stories focused on her "simple" life or they reminded the world that she had written a cookbook containing 400 recipes using pumpkin. "Writers wanted a rich woman who on a whim was building 'pumpkin palaces,' " Caroline observed later. "Those are some of the words they used—because that's copy."

Tolerantly, Caroline kept granting interviews. But she also began to take a more active role in business-related activities, such as hosting and chairing many charity benefits in Dallas and in other cities where her hotels were located. She continued to be active in her church and in the affairs of Mary Baldwin College, where she was serving on the Board of Trustees, but she enlarged the scope of her interests substantially. The more she did, the more confident she seemed to become that she could do still more.

Consequently, her involvement in her business affairs, especially in the hotels, became more active. The first hotel, The Mansion on Turtle Creek, had been almost intimidating to its own financier. But this was changing. When Rosewood decided to enter the Houston market with a hotel built from the ground up, rather than renovating an existing structure, Caroline found she was comfortable with the $200,000 or more spent on each room—an industry high—plus the investment of a million dollars in original and high-quality works of art.

By the time Rosewood returned to develop a new site in Dallas, Caroline was ready for an even more dramatic investment in what was to be the Crescent project. The *New York Times* described the Crescent as a $250-million study in Texas superlatives. "Designed in French chateau-style by Philip Johnson and John Burgee, it required more limestone than any structure since the Empire State Building in 1931. The four-level parking garage sits in the biggest hole ever dug in Dallas. It includes 1.2 million square feet of high-quality office space in a 17-story, crescent-shaped tower, 750,000 square feet of retail space and a 240-room hotel."[25] Like The Mansion on Turtle Creek, the Crescent Court Hotel offered extreme luxury, with fabulous flowers and antique furniture and so much brass that a full-time metal polisher was hired. The office spaces were grand and striking. Even the retail shops were top-of-the-line, ranging from "high end" to "extremely high end," with outposts of Rodeo Drive and Trump Tower shops filling their elegant spaces. Moreover, the Crescent was built in a relatively undeveloped quadrant of the city and appeared destined to "redefine the borders of downtown Dallas."

As Rosewood grew in grandeur and scope, constantly involving Caroline, there was still a quiet and modest side to her life. She continued to refer to her children as the driving forces in the business. "I refer to my business as a *we* business," she said. "Many things we did were my children's decision and I went along with them. I would never have built the Crescent on my own. It's really *their* venture and I've done what I can to *promote* it. I do have personal ventures such as my antique shop at the Crescent, Lady Primrose's, and a helicopter company, Silver Air Aviation, which provides emergency medical helicopters for hospitals in nine states." And she still maintained a traditional married life, accompanying Buddy on trips he planned, doing what he liked to do. "I always made their activities my activities," she said, referring to her life with each of her husbands.

But finally, modest life and all, during the years between the *Fortune* article and the Crescent opening, Caroline simply became a force that could not remain hidden behind Buddy and her children. A 1983 *Town and Country* article described how people in Dallas were talking about "the blossoming of Caroline Hunt Schoellkopf. She's more outgoing, she's more confident, she's more attractive." Caroline began to feel—to her initial consternation—like the American equivalent of British royalty: gracious, available, and, above all, visible. "It's not something I ever sought," she mused. "At first I didn't feel quite comfortable. But I'm enjoying it. . . . Every [time a] king comes to town I'm invited and they sit me right next to him. I had dinner with the President of Nepal Monday night. And there I was, sitting next to him. . . . Sometimes I'd rather be sitting at the *bottom* of the table, where I don't have to make state conversation. But being forced into that, I have developed a lot more social ease."

By 1987, Caroline, in her early sixties, was epitomizing a part of her legacy that had long been under wraps: the enthusiasm for new things, the interest in the world, the *joie de vivre* that she recalled as characterizing her father. It had all been there all the time. The quiet, self-effacing woman who had modeled herself on her gentle and accepting mother was blossoming irreversibly into a more complex and appealing person, with a range of interests and a set of social skills that seemed to surprise her most of all.

But then, Caroline's successes seemed to lead to something that others might have been able to predict all along: she and Buddy separated, and then divorced. Although Caroline was unwilling to comment publicly on the source of the breakup, other family members suggested that her increasing visibility was perhaps more than Buddy had bargained for when he married her fourteen years before. She had changed in a very positive direction, but these changes had brought their own strain to her most personal relationship.

Whereas her mother had, at almost the same age Caroline was at the time of her second divorce, finally given up on life and emotionally resigned herself to an early death, Caroline was able to draw on the strengths she had developed during her difficult first marriage and through her increasing involvement in the larger world beyond family and children.

In a 1987 interview, after her divorce, Caroline talked about her view of her past and her plans for the future. "I don't know about the rest of my family," she observed, "but I have a sense of eternity. One reason may be that I'm very interested in ancient history. I think that when you think about the pyramids and 5,000 years ago, and if you're religious and you think about eternity, all the little failures don't seem that important."

But there were still active demands to consider, including participation in managing her fortune. Caroline had lived a relatively modest life, though not as simple as some portraits of her would lead readers to assume. But becoming more involved in managing her own money, being a guiding light in certain investments that were not only reasonably successful but also highly visible, had gradually led her to become comfortable with her wealth and the effect it had on her position in the world and her relationships with other people.

She observed: "When my children moan and groan and say, 'It's so awful to have all this money. You'll never know if anybody loves you for yourself,' I say, 'Everybody likes somebody for some reason. Looks, personality. Just look at it this way: money is an asset. You might as well treat it that way and think of it that way. It doesn't matter if they like you for your money. *That's okay*. That's their problem, not yours. You just enjoy them for what they can bring to your life.' "

It was as part of her grappling with the active demands of her single life that Caroline had decided to lease her house, which she had designed, which she loved, and where she had lived for thirty years, and move into the hotel at Crescent Center. "I gained an hour a day," she said, sounding more like a yuppie career woman than a sixty-four-year-old builder of pumpkin palaces. "It took me an hour a day to get from home to the office and back again."

And what now of her inherited past? She was facing and coping with marital problems, which were her version of those her parents had side-stepped—not very successfully. How did this affect her perspective on her parents' choices?

"My father was a man caught in whatever his weaknesses were," she said from the vantage point of her own maturity. "He was not a bad man. Most men wouldn't even have worried about marrying those other women. He had his streak of eccentricity and strange beliefs, I'm sure. He did believe in his own genius, I think. Which he had. But he had his lacks also."

And Hunt's other families? "I really forget all about it," she continued. "I'm friends of the third family. And very good friends with Ruth, too. I was always kind of sorry for Ruth," she said pensively. "Supersweet—but I don't think it's fake. I think she just is supersweet."

She had become the shy girl who sits with kings; the woman who replicated her mother's life of acceptance but who was now living alone at the elegant Crescent Court; the favorite daughter who grappled with the inner life her doting father could never face. "I have a fabulous life ahead of me that I wouldn't have had if I'd stayed married to my husband," Caroline concluded in the 1987 interview, speaking with only a touch of wistfulness. She looked out the elaborate windows of her magnificent Crescent Court office for a long moment. "So you see," she finally added, "one door shuts and another door opens."

SEVENTEEN

RAY Hunt had progressed during the 1970s from membership on Hunt Oil's board to sole executor of his father's estate to president of a Hunt Oil Company whose board included representatives of his half-siblings. In July 1978, when the intertwined Hunt empire was dismantled and each part of the family went its own way, when Bunker and Herbert resigned finally from the board of Hunt Oil, Ray was at last on his own. From that point forward, he was almost solely responsible for the strategic direction of Hunt Oil and for its ongoing operations.

A few months before he attained his final independence, he was called on to act as titular head of the family when the Hunts were faced with the lawsuit initiated by Frania Tye and her family. It was in January 1978 that this case went to court.[1] Frania had begun her legal actions on November 11, 1975, just a year after Hunt's death. By then, it had become completely clear that Hunt had not, as Frania had expected, either fully provided for her family in his will or even acknowledged their existence.

During the two years when depositions were being taken and evidence gathered by both sides, the two parts of the Hunt family whose inheritances and rights were being challenged—Lyda's children and Ruth's children—appear to have been relatively unconcerned about Frania's suit. It was not clear for some time whether the case would actually go to trial. Furthermore, the two families had been distracted by working out their relationships with one another, particularly by the details of separating their financial holdings. Because Frania's suit was filed against the estate of H. L. Hunt, of which Ray Hunt was executor, it could be seen as not having a significant effect on any individual's holdings, except perhaps those of Ruth Ray Hunt.

But once an actual trial date was set for the case, the two families decided that their personal holdings might ultimately be in jeopardy and that they should make a concerted effort to head Frania off. Consequently, when court convened on January 9, 1978, in Shreveport, Louisiana, Ray, his wife, June, Helen, and Swanee, as well as Bunker, Herbert, Lamar, and their wives were all present in Shreveport.

Frania's family, in contrast, had few representatives. Her oldest son, Howard, had died in 1975 of cancer. Her oldest daughter, Haroldina, was not well enough to attend the trial. In taking her deposition, attorneys for both sides had agreed that she was, owing to her psychiatric problems, unable to provide meaningful testimony.[2]

Frania's other daughter, the first of Hunt's two daughters named Helen, was also dead. She and her husband had met a tragic end in 1962 when a chartered plane they were on had crashed at Orly Airport, outside Paris. The flight had been part of a trip for Atlanta art patrons; more than 100 people had been killed.[3] Helen had left her two-year-old son, Ron Cartledge, with Frania. After the accident, the child had been raised by his grandmother, and now appeared with her in court.

The last family member with Frania was her youngest son, Hugh. One attorney who participated in the proceedings believed that he was actually the driving force behind Frania's charges. He not only may have been trying to resolve his self-described identity problems by leading Frania to file suit, but may also have been hoping to participate much more substantially in Hunt's financial estate. By this time, Hugh, who was married and the father of a large number of children, had reportedly pursued numerous investment opportunities that had used substantial capital while generating little income in return.

Even before the trial began, Frania's suit had generated interest and publicity. One of the Shreveport papers ran a detailed series of articles a month before, which described findings in the depositions the attorneys for both sides had spent several years obtaining. The three-part series set the dramatic tone the trial would assume. "Haroldson Lafayette Hunt, the late Texas oil billionaire, maintained the wife of a bigamous marriage in Shreveport for years in the 1920's, according to testimony piling up in the federal court in Shreveport," the first article began, going on to say that there was evidence Hunt had spent more than a million dollars to keep the union a secret. By the time the trial opened, reporters from all over the country were present, and papers, not only in Shreveport, but in Dallas and Atlanta, Frania's hometown, were giving the story front-page coverage.

The jury selected consisted of six men and women from typical middle-class or working-class families. On the first day of the trial, there was dramatic testimony: Ray Hunt, as executor of his father's estate, was called to testify and stated that he was "of the impression that H. L. Hunt is the father of [Frania's] children." Frania's attorney, in his opening statement, had promised even more excitement: proof that Hunt had married Frania, that Hunt had presented himself under a pseudonym, and that through it all his client was simply an innocent woman who was ultimately forced, under duress, to sign away her morally defensible claims to Hunt's wealth.

Testimony followed, by innumerable individuals who had known Frania and Hunt during the time they had been together. This was capped on the third day of the trial when Frania took the stand. She appeared composed, well groomed, and attractive, but also somewhat frail and decidedly elderly. She unstintingly provided detailed testimony about her time with Hunt, recalling with great clarity specific incidents and their emotional overtones. She did not condemn Hunt in her testimony, but reiterated that she had loved him and that she had tried to do her best to balance her feelings for him with the needs of their children.

Legal issues in the trial were somewhat complex. Whether a marriage ceremony had in fact taken place was hard to determine: a marriage license had been issued but documentation of the actual wedding was lacking. Whereas defense counsel was able to raise some important questions about precisely when Frania became aware of Hunt's other family, they were hampered by a need not to appear to be browbeating a dignified grandmother even while casting doubts on her story.

By the end of Frania's testimony, the Hunt lawyers apparently began to feel that their clients were vulnerable. During the lunch break, news stories later said, they offered Frania a substantial sum—reported variably as $3.5 or $5 million—to settle the case out of court. Apparently Frania's lawyers felt their case was strong: they refused the settlement.

Over the weekend, negotiations continued. Frania's family and legal entourage were ensconced at a motel on one side of town: Ray and his group were at a motel nearer the courthouse. The attorneys acted as go-betweens, but the ultimate decisions had to come from the principals: Frania and Ray. As of Monday morning, they had not reached a settlement, but after spending the morning in the judge's chambers, negotiating head-to-head, a final arrangement was worked out.

The settlement granted Frania $7.5 million, or half of H. L. Hunt's estimated community property at the time he and Frania had made their final break—the 1942 agreement. The trusts of Lyda's children and of Ruth's children would put up equal amounts of the settlement. Further speculation about Frania, her family, and her history with Hunt was cut off by the terms of the settlement. No one was allowed to discuss the agreement with outsiders, and the judge sealed all records of the proceedings, including the depositions taken during the two years prior to the trial.

The actual transfer of Frania's settlement was held up for years by Frania's son Hugh, who had second thoughts about its fairness.[4] But for all practical purposes, once the initial settlement was reached, the way was cleared for each of the half-siblings to return to his or her own life and for the final separation of the holdings of Lyda's children and Ruth's children. Except for occasional attempts to have the settlement executed, neither Frania nor any of her children had any involvement with the other two parts of the family for the next decade.

Now Ray was left to concentrate on managing Hunt Oil. His mother and sisters held a significant shareholder position, but Ray became their fully empowered representative in actually running the company.[5] Ray's independence stemmed from the fact that his mother and sisters had decided not to participate in management of the company on a day-to-day basis. This apparently fit well with Ray's preference. "You need to be in [the company's management] sixty hours a week," Swanee said in 1987. "You can't piddle around in the company without getting into some problems. So we have very much respected Ray's desire and his love of management."

Swanee had no regrets about her brother's decisions; she believed he worked hard and had a certain gift for management. "Ray's done a phenomenal job—and he's been very lucky with certain timing of various deals," she observed. "But luck happens to those who are prepared for it and ready for it to come along."

The three sisters' lack of involvement in the day-to-day management of the company stemmed from two things. First, they had not been given the same opportunities as Ray had to learn the business or to develop an interest in management. While Ray had been out in the field writing oil leases, June, Helen, and Swanee had been working on the Hunt Oil switchboard or doing little jobs around the offices.

Helen, in particular, felt that she had been given so little information about the business and what role she could play in it that she had become something of a financial cripple. In a 1985 interview, she described how her father had never dreamed that she might be interested in business or financial matters. "So he never mentioned the subject to me. . . . He never did sit down and talk to me about how I could connect [his ideals in business] to my financial resources." Helen recounted how she still didn't know what she and Randy Kreiling lived on when they were first married, whether her parents gave them money or not. She had been that detached.[6]

More important than the lack of opportunities was the second factor that led to their choosing Ray to lead the company. Each of his three sisters had developed an early interest in some area completely outside the business. For June, it was religion. For Helen and Swanee, it was social action. As each woman developed her career, there was little drive to become involved with Hunt Oil.

June's interest had begun to take most of her time almost immediately after college, when she went to work for First Baptist Church as a youth director. She had begun to refine the focus of her career after her USO tour in the early 1970s, when Ray was first assuming a position of major responsibility with Hunt Oil. It was then that she detached herself from the traditional structure of the positions she had held at First Baptist and became a more independent teacher.

At first, June made appearances at assemblies around the country, going wherever she was invited and following the same format she had developed in Vietnam. She spoke about her views and sang songs that illustrated them. Although in retrospect she considered this a time of growth, especially because of the many different people she met in varied surroundings, the better she was at what she was doing the more out of touch with her own spirituality she felt she became. "You can polish something quite well and perhaps not grow," she said of this period in her life. "You can actually be stagnant. What you are giving out is new to the audience or enlightening to them but you may not be growing. I saw the inherent danger in being a traveling guest speaker without having accountability for where you are."

As a response to this situation, June began spending more time in Dallas, where she made a commitment to teach Bible-studies classes to single adults. One set of classes, on Sunday morning, was held at First Baptist, but she gradually developed a series at her own house, held on Monday evenings. These became increasingly non-denominational as she focused on the Bible and its meaning, rather than on the dogma of any particular religious group. The classes also expanded to include anyone interested; in June's words, "it grew into just a mixed bag, a mixed class of married, singles, any age."

As she gained confidence and competence in her teaching, June began to extend the reach of her work beyond Dallas through a series of radio shows called "Help for the Heart." She and a partner, Jan Silvious, wrote, produced, and recorded daily shows for broadcast under the auspices of Cornerstone Christian Outreach. These shows were carried on Christian radio stations across the country. They lasted fifteen minutes and were supported by a regular newsletter. "Help for the Heart" described itself as addressing "the struggles, pressures and challenges believers have experienced. Jan and June offer compassion, assurance, and optimism. They also offer straightforward answers and guidance [in] a program with the blend of encouragement and practicality you've been looking for."

The co-hosts covered a variety of topics. Many episodes gave help with specific problems, such as how to have a successful marriage, how to live a fulfilling single life, how to cope with alcoholism or death of loved ones or even incest. Some of the programs were more generally inspirational, such as "Loving Your Enemies." A number of others addressed issues specifically relating to Bible interpretation, although all three kinds of program were Biblically oriented, with the messages offered by Jan and June drawn from a conservative, even fundamentalist, interpretation.

In the classes, which usually numbered fifty people or more, June took a somewhat different tack. She chose a theme from the Bible and followed it through various texts in the Old and New Testaments. Her approach to Bible study in these classes was detailed; sometimes she even focused on a particular word or phrase and traced its origin to the culture of the period when that part of the Bible had been written.

Just as important in the Bible-study classes, though, was June's work after the formal teaching section. During this time, she would talk with people who had attended the class and who sought her out for personal help and support. After one class, for example, she counseled an alcoholic woman who was having trouble staying dry, a man who was helping a friend with a suicidal son, and an entertainer who was trying to correlate her desire for financial success through her work with her need to lead a more balanced life. "I protect my Sunday mornings and Monday nights," June said in a 1987 interview, "because I need to be accountable in dealing with real issues and it's for my benefit that I not be detached from where people are hurting."

June felt that it was vitally important for her to maintain close contact with people in pain in order to do the kind of "sharing" that she felt constituted the work she was called to. "It's good for me to help," she said, adding, however, that "sometimes you don't know how helpful you're being. You can present truth and if the soil of their hearts is ready to take the seed, it's amazing how *anyone* can be useful in another's life. The focus of attention here, in what I do, is that God has created us. . . . He says, 'I know the plans I have for you, plans to prosper you, *not* to harm you, plans to give you hope in the future.' "

Although June's teaching was focused on a traditional interpretation of scripture, there was a positive aspect to what she said that kept her focus from being harsh or condemning. "God's not sitting there trying to beat you over the head just because you chose something wrong or acted indiscriminately. What I want people to understand is that no matter how *dark* their situation is, no matter how hopeless-looking a situation may be, there is hope, not because of your intelligence or your experience, your capability, but because of Him, the Creator, who knows how to give hope in the midst of hopelessness and how to make masterpieces out of messes. People who really have a sense of deeper values—they know what it is like to have gone through the valleys."

By 1987, the only unresolved area of June's life was her singleness. "I know my mother would love for me to be married, because I think she worries about me," June observed. "Yet it would only be because she cares that I am happy." Despite the problems she had seen in her parents' marriage, June said that she was "not putting any barriers up" and would be "more than happy to be married. If God wants to bring somebody for me to marry where He would be the initiator, I have no closed doors."

While June had found her own ministry and her own identity in her conservative religious leadership, Swanee and Helen had gone in quite a different direction, though they too were involved in working with other people and their problems. By 1987, the two were focusing their work lives on philanthropy, particularly in areas that would traditionally be considered politically and socially "liberal." Initially, they had created a nonprofit foundation called Hunt Alternatives and used this as the starting place for their contributions of both money and time. Gradually they had then expanded their interests to include setting up a group of "women's foundations" whose reach would extend far beyond the kind of philanthropic activities the two women alone could undertake.

Swanee's interest in liberal social issues had begun during her marriage to Mark Meeks. After four years in Germany, the couple had moved to Denver, Colorado, where Mark was pastor to an unusual church, which combined Catholic and Presbyterian congregants, most of whom Swanee characterized as social activists. Swanee had also worked there, serving as the minister of pastoral care, and had begun attending the Illif School of Theology, where she earned a master's degree in theology and ultimately a doctorate in philosophy.

Besides working at the church, Swanee and Mark set up a halfway house for mentally ill young adults, located about a block from their house in a respectable but modest section of downtown Denver. Their involvement in the church and the halfway house, as well as Swanee's studies in what had originally been Mark's field, made for a kind of intensity in their relationship that went beyond that of a more traditional marriage.

"Mark and I worked together throughout our marriage," Swanee said about this period of her life. "Even my schooling—which he was, of course, very, very close to, because of his interest in philosophy and theology. We would get together and have lunch and talk about what I was reading for a class and we'd talk about what he was reading just on his own independent time. He would get up at 4:30 to read Martin Buber because it was quiet then. And then at breakfast we would *talk* about Buber. It was real heady stuff! We were incredibly close in terms of our interests—which is what held us together a long time. And we were married for fifteen years."

Although they were extremely close in terms of interests and work, as early as their time together in Germany the couple apparently had problems in other aspects of their relationship. In retrospect, Swanee did not enlarge on these problems other than to say that "everything personal wasn't wonderful" and "there were other parts that didn't work—as happens." Relatively late in their married life, Swanee and Mark had a child, a daughter, but the problems remained. Finally, they separated, and divorced in the mid-1980s.

Swanee planned, after the divorce, to spend some time on her own. However, within a short time she met the man who was to become her second husband, Charles Ansbacher. He was the conductor of the Colorado Springs Symphony Orchestra, in Colorado Springs, 115 miles from Denver. He had grown up in New York City, the youngest of four sons of two well-known psychologists. He shared some of Swanee's interests in social issues; he had spent a year as a White House Fellow and had a good understanding of politics and what Swanee called "the way things work." And Swanee shared Charles's interest in music; she played a number of musical instruments and had composed some works that had been publicly performed in Denver. Despite the fact that each had strong commitments in distant cities, Swanee and Charles carried on an intensive courtship and then were married. By 1987, Charles had taken a job that allowed him to live in Denver.

While Swanee had settled in Denver, Helen had also moved away from Dallas—to New York City. After her marriage, a year before Swanee's, she and her husband, Randy Kreiling, had continued to live in Dallas, where Randy worked closely with Bunker and Herbert Hunt. During this time, the couple had two children, and Helen did not pursue her teaching career beyond the birth of the first child, though she did continue her education, eventually earning master's degrees in both liberal arts and counseling.

When Bunker and Herbert became involved in commodity ventures during the early 1970s, Randy joined them. He was very successful in his personal commodity investments, reportedly building a $10,000 gift from his father into holdings of over $1 million. Then, in 1976, there was a falling-out between Randy and his half-brothers-in-law. According to Harry Hurt, Bunker and Herbert believed that Randy had used information about their dealings to benefit himself in ways that were damaging to their interests. Randy was "fired" by the two brothers.[7]

Shortly after this, when Helen was twenty-six, she and Randy were divorced. She has not commented on the reason for the breakup, though in 1987 she did say that their children continued to see their father regularly and that she and Randy still maintained a friendly relationship.

After Helen's divorce, she found the opportunity to leave Dallas, a step she had felt was important for herself ever since her high-school years. She and her two children moved to New York City. There, Helen, on her own for the first time, became interested in learning more about managing her life, particularly its financial aspects. "I suddenly looked around and thought, wow, I have responsibility for something and I am not very comfortable yet talking about money," she recalled in a 1985 interview. "I'm not as knowledgeable as I should be, so I'd just better start getting knowledgeable."[8] In the late 1970s, Helen began following the financial and business news and working with a broker who was willing to explain the ins and outs of financial investing to her.

While Helen was beginning to understand the role money played in making the world go round, Swanee had been developing a similar perspective. "Everybody has certain tools that they bring into a situation: their time, their intelligence, their experience. They try to figure out how best to use what they have," Swanee observed. "The tools that I have to use, to shape whatever I want to influence, happen to be heavy on the asset side. I have a lot more money than I do time compared to other people. So it's just a matter of strategizing what you can do best."

It was in 1981 that the two sisters—who were now living on opposite sides of the country, who still had quite different life experiences, and who, until this point, had been more competitive than close—arrived at almost the same place at the same time. They both were interested in social change. They both were becoming comfortable with being "heavy on the asset side." They both were old enough, at thirty-one and thirty-two, to be ready to look for their life's work, rather than to wait to see where life would take them next. It was then that they decided to work together.

It was not easy at first. "We argued the whole first year," Helen said from the comfortable vantage point of 1987. "It was almost impossible for us to work together. First there was the name, then the logo. We were so competitive." It was almost as if the two had never before confronted their personality differences and the stresses and strains that being "the babies" together had placed on them. "But once we worked out the persona issues," Helen continued, "we never had another problem. Where the money goes, special projects, how to handle involvement in three cities [Denver, Dallas, New York City] by two different people—we've been able to work everything out."

After five years of working successfully together, the two sisters talked about each other with tremendous respect and caring. Each saw the other as providing important leadership for their work, as having valuable insights. "I'm just crazy about Swanee," said the usually reserved Helen. "I love all of my family, but she's just . . . The most valuable part of Hunt Alternatives is working with her."

The scope of Hunt Alternatives proceeded, after its official beginning in 1982, to expand rapidly. At first, the money the foundation gave away was contributed in modest amounts. There were several reasons why it began small. Swanee described how at first she and Helen felt themselves to be very inexperienced as philanthropists, so they didn't want to make any big mistakes. Helen talked about how they wanted to highlight the work of others in the community, rather than overwhelm projects with large gifts that would change their nature and focus. In addition, Helen continued, "we wanted to show other people what $1,000 might mean . . . how little it takes to preserve or enhance life."

The projects Hunt Alternatives supported were not those usually favored by the wealthy. Many of these projects were small, lending credence to Helen's concern about swamping them with large grants. For example, the 1985 Hunt Alternatives report described a grant of $4,000 for equipment for the Dallas West Child Care Agency, a day-care program for 100 children, and a grant of $1,000 to the Eden Theatrical Workshop, a "living theatre" in the inner city of Denver.[9] Other grants were to programs that were larger but totally lacking in glamour, being focused on the poor, the aged, members of minority groups, or those outside society, such as the mentally ill. Many organizations that Hunt Alternatives supported offered services primarily to women and children. Traditional and highly visible charities and elaborate events such as spectacular charity balls were generally not on the Hunt Alternatives list of grants.

As Swanee and Helen got involved in organizations that could use their financial support, they also found themselves making commitments to their continued functioning. They spent time with the people running the organizations and met their clients. Both began to develop enormous respect for the kind of people who were able to go out day after day and keep helping others, often with little hope of large successes and frequently with not enough money.

The sisters gradually concluded that Hunt Alternatives provided a valuable opportunity for them to educate themselves in depth about the social problems around them. As a result of this, beginning in 1985 they chose one theme for Hunt Alternatives grants each year. The first year it was "women of color," the needs of women from a wide range of minority groups. In 1986, the focus was on issues related to making affordable housing available for anyone who needed it; in 1987, the focus was on youth, with issues covered ranging from child abuse to educating New York City children about AIDS.

As Helen and Swanee learned more about philanthropy, they became interested in a movement that had begun in the late 1960s, during the burgeoning of the women's movement, with the establishment of the Ms. Foundation. This was the development of various "women's foundations" or "women's funds." By 1985, twenty-eight of these funds, located in eighteen states, had been organized into a National Network of Women's Funds.

The following description of these funds appeared in the 1985 Hunt Alternatives *Annual Report*: "In the last five years, a new wave of activism has come onto the American scene. Women have begun to organize themselves and their resources—in a way unlike any other time in history. . . . The formula is simple—women helping women. Communities of women have been raising monies and then redistributing them back into the community into organizations that benefit women and girls. Essential to the formation of each fund is the coming together of women from varieties of histories and contexts, each contributing her perspective and resources to the building of the fund. Working together, women hope to move from positions of dependency into self-determination."

The women's foundations Swanee and Helen helped develop were located in Denver, Dallas, and New York City. Besides giving women an opportunity to make charitable contributions to issues that benefited other women, these foundations offered information about managing assets to the women who had the money to give. Swanee described how important it was for women to develop a sense of empowerment around their money. "One of the eternal transformations [of the women's movement] is women feel more comfortable succeeding, having power, breaking out into new areas," Swanee said in 1987. "You either take your assets and use them or you deny that you have them. [The question is] will I take on the burden of trying to use what I have." By this time, the answer for both Swanee and Helen was clearly yes. For each, their philanthropic activities amounted to a full-time job, and even more as they learned more about the needs of the people around them and how they could address these needs.

By the time Hunt Alternatives was five years old, and the women's foundations were underway, Swanee was beginning her single-household life with Charles, and Helen was juggling an even more complex family situation. She had been remarried in the early 1980s, to a psychotherapist named Harville Hendrix whom she had met in Dallas. They had known each other for five or six years before they began to go out together; their marriage followed five years later.

Gradually Helen's two children and Harville's two children from his first marriage had come to know and care for one another, so by the time the marriage took place, Helen and Harville had a kind of instant family. They built on this, having two children together. By 1987, the family ranged from a toddler to a college student. Harville and Helen had separate offices in the same large space within a brisk walk of their large but homey New York City apartment, and, like Swanee and Charles, each took an interest in and had a great deal of respect for the other's work.

The challenge for Swanee and Helen by then was not different from that facing most women with deep professional commitments and families as well: how to do everything well and not shortchange husband, family, community, or oneself. It was a difficult challenge, but one both women welcomed since it gave full range to their talents as well as their asset base.

While his sisters had found the work they wished to pursue in their lives, Ray had become more and more involved in the arduous process of bringing Hunt Oil into the mainstream of the late-twentieth-century oil business. He had worked hard to determine the "principles" his father had developed to build a successful company, but he also believed that the way those principles were applied had constantly to change in a changing world. "I'm a big believer that a company is like any other living organism," he said in an Associated Press interview. "It is constantly changing. If it ever ceases to change, it's dead."[10]

When Ray had looked at the oil business as it was evolving in the late 1970s, he had decided that Hunt Oil needed to do a number of things if the company was to live. Perhaps most important was to increase oil exploration in the United States, offshore, and particularly in foreign countries. Although Bunker had developed producing wells in Libya, and Placid Oil had been involved in other overseas areas, Hunt Oil had remained largely a U.S. company.[11]

One of the first areas Ray became involved in was a field in the North Sea. One of the participants in a consortium there had dropped out, leaving an opportunity for Hunt Oil. The majors had looked at this particular area, the Beatrice Field, and concluded, after a number of dry holes had already been drilled there, that it was nonproductive. However, Hunt Oil's chief geologist was familiar with the area and believed there were good but subtle indications that a strike was likely. Following his "principle" of delegating responsibility to the best people possible and then taking their recommendations, Ray listened to the geologist and within a week had committed the company to participate in the drilling site.

The field was a producer. Reserves were not of giant dimensions, but were quite attractive: 160 million barrels of oil, of which Hunt Oil owned twenty percent. It wasn't just the strike that pleased Ray; it was also the fact that Hunt Oil's involvement gave the company what he described as "credibility" in doing further overseas exploration.

The second thing Ray identified as important to the company in the late 1970s was to strengthen Hunt Oil's domestic presence. This involved both conducting aggressive domestic exploration and filling in some of the gaps in Hunt Oil after the first family's holdings were split off in 1978. For example, in 1978, Hunt Oil bought a company that gave Hunt Oil a presence in drilling and well servicing, areas that Penrod had covered before; in 1981, Hunt Oil added another drilling operation. Ray also spearheaded investments in increasing yields from the old fields that constituted part of Hunt Oil's holdings after the separation and in regenerating production and refining facilities that were showing their age.

In both the domestic and the international exploration and development efforts, Ray began to emphasize what he had identified as another important element of his father's strategy: decentralization. Prior to H. L. Hunt's death, more and more decisions had been made in Dallas. But Ray believed that the people in the field needed to be in a position to develop great expertise in a particular geographic area, and also had to be able to move quickly when there was a deal available. In fact, he saw this as one of the major strengths of being an independent oil producer: the man in the field for Hunt Oil had to have more authority than an executive vice-president at Exxon. As a result of his beliefs, Ray set up more exploration offices through the late 1970s, giving them permanent staffs, in contrast to his father's approach of constantly moving people. He set up a London office to focus on international opportunities. This move was to pay off in a big way only a few years later.

In addition to his attempts to revitalize Hunt Oil as an independent producer, Ray continued to lead the company in the direction in which he had developed a strong interest before his father's death: real estate development. The real estate subsidiary, Woodbine Development, had begun its first big project, Reunion, in the early seventies. In 1978, its first segment was completed, on budget and on time. This was a 1,000-room Hyatt hotel and skyline-altering restaurant tower. By 1980, the next major facility, the $24-million Reunion Arena, was completed. Ray apparently felt that Woodbine was a capable and potentially profitable arm of the corporation, and authorized it to do more development from the late 1970s on.

Other areas into which Ray took Hunt Oil were an echo of some of his father's wilder investments. He began to diversify. An associate came to him with an idea for a new magazine, to serve the city of Dallas. Ray liked the idea and agreed to finance it under the Hunt Oil umbrella. The result was Southwest Media Corporation, which went on to publish not only *D*, the Dallas magazine, but also *Houston City* and *Texas Homes*. In 1981, Ray took the company still farther afield when he purchased Union Life Insurance Company, a Little Rock, Arkansas, insurer with $100 million in assets. He planned to use the insurance company as "the basis of a very sophisticated financial services operation." Ray also continued to support what remained of his father's agribusiness investments, which included both cattle and producing farms.[12]

In late 1980, Hunt Oil became involved in a project that represented the culmination of Ray's development of the company during the initial period in which he was responsible for its management. Dr. Ian Maycock, manager of Hunt Oil's London office, learned from a friend and former colleague of a new study focusing on an interesting area in North Yemen, a country abutting Saudi Arabia. This area had been studied and dismissed as not likely to be rich in oil, but Maycock and his friend, on looking over the new information, decided that North Yemen might be promising after all. Their thoughts were not part of the conventional wisdom: "Some of our people [had ideas] that were very, very high risk," Ray said in retrospect. "I believe firmly that in the vast majority of other companies in the industry, [their approach] was so unusual and high risk that it probably would never have survived the first meeting."[13] But Ray still believed in his principle of delegating authority and letting the experts follow their beliefs. He told them to go ahead.

In early 1981, Maycock and two other men went to the capital of North Yemen to try to obtain permission for Hunt Oil to study the surface geology of the area. According to the company history, "Hunt Oil was an unknown to the government of North Yemen, so a considerable amount of time was spent explaining what the company was and how it operated. The North Yemen officials were interested in a company that had expertise and could act quickly, something on which Hunt officials prided themselves."[14] After obtaining permission from the government to move ahead, the team began to investigate the political climate of the country; Bunker's experience with Libya was still fresh in every Hunt Oil employee's mind.

Concluding, after quite a bit of research, that the country was stable and interested in joint exploration, Hunt Oil officials went on to do some politicking that gave them more opportunities to get acquainted with the North Yemen decision-makers and to make a good impression on them. By September 1981, Hunt Oil had a signed agreement allowing them to explore and develop resources in North Yemen. After three years of exploration, the final word on the field came in. It was a "giant," an "elephant," with 400 million barrels of reserves in an area that no one else believed would yield any oil whatsoever. Although in the next year Hunt Oil sold forty-nine percent of its holdings to Exxon, in return for substantial capital for development costs, the field promised eventually to produce 400,000 barrels of oil a day, beginning in late 1987, when oil prices hovered close to twenty dollars a barrel. At full production, Hunt Oil's share in these sales would be a gross of almost $1.5 billion a year.

Some of Ray's decisions, however, were not as fortunate as his energetic go-ahead in the Middle East. In late 1986, he had sold Union Life, for $16 million less than he had paid for it in 1981. "It was profitable for us, but not a home run," he was quoted as observing in *Forbes*. "We just didn't have the sophistication in an industry changing so much so fast."[15] Two of the magazines had also proved to be beyond his ability to make profitable. After watching modest but unremitting losses, Southwest Media put *Houston City* on the market during the summer of 1986; the future of *Texas Homes* was being reviewed.[16]

Overall, however, Ray's oil successes counted for more than his relatively modest losses in the diversification areas. In 1987, in part because of North Yemen, Hunt Oil was generally a strong company, well positioned to expand further from a firm economic base. *Forbes* estimated the Hunt Oil fortune at over $1 billion; at H. L.'s death, Ray and his family's holdings had been estimated at around $250 million.[17]

This substantial increase in the company's value might have been the norm in the days of the great oil boom, which had taken place in 1979, 1980, and early 1981. But by 1986, many energy-based fortunes were in disarray. Problems had begun suddenly in 1981, when oil prices declined sharply. Whereas they had nudged forty dollars a barrel off and on during 1979 and 1980, in 1981 they fell to slightly over thirty dollars a barrel and stayed there. The Texas oil economy began to put on the brakes. But, like one of the enormous oil tankers that was transporting black gold across the oceans, the boom was so big that it could not suddenly grind to a stop. Buildings had been started; it was better that they be completed. Wells had been spudded; they should be brought in, even if only to be capped for later production. Contracts had been signed to go on and on, in one economic undertaking or another; they had to be honored.

By the time the Texas economy slowed, things began not to look quite so bad. Oil prices were down but became relatively stable at somewhat under thirty dollars a barrel. Breathing a sigh of relief, everybody went back to doing most of what they had been doing a short time before.

Until, that is, what was probably inevitable occurred. Oil prices took another nose dive. At one point in 1986, the same oil that only months before had been selling for around twenty-seven dollars a barrel was worth only nine dollars. And this time, after the fall, the economy didn't pick itself up and dust itself off. Rather, a real and deep recession began to roll over Texas, beginning during 1985, becoming absolutely critical during the summer of 1986, and continuing into 1987 and the foreseeable future. Only the strongest and most farsighted companies escaped intact. Ray Hunt's company was one of these. And Ray, though by now the seasoned leader, since his election as president of Hunt Oil in 1976, was still, in 1987, only forty-four years old.

In discussing how he'd kept Hunt Oil on course during the troubled 1980s, Ray recounted how his father had once told him, "Ray, I've never made a decision that if everything went against me I couldn't keep right on going." "That really stuck with me," Ray said in a 1987 interview. "That is one of the guiding principles that heavily influences and controls our operating philosophy."[18] Elsewhere he enlarged on this: "You minimize your risk by doing as much homework as possible, and by spreading risk. Then, every once in a while, you'll stumble onto something that makes you go *boom!*" as, of course, North Yemen had done.[19]

Besides taking an aggressive and yet manageable approach to corporate risk, Ray had done one other thing during the late 1970s and 1980s, which only indirectly contributed to Hunt Oil, but which played a direct role both in enhancing his management skills and in maximizing his and Hunt Oil's position in the community. Ray become heavily involved in civic and community affairs and had supported his employees in doing the same. "I really encourage a young person to take every opportunity to become involved," he said. "The sort of standard I've got here is I'm very willing to let people make a contribution. I don't care if they accomplish whatever responsibilities they have [at Hunt Oil] at 2 o'clock in the afternoon or 2 o'clock in the morning so long as they get the job done. When people undertake civic activities, social responsibilities, I encourage them, just so their business responsibilities don't get short-changed."[20]

Ray followed very much the same guidelines himself. He assumed an almost daunting number of responsibilities, including high-level involvement with the Dallas Chamber of Commerce, the Dallas Museum of Art, the Dallas Central Business District Association, the North Texas Commission, Southwestern Medical Foundation, and a church foundation, as well as serving as president of the prestigious and historically powerful Dallas Citizens Council. "I don't think I have any greater talents than anyone else," he said in 1987. "I do believe strongly that if you belong to a community you have to put something back."[21]

It was during 1987 that Ray served in one of the most nationally visible positions he had ever held: he headed the search committee for a new president of SMU, during a time when the university was receiving intense negative publicity due to a major football scandal. In approaching this job, Ray demonstrated a tough business sense and a strong need for integrity that some people believed characterized how he conducted his oil business as well. "Part of the negotiations were that if I were to chair this thing, that it would operate with total integrity of process," he said in a newspaper article describing "Ray Hunt's wealth of influence." "In other words, it wasn't going to be a public relations ploy. The committee would function and would select the next president. It wouldn't be out there as a sort of stalking horse while two or three trustees went out and picked their person."[22] A. Kenneth Pye, the person whom the committee eventually picked, said that his decision to go to SMU had been strongly influenced by Ray and his approach to the invitation he offered.

Throughout all this, Ray Hunt maintained a great separation of his public persona as chairman of the board of Hunt Oil, and his private self as husband and father, though he was not hesitant to grant interviews or to step into the public eye. But even after years of his being in the limelight, ever since his father's death in 1974, most people could not have named Ray's five children or said exactly where the family lived, could not have described Ray's hobbies or where he vacationed, and rarely saw his name on the society pages in any but the most public context.[23] His sisters all described him as a wonderful man, thoughtful and sincere. His mother freely told stories of his love, support, and attention. But Ray himself led his own version of the quiet life, apparently successful at marriage and fatherhood, apparently winning enough respect from those around him to be left alone to value his privacy no matter how newsworthy such an exposure of that privacy might have been.

As Ruth Ray Hunt, mother of Ray, June, Helen, and Swanee, reached an energetic old age, she could look at her four children, with their romantic origins and unconventional family circumstances, and see each settled into a life's work that was meaningful and rewarding. "We're really much more alike than we are different," Swanee explained. "We *look* real different—Helen and me, and then June's more conservative religious emphasis and Ray's more conservative political emphasis. But actually what drives us all is very similar. We all tend to be very oriented toward looking at the world around us and trying to figure out how to impact it. . . . Philosophically it's different, but not in values, in that sense. And that allows us to have enormous respect for each other."

EIGHTEEN

BUNKER and Herbert Hunt had made some big mistakes in the extent and nature of their involvement in the silver market prior to 1980's Silver Thursday. But as they confided to the *Fortune* reporter that year, they could survive their losses.[1] Not only was there the possibility that eventually the price of silver would return to what the brothers saw as its logical value in relationship to gold and other investments; but there was also the fact that other holdings the brothers continued to control, particularly those in energy and real estate, had such an enormous absolute value that even if the silver debts were simply paid off outright, the Hunts would still be very, very rich.

The two brothers probably could, in fact, have liquidated some of their other holdings and retired their debt relatively quickly. But while this might have made it easier for them both to sleep comfortably at night, this option was not very attractive overall. First, any property that they sold at a profit would be subject to heavy taxation, and paying taxes was something that the Hunts, like many other wealthy Americans, chose to avoid whenever possible. Second, once an asset was sold, it was gone forever, and Bunker and Herbert could no longer benefit from any future appreciation that asset might realize.

During the period immediately following the silver crash, expectations of major appreciation throughout Texas were the norm. There was a big oil boom, and everybody was participating in it. Not only were oil prices high, generating enormous levels of absolute income, but also the funds pouring into the state were fueling all kinds of development, which promised to go on indefinitely. Farmland, ranchland, commercial and residential real estate development, retail sales, tourism and business travel, leisure activities— everything was going up. Bunker and Herbert were not the only Hunts who participated in the boom. Ray was involved in his real estate developments and his magazines; Caroline was building her hotels. All of Texas was on a rocket ship to wealth and there was no end in sight.

Unfortunately, it was not long after Bunker and Herbert took out their loans that things took a turn for the worse. Throughout the 1982–1987 period, the brothers saw a drop, temporary stabilization, and then massive decline in oil prices. For wealthy individuals like the Hunts, a large proportion of whose assets were in the form of oil that hadn't been brought to the surface yet, the sharp ups and downs of the oil business during the seven years after Silver Thursday meant that the value of their holdings followed suit. A reserve of a million barrels of oil at thirty-eight dollars a barrel was worth a lot more than the same reserves when oil was selling for nine dollars a barrel.

For the creditors of these wealthy individuals—such as the consortium of banks who had loaned Bunker, Herbert, and, to a lesser extent, Lamar, a great deal of money—loans that had looked well secured began to look a lot less safe. And then, as the recession sweeping across Texas led to huge devaluations of real estate holdings, a secondary Hunt investment, things looked worse and worse indeed. When a Texas bank president considered where he stood with the Hunts and placed that against the backdrop of where he stood with all his other energy-dependent clients, that man probably became very worried.

Reflecting the changes in the oil economy and the bankers' responses to them, pressures grew on the Hunts to lower their absolute level of indebtedness and to keep coming up with guarantees to the banks that they were good for the money they had been loaned. According to a 1986 *New York Times* article, in January 1982, during the first oil-price declines, trustees of some of the Hunt holdings sold off oil properties partially owned by Placid, the Hunt corporation that had signed for most of the debt, in order to make payments of $410 million on the silver loan. Then, a month later, the Hunts and the banks, probably reflecting the continuing changing environment, restructured $1.1 billion in debt. The new agreements were detailed, calling, for example, for an orderly sale of the silver the Hunts were still using as collateral.[2]

At the time of the 1982 renegotiations, although Bunker, Herbert, and Lamar were the family members who had actually lost money in the silver market, the holdings of these three men were still heavily intertwined with the holdings of their two sisters and their brother, Hassie. During 1983, Margaret, who was primarily responsible for Hassie's trust, and Caroline took significant steps toward separating their holdings from their other three brothers'.

Margaret and Caroline may have been motivated by the fact that in addition to the financial problems the silver debacle was causing, Bunker and Herbert appeared unable to resolve their legal situation regarding their silver dealings. In 1982, the brothers had settled an SEC complaint stemming from their position in Bache stocks during their silver investing. But there was to be more. In March 1985, the Commodity Futures Trading Commission capped a five-year federal investigation with charges that the two men were part of a group of international businessmen who had developed a "manipulative scheme" to inflate silver prices to their benefit in violation of com- modity trading laws, and that their scheme had led to the crash of the silver market. Each day of "scheming" could be considered a separate offense, with each violation capable of generating a fine of $1,000. If the plotting had gone on over a period of nine months, as alleged, and if each man were found guilty, these fines alone could mount up to over half a million dollars for the two brothers. As of November 1987, these charges had not been resolved.[3]

Caroline and Margaret were probably also aware that the silver- related deals were not the only economic pressures that Bunker and Herbert were facing. In early 1984, Bunker's Libyan situation had finally been resolved, but the judgments had cost him a great deal of money. A U.S. district court judge ordered him to pay close to $41 million to BP, upholding the findings of a British court of appeals and denying Bunker's countersuit against BP. The judge also dis- missed Bunker's claim that he and BP had agreed to submit any disagreements to arbitration; Bunker was now left with little recourse except to pay.[4]

There was also the continuing erosion of Bunker's and Herbert's position in Great Western.[5] Great Western United had never made money for the two men. First, there had been the losses in sugar, which they had attempted to offset by trading in other commodities. Then, there had been the poor performance of their unlikely subsidiary, Shakey's Pizza Parlor, which the company managed to sell. At times the company considered intriguing possibilities for the future: there was a plan, for example, that involved international trading between the Philippines, the Middle East, and Great Western, utilizing various combinations of sugar, oil, and cash. But this plan was never executed, and the company's financial situation did not stabilize. Bunker's and Herbert's problems with Great Western were aggravated by the rigors of reporting required of publicly held companies; the brothers had never been required to run their businesses with anyone but themselves in mind before. Finally, in frustration, the Hunts bought more company stock and took Great Western private, renaming it Hunt International Resources.

HIRCO continued to have problems, some of the worst being in its sugar subsidiary. Great Western Sugar Company had originally been the major component of Great Western, and after the Hunts got the company out of silver, it became important again. A 1985 *Fortune* article described how the company had lost volume when U.S. soft-drink manufacturers had begun using corn sweeteners instead of sugar. When sugar prices consequently fell violently during 1981 and into 1982 and 1983, the company, rather than negotiate new contracts with valued customers, infuriated them by insisting on keeping the old contracts and suing when the contracts were not honored.[6]

At the same time that the company was alienating its customers, it was alienating its suppliers. Growers maintained, in the words of the article, that the Hunts "muscled them to accept a sharp cutback in their contract to supply beets to the company." The growers retaliated by providing their own cutbacks, in some cases to nothing.

By 1984, Great Western plants consequently sat underutilized or even completely idle. The economic effects were devastating. Just how devastating began to be clear in October of that year. It was then that HIRCO creditors began writing off loans to HIRCO subsidiaries, including Great Western.[7] The Hunts began trying to sell the sugar companies, but were unable to find a deal that would satisfy the creditors. The lenders who had not given up on collecting their loans from the Hunts took control of operations in early 1985, and in March, all of Great Western's operations were shut down, and more than 300 employees were furloughed indefinitely. A few days later, the company filed for bankruptcy, citing loans of $295 million, which it was unable to repay, and informing the Securities and Exchange Commission that in its fourth quarter, which had ended six months before, it had lost money at a rate of $1 million per day, leading to a negative net worth of $112 million.

By the end of March, the lenders had accepted the reality of their loss, and deals had been worked out to sell the assets of the sugar companies. This reportedly left HIRCO, which once had had a national restaurant chain, a community-development company in California, and oil and gas exploration-and-development enterprises, with depleted assets consisting of two offshore oil rigs. And in March 1985, offshore rigs just weren't worth what they used to bring: half the rigs were idle, and those being used were renting at bargain-basement rates.

By December 1986, Great Western was still around, with a negative net worth of $49.14 million. The sugar subsidiary was still involved in lawsuits, which Great Western hoped to benefit from, though the one suit that had been settled had gone against it. In August 1986, the company had paid $5.5 million to claimants, whom the *Wall Street Journal* described as "some disgruntled sugar-beet farmers." Meanwhile, as creditors continued to seek payment of Great Western's debts from the parent company, HIRCO had been pulled into Chapter 11 only a month after the sugar companies, and then, in November 1985, had been removed from the control of the Hunt brothers. Total HIRCO assets had dropped in value by nearly $500 million since 1982, according to documents related to the bankruptcy proceedings. HIRCO itself had a negative net worth of more than $167 million. Even the IRS got in on the kill: it claimed that HIRCO owed almost $20 million in back taxes, a claim that, needless to say, HIRCO disputed actively.

As it turned out, HIRCO was a precursor of what began to happen to Bunker and Herbert in other areas of their business empire, specifically those that had provided the collateral for more than a billion dollars in loans. By late 1985, silver was no longer much of an issue itself. During the year, the brothers had quietly sold off their silver holdings, probably to generate cash to meet their debt obligations. A *Wall Street Journal* article in October said they had sold 59 million ounces of silver, the bulk of their holdings. At the average 1985 price of six dollars an ounce, this would have generated over $350 million. But as the article went on to report, "the sales represent a loss of about $1 billion, largely interest costs on loans used to finance the cache."[8] This was in addition to the out-and-out loss of $1.1 billion on Silver Thursday due to the Hunts' futures positions.

With silver aside and the reality of the HIRCO disaster beginning to be fully visible, the Hunt lenders now began looking very carefully at other parts of the brothers' holdings to make sure they could collect the money owed them if need be. What they saw, as the energy recession in Texas began to develop and then gather momentum, was not reassuring.

There were two problems. One was that all along the banks lending to the Hunts had thought in terms of loans to extremely wealthy individuals; if one part of these individuals' holdings lost value, there was always another part that would be stable and that the lenders could go after for debt repayment.[9] What happened while the details of the loans were first being worked out contributed to this reassuring belief: Bunker, Herbert, and Lamar had graciously listed personal assets, such as Rolex watches and race horses, when they provided lists of collateral to the banks. But as the problems with insolvency surfaced in HIRCO, the Hunts appeared to change their stance. The message they began to communicate was that certain corporate entities had signed for the loans stemming from the silver losses. If these entities ran into problems, the brothers would not come running in with funds drawn from their other holdings, including their personal asset bases, either to bail out the companies or to pay off the debts. Perhaps the Hunts had always thought in these terms. Clearly, however, the banks hadn't.

The other problem was that even if the banks succeeded in having the Hunts tap their other holdings, these were not unencumbered. The situation at Penrod Drilling, one of the biggest Hunt companies, was typical. According to a 1985 *Fortune* article, Penrod had borrowed a great deal of money during the oil boom to finance sophisticated offshore drilling rigs. Some of these rigs cost as much as $30 million and, during good times, rented for $45,000 a day. By early 1985, even before hard times had really hit the oil industry, rents had plummeted to one-half their former value as fewer and fewer wells were begun. Penrod's land rigs, of which it had seventy, were also facing an inability to generate income. The article estimated that the company had $800 million in debt, with principal and interest of $130 million a year coming due. Penrod was just barely breaking even, and if things got worse, it could face a serious financial crisis. Although the *Fortune* reporter did not know it at the time, this was, in fact, already the case. A subsequent *Dallas Morning News* article described how even in late 1984 Penrod was running behind on interest payments to its lenders, and the banks were refusing to renegotiate loans to let the company off the hook.[10]

Then there was Placid Oil, described as the "bedrock of the Hunts' castle." Placid still had extensive reserves of gas and oil, which it could tap to generate cash to pay its debts and those related to silver. But with declining oil prices, it took more and more depletion of reserves to come up with the same amount of cash. And it also became harder and harder to produce enough oil to come out far enough ahead to finance *new* exploration. Without new exploration—as Ray Hunt had seen when he took over Hunt Oil—the company would slowly go downhill, until finally it had depleted everything it had, and its value as a going concern reached zero.

By early 1986, Bunker and Herbert recognized only too clearly that their empire was in trouble. Whether they looked to Placid, Penrod, real estate, or race horses, they still needed a little more room to maneuver. According to the recollections of the brothers, the banks had assured them all along that they could be flexible regarding exact terms of repayment; the banks would be willing to restructure agreements to reflect the expected cash flow of the various Hunt enterprises. Their recollections might well have been correct at one time. But by 1986, the banks were seeing the Hunts start to draw lines between holdings, to protect personal assets, to shield their trusts. Consequently, they may already have been moving toward less flexibility just when Herbert and Bunker needed a more free-flowing arrangement.

Regardless of the sources of the conflicts, conflicts there were. Banks that had traditionally reviewed loans like those to the Hunts once a year started to reexamine the Hunts' collateral weekly or even daily. The Hunts themselves had constantly to reassess their cash situation as the value of their empire fluctuated wildly.[11] The days of borrowers and lenders meeting informally at the Petroleum Club to make agreements sealed by a handshake were coming to an end throughout Texas. The brothers were beginning to mistrust the bankers who had seemed so friendly just a few years before, and the bankers were beginning to have no confidence at all that Bunker and Herbert, as Texas gentlemen, would do everything possible to honor their commitments. The world of bottomless oil reserves and uncapped oil prices was crashing around bankers and oilmen alike, and the Hunts' deals suffered from the fallout.

On June 24, 1986, all the uncertainties, insecurities, and bad feelings finally erupted into front-page headlines. "Six Hunts sue 23 banks for $3.6 billion" was the lead story in Dallas the next morning.[12] Bunker, Herbert, Lamar, three of their sons, plus affiliated companies and family trusts were suing the banks. They charged that the banks used fraud and deceit in attempts to obtain repayment of the $1.5 billion in loans they had made to the Hunts. Specifically, the banks had tried "to dismantle and ultimately destroy" Penrod and Placid and had used credit terms as a "club" to force the family to use personal resources to repay loans to the corporations. The Hunts requested $3.6 billion in damages, plus punitive damages.

The Hunts were being represented by McCabe/Gordon, a young and extremely aggressive law firm located in Boston. Its two principals had a history of "stirring up trouble," as the *Wall Street Journal* put it. The *Journal* described their break with their previous firm as "acrimonious," and reported that Stephen Gordon had been in trouble with a federal court for "intentionally discarding" important documents in a case and that he had been disqualified from "all or part representation of a client in a bankruptcy case, in part because he violated bar standards governing conflict of interest." "You'll find lawyers and courts who don't like us, but you won't find a client who doesn't think we did everything we could for him," Gordon was quoted as saying.[13]

The banks sued by the Hunts were caught somewhat unaware. After all, the money they had loaned was bank money, and they were supposed to get it back. Weren't they? The bankers were positive that they were wearing the white hats here, having been more than generous to Bunker, Herbert, and Lamar during hard times. But a challenge was a challenge, even to nice guys. On July 17, the first bank countersued, with the twenty-two others following suit shortly thereafter.[14] Claims against the Hunts totaled $1.28 billion, and all highlighted the banks' belief that the Hunts were "personally liable" for the debts they had incurred.

Immediately, the Hunts escalated their attack.[15] They filed a second suit, claiming that the banks violated antitrust laws by conspiring to gain control of the offshore-drilling industry. They cited an internal bank memo, circulated some months before, that outlined the possibility of taking advantage of the disarray in the offshore-drilling business to create a joint venture, with the oil rigs as assets and the lending banks as manager and beneficiary of that business. As part of this suit, the Hunts requested treble damages, which would bring the total amount at stake to $13.8 billion.

Now it was the banks' turn to respond. They began taking steps to gain control of specific assets held by the Hunts by foreclosing on properties. The Hunts asked the court to restrain the foreclosures, which the court bluntly refused to do. The banks chose specific properties and set the date for auctioning them off. On August 30, the day the sales were to begin, the Hunts again grabbed front-page headlines, by doing what a short time before would have been unthinkable when it came to the basic Hunt empire: they filed for bankruptcy.[16]

In a business situation as complex as that of the Hunts, even declaring bankruptcy was a multifaceted undertaking. The actual entities that sought protection were Placid Oil Company and Placid Building and Service Company, one of its subsidiaries, which held an interest in Thanksgiving Tower, a Dallas skyscraper where the first family had offices. Two days later, the William Herbert Hunt Trust, which held the next property the banks threatened to sell off, also filed for Chapter 11 protection.

Putting these holdings under Chapter 11 in no way negated the claims the various banks held against the Hunt assets. When a corporation, or, for that matter, an individual, files for bankruptcy, it does not mean that that company or person owes any less money. It simply provides time during which a plan can be worked out for paying off its debts. Without this protection, secured lenders can start taking assets that were provided as collateral and selling them for whatever they can get. In the case of a corporation, this could, and often would, mean the end of the corporation's existence.

Bankruptcy protection originated as a way of protecting others in addition to the borrower. In most cases, not only are there lenders who have made collateralized loans, as the banks had to Placid Oil, but also there are other people or companies who are, in effect, lenders whose claims against the insolvent company would be unmet completely if the big secured lenders liquidated it to meet their own interests.

In the case of Placid, for example, there were companies that had drilled wells and had not yet been paid. The money owed to them was not "secured" or guaranteed by anything except the ongoing functioning of the business. If the banks sold off everything, including the new wells, the drilling company, as a creditor, would receive nothing.

There is also the possibility that in the long run even secured creditors will be better off if a company is allowed to go on functioning in a restructured form. Sometimes corporations are able to overcome their problems and pay off their debts fully from operations, whereas if they are liquidated, even secured lenders will have to settle for less than a total return of their loans.

Because of the usual complexity of debts a corporation holds, once it files for bankruptcy protection it is no longer completely on its own, either in creating a plan to pay off its debts or in continuing to do business. The operations of the company begin to be supervised by a court-appointed official, whose job includes insuring that the company has enough money to keep going but does not spend money that could otherwise be put aside to satisfy debts. During this period of "receivership," the regular corporate management loses a great deal of autonomy. At the same time, this management, as well as each set of creditors, has the opportunity to come up with a specific plan for paying off the debts as fully as possible. It is ultimately up to the court to sort out these plans and find one that everyone can agree to. The court also has the right, after a reasonable length of time, to override the wishes of the corporation and its creditors if they cannot come up with an acceptable plan, and to force them all to accept the court's plan for settling the debts.

In the Hunt case, the bankruptcy issues were separated legally from the issues of whether the Hunts really had to repay the banks or whether the banks would end up paying damages to the Hunts.[17] Two different judges in two different courts oversaw the two different legal proceedings. When there was an issue that affected both cases, such as whether Placid, under its Chapter 11 protection, had to keep making payments to the banks—payments in dispute in the other case—the judges had to work it out between them.

Since the Hunts and their lenders were involved in two massive and closely related legal proceedings at the same time, the two cases proceeded very slowly. The fact that the Hunts were represented by such aggressive legal counsel in their suit against the banks did not help. Hunt attorneys used every opportunity to create conflict, beginning with repeatedly trying to remove the judge appointed to the case. (They were not successful.)[18] In the bankruptcy proceedings, there was also a lot of legal jockeying, particularly regarding in what state and under what legal system the filings would be made; the banks wanted everything centralized in Dallas; the Hunts tried to fragment the proceedings by filing in another area where they held substantial property, Louisiana, where many laws were different from those in Texas, due to the use of the Napoleonic Code. The banks won on this issue, too.[19]

In fact, during the early months of the two cases, the banks seemed to win on everything. Even the bankruptcy protections did not work out completely to the Hunts' advantage. On October 7, the banks managed to sell, from the steps of the relevant county courthouse, a piece of property that had been held by Herbert's trust. The only thing that saved the Hunt brothers from total humiliation in this instance was that the winning bidder for the property was none other than Mrs. Albert G. Hill—sister Margaret.[20]

Then in December, the Hunts fired McCabe/Gordon.[21] The reasons were unstated, though one newspaper article mentioned that Judge Barefoot Sanders, the man the lawyers had been unable to have disqualified, had recommended that the firm step down. After some heavy skirmishing in the other judge's court about the firm's charges, as well as those of the new attorneys, McCabe/Gordon retired to Boston to assess their loss. Five months later a quiet article in the *Wall Street Journal* noted that the law firm had dissolved. They left behind their "lavish new offices overlooking Boston's harbor," where they had thrown a $25,000 open-house party for 500 guests only the summer before.[22]

Back in Dallas, the lawsuits and bankruptcy proceedings continued. The Hunts' new lawyer, Stephen Susman, a Houston attorney, managed to negotiate a high fee of $600 an hour for himself; what the corporations in Chapter 11 were not allowed to pay, the Hunts picked up personally.[23] By now estimates had the banks paying as much as $6 million a month in legal fees in both cases, and the Hunts a million a month or even more.

In early 1987, both legal proceedings were focused on what some people had believed was the beginning of the conflict between the banks and the Hunts all along: Green Canyon. Green Canyon was an offshore area in the Gulf of Mexico where Placid Oil had obtained rights to drill. However, the land mass where Placid hoped to find oil was located very deep below gulf waters, more than 2,000 feet down. To drill there required a new technology, which had been developed using a drilling rig belonging to Penrod Drilling. The Hunts said that they had to drill Green Canyon if they were to keep Placid alive as a business; to be able to drill, they had to spend more money adapting the Penrod rig, putting it into place, and actually sinking the well. The banks said that it was ridiculous for Placid to spend enormous amounts of money on an untried technology in an unproven area when that same money could be set aside for paying off Placid's debts to them.[24]

Finally, the Hunts succeeded in raising money from outside investors, including other family members, to finance Green Canyon.[25] The modified rig was more or less held for ransom for a while, but it was finally released, and work went forward. By late 1987, whether or not Green Canyon would produce gas and oil was still unknown; even if a major strike came in, there was always the possibility that depressed oil and gas prices would mean that the well would never succeed in paying off the investments that Penrod, Placid, and the other investors had made in it.

Once Stephen Susman became the Hunts' lead lawyer, there seemed to be less acrimony between the two sides in the cases. The Hunts accepted Barefoot Sanders, although he later removed himself from the case anyway, and they had to start over again with another judge.[26] Various rumors circulated about possible agreements between the two sides, about the Hunts negotiating secretly with one bank or another, about plans that the two sides were considering submitting to the courts for Chapter 11 reorganization.

By late September 1987, Susman had succeeded both in convincing the Hunts to let him drop some of the charges against the banks, which he had come to feel he could not substantiate, and to reestablish some of the contact the family had let slip with the outside world during what they seemed to see as their period of being besieged. That was the month in which the *New York Times Magazine* ran a cover story on Bunker, Herbert, Lamar, and their families, which discussed their legal situation and how they saw what was going on, a story with which the Hunts had cooperated fully.[27] The article described Susman as recommending to the brothers that the story would help their chances if their case against the banks went to a jury trial; it also featured a full-page picture of the attorney lounging against a desk topped with legal documents, looking at ease and wearing a ten-gallon white hat.

Even Stephen Susman could not change the Hunts, however. They remained both combative and publicity-shy. For example, Susman had reportedly said in a September 1 hearing before the new bankruptcy judge that his side was willing to try to work out a way of repaying the banks to whom the Hunts owed money. The formal plan Placid had submitted some time before had not allowed for a prompt repayment. A week later articles appeared in the *Wall Street Journal* and other papers about the details of a new plan; it would involve selling off part of the Hunts' holdings and settling some of the legal battles out of court. But almost at once the Hunts said that due to too much publicity and too many leaks, all proposals were withdrawn. Later the *Wall Street Journal* reported that the investment banking company that had been most instrumental in developing the new settlement proposal, First Boston Corporation, of New York, had been "dumped" by the Hunts.[28]

By late 1987, it was clear that there were going to be no easy answers to the questions faced by the Hunts and their twenty-three banks. With the stock market crash of October, the perpetually uncertain future of oil prices, and the continuing depression in the Texas economy, an easy solution was becoming highly unlikely.

In early November, Bunker announced that he planned to sell his entire stable of thoroughbred horses (many of which were prize-winners), worth perhaps as much as $60 million. He had created his stables from a combination of a great deal of wealth and a real nose for a good horse; he could quote bloodlines, win records, and sale prices with equal fluidity. For thirty years he had traveled around the world to buy and sell horses and to watch them run. But now the horses had to go. "You can always use a little money, especially in the oil business," Bunker said about the sale. "I like 'em, but you know it's not like they're family."[29] Perhaps, in the end, it all came down to that. Family sticks together through good times and bad, thick and thin, wins and losses, but if they're not family—and sometimes even if they're only half-family—they can always go.

NINETEEN

THE rapidly fluctuating economic realities of the late 1980s called on almost all twelve living children of H. L. Hunt to manage and shape their resources in constantly changing ways. The vagaries of the energy market that had begun in the 1970s and the disruptions of the traditional position of the United States as industrial and fiscal world leader not only affected the Hunt economic power base—the oil business—but also demanded that the children who drew their wealth from energy consider alternative methods of building or at least protecting their already accumulated assets. Whether it was Bunker making commodities investments or June using her share of Hunt Oil's North Yemen earnings to finance Christian radio programs, all of Hunt's children were faced with problems that even H. L. Hunt himself, dead now for close to fifteen years, would have found daunting.

As the children and their own now maturing children coped, they displayed one set of similarities after another, across family segments and across generations. These similarities could be seen as the ultimate flowering of the legacies H. L. Hunt had left to them—the legacies not stipulated in any legal document, not argued over in any private financial agreements, but legacies that nonetheless were just as real.

Hunt's legacies to his descendants appeared to fall into two sweeping categories. The first had to do with how the children and grandchildren did business and handled their money; the second, with how each family member dealt with being a Hunt and managed relationships with all the others who shared his or her last name.

Almost every Hunt business undertaking was characterized by one recurring theme: a love of the grand scale, the big gesture, even the flamboyant stance. Just as H. L. Hunt had sunk his last few hundred dollars in the all-or-nothing challenge of Dad Joiner's "pig in a poke" field, so his descendants went after the big stakes in a big way. There was nothing modest, for example, about the way Lamar went about entering the sports business. He not only started his own football club but also set up his own football league, followed by taking a high-profile leadership position in professional soccer and professional tennis. And Lamar's dramatic business undertakings were, of course, rivaled and even outdone by those of his older brothers, Bunker and Herbert, as they bought, sold, and ultimately were nearly bankrupted by silver.

These were the obviously dramatic Hunt business undertakings. But even in areas that attracted less attention, the Hunts did things in a big way. When Caroline and her children began building hotels, they built dramatic ultraluxury facilities that catapulted Caroline's whole family into the public eye. When Ray Hunt moved Hunt Oil into the mainstream of high-competition energy production, he did it by authorizing exploration in an area nobody else would even think of touching; when he struck oil there, he brought in a giant field. When Swanee and Helen became interested in philanthropy, within a few years they not only were giving away well over a quarter of a million dollars of their own each year but also were playing major roles in setting up women's foundations with endowments targeted at hundreds of millions of dollars.

Closely related to the dramatic scope of the Hunt undertakings was their almost universally high risk. The shadow of H. L. Hunt's lonely high-stakes card game with the Mexican railroad workers or impetuous desertion of his family to invest borrowed money in the El Dorado oil fields fell consistently and sometimes darkly over the next seventy-five years to color the undertakings of his progeny. To begin with, as Hunt's children maintained and built on his energy endeavors, their business activities, by the standards of any ordinary person, presented enormous and almost paralyzing risks. Oil wells are tricky undertakings: some wells can't be completed; many are dry holes; others fizzle out after minimal production; and even if all goes well, oil prices may plummet, making a nominally productive well a money-loser. With almost all of the Hunts directly or indirectly in the oil business, there was always this basic sense of risk to almost everything they did. And these risks were constantly being leveraged, as, for instance, when Bunker and his part of the family sank millions of dollars into an unknown technology in an unknown field in Green Canyon, and when Ray sent his exploration team off to an undeveloped Middle Eastern country better known for its political uncertainties than its energy production.

The Hunt legacy continued to manifest itself as H. L.'s children and grandchildren constantly went beyond the risks of the energy business to undertake other investments and pursue other career opportunities. In fact, the flip side of almost every high-profile Hunt venture was the large risk—economic or otherwise—it presented. June put herself and her beliefs on the line five days a week as she wrote, recorded, and distributed radio programs focused on her own unique and transdenominational perspective on religious and spiritual matters. Margaret's son, Al Hill, Jr., followed his involvement with Lamar in World Champion Tennis with an almost single-handed attempt to interest Dallas in the remarkably high-risk business of movie production and distribution, beginning with the $2.8-million film *Hostage: Dallas*, a 1985 B movie, which Al was certain would pay out through sales of cable, pay-TV, and video-cassette rights.[1] Margaret's daughter, Alinda, leveraged what had begun as a modest interest in flying, while she was raising a family, into a buyout of Jet East, a small entrant in the highly competitive and expensive air charter business.[2]

Another business legacy that Hunt's successors seem to have inherited was a desire to run their own show, a persistent and even driven kind of entrepreneurism. The family members who did enter an established business largely chose some aspect of the family business. But even there, entrepreneurism prevailed. As of late 1987, the most complex family business, Hunt Enterprises, the holding company for Hunt's children of his first marriage, was not a company in the traditional sense of the word. Rather, as an article in the *New York Times Magazine* put it, "each man runs what amounts to a separate business entity."[3] The men—the three brothers and a number of their children and sons-in-law—shared information and looked at deals together, but made their own investment decisions.

Other members of all three of Hunt's families were even more clearly entrepreneurial. Among Hunt's original family, there were

Margaret's two independent children, Al, Jr. and Alinda. Caroline's daughter Laurie had started out, completely on her own, buying and remodeling houses for resale before joining three of her brothers in the hotel business. Caroline's youngest son, Patrick, decrying his position as, in his sister's words, "the fifth child on the rung—who's going to listen to me?" had moved out of Rosewood to learn the wine business, in which he planned to make his own niche.[4]

In Frania Lee's family, son Hugh had made a career of moving from one independent interest to another, from energy businesses to starting Montessori schools. Howard, before his death from cancer, had also been involved in a number of business ventures. And in Ruth's family, Ray, although considering himself very much a corporate man, was in a nontraditional corporation, where he was clearly first among equals. His sister June, with her own style of religious teaching, could be seen as a kind of entrepreneur of souls.

By the third generation, however, there were clearly some individuals who were beginning to lay aside the legacy: they were either not in business or entrepreneurial enterprises or had chosen to go into someone else's organization. Several of Hugh's children and one of Haroldina's daughters were pursuing professional careers: lawyer, doctor, economist. Lamar's oldest son had become a professional musician, playing flute in a symphony orchestra; his brother was training to be an investment banker. Quite a few of the daughters of Hunt's various sons had chosen not to pursue careers at all, at least while they were in their twenties and thirties, but, rather, were married and raising children full-time.

There was one more legacy related to H. L.'s success that appeared, although sporadically, in the second and third generations. This was Hunt's intuitive style of decision-making, of running his business. During the waning days of his power in Hunt Oil, his ability to walk into a room and say "I want that one" and have "that one" pay off hugely had given him an almost mythical staying power. Which of his children inherited that ability, or even that propensity?

This is not an easy question to answer. Whereas Hunt's children and employees and even Hunt himself had talked extensively about how he made the choices he made, nobody has ever said much about how Bunker or Ray, much less Margaret or Alinda or Laurie, make decisions. From an outsider's perspective, it certainly looks as if some of the Hunts follow their instincts rather than a more rational approach: there was Bunker's and Herbert's continued faith in silver, for example, faith that went counter to that of just about everybody else in the precious-metals market.

It is Bunker, in fact, among all Hunt's legatees, who appears to have evolved into a highly intuitive decision-maker. A strong picture of Bunker's style appeared in the *New York Times Magazine* article on the Hunts. In describing a deal the brothers were considering at the time the reporter was visiting their office, the article quoted one of the company geologists as calling Bunker a "big-picture guy," and told what happened after Herbert had presented a set of cut-and-dried facts related to a specific deal to Bunker. In a style strongly reminiscent of that of his father casually walking around a room posted with geological maps, "Bunker, seemingly uninterested, arms drooping alongside his chair, said nothing at first." Then he asked a single, almost careless question, which focused the decision-making process. Everyone else seemed to take it seriously and to plan to act as his question implied they should. Whether Bunker Hunt is as *good* an intuitive decision-maker as his father is, of course, open to debate; evidence to date indicates that he is not. But it seems that this is his style, and that he inherited it straight from his father.

Ray Hunt, the other son about whose business dealings the most observations have been made, has declared that he is not a highly intuitive person. Rather, he characterizes himself as "a fast learner" and a person who takes every opportunity to benefit from the experts with whom he has surrounded himself. But even if Ray does not follow his own intuition, the kinds of investments he has made in high-risk situations on the gut feel of his employed experts indicate some comfort with what he characterizes as a "sixth sense" that is unusual in most businessmen.

Any discussion of the Hunt family and how they do business naturally leads to another legacy Hunt seems to have passed on to his children: his attitude toward spending money. Over and over again, what was characterized as H. L.'s "frugality" was written about during his lifetime and even after. His worn suits, aging cars, sack lunches crept into almost every story about him. Not unexpectedly, it appears that, when it comes to spending money, shades of H. L. have permeated the lives of almost all his children, and their children as well.

In terms of style of dress and general physical appearance, practically all Hunt's children tend to be as far from high fashion as is possible without approaching out-and-out disrepair. Ray, whose big bones and ruddy complexion are strongly reminiscent of his father's, favors unobtrusive business suits and has been known to appear outside work in blue jeans or shorts. Margaret once expressed a certain amount of regret that she had promised some thirty-year-old evening dresses to a clothing museum when she found they still fit her. Even Caroline, who by the late 1980s owned a fancy retail clothing store, located in the Crescent development, likes to buy dresses for special occasions from a Dallas designer whose claim to fame is quick copying, at greatly reduced prices, of the latest European couture outfits.

In some contrast to the quiet personal appearance Hunt's children generally maintain, they almost all live in large houses located in upscale neighborhoods. Yet compared to how they could be living, the houses are relatively modest. Herbert's large two-story house, for example, is located on a corner lot on a rather busy residential street in Highland Park, an exclusive Dallas neighborhood. But the house fills most of the lot, and it presents an unassuming face and formal, even stuffy, appearance to the passer-by; there is nothing flamboyant or fancy about it. And whereas some of the other Hunts have bigger or fancier houses—Lamar's recently sold estate looked indisputably like the home of a millionaire, and Ray's suburban house is reportedly over 10,000 square feet—many of them live more modestly than Herbert. Swanee owns an average-size house in a redeveloping neighborhood of downtown Denver. Inside, the largest space is a living room that she added to within the last few years and that, she claims, still makes her terribly nervous, because its size perhaps puts off people from more modest circumstances. The room, about twenty by twenty-five feet, is probably smaller than the eat-in kitchens of the average tract houses being built in Denver's suburbs.

Hunt's children frequently don't make up for their relatively modest clothes and homes by embracing other status symbols: they tend to drive average American cars, go to cafeterias, and frequently take commercial air flights, even in the economy section. In fact, many of the children often demonstrate an element of almost otherworldly unconcern for money and disinterest in what it can buy. "Those red lights that come on and warn you the [car's gas] tank is getting low have been a big help," Lamar was quoted as saying in a 1984 article about him.[5] He explained that before the lights, he'd almost run out of gas as he drove around town in the six-year-old Detroit car he'd received as an NFL perk. Sometimes, like June with her seven-cent tip, he'd drive into a gas station and ask for something like thirty-one cents' worth of gas—all the change he happened to have.

Occasionally, Hunt's children, particularly those he had with Ruth, have gone even farther in distancing themselves from spending their money. In a 1987 interview, Swanee described how she recently asked her husband to help her stay out of what she saw as the trap of "eating at fancy restaurants four nights a week and getting a plane and flying all over the place from one vacation to another.

"It's insidious," she explained. "It's seductive. You add one thing, and you add another little thing and you get used to spending more and more money until you just don't notice it. . . . It is absolutely nothing to add $30 to a dinner bill by ordering this and this and this. . . . And that $30 to a woman who is living on Aid for Dependent Children with three kids—I guess I live with a tear inside all the time which I'd rather live with. . . . I believe in living with a certain discomfort toward the privileges. I think that's important."[6]

On the other hand, there are times when even the most modest-living Hunt son or daughter spends money like a rich Texan is expected to. June has a complete recording studio in her house, and Ray conducts business, though only business, with a private jet. Lamar drives his old car, but his wife has a new Mercedes. Caroline lived for many years in a house that looks extremely modest from the outside, but which she describes as "more splendific" than it appears, with beautiful views of a stream and ancient live-oak trees from the sweeping back windows. And many members of the family give away money in large sums for large projects: a new wing for the Highland Park Presbyterian Church, a new dining hall for Mary Baldwin College, over half a million dollars to Oliver North's Contra-support mission.

As with the entrepreneurial tendencies, which are beginning to lessen somewhat in the third generation of Hunts, the tendency to spend money modestly also is lessening—although not abating entirely—in the persons of Hunt's grandchildren as they become adults. Several of the grandchildren have earned the approbation of "jet-setters" in articles written about them or their families. Caroline's daughter, Laurie, discussed the third generation's ambivalence about money in a 1987 interview: "I have friends who grew up in Highland Park who dressed in couture clothes to go to high school. They had BMWs and Mercedeses when they were sixteen. We weren't given those kinds of things. I always had a lot but I wasn't spoiled like that; I had my brother's hand-me-down car first. It teaches you something. It's no good to get everything in the beginning. Good things come to those who wait. I really would love to have a big beautiful house on Lakeside Drive [one of the best streets in Highland Park], but I know I shouldn't really live there until I'm forty. You need to make the steps. It's kind of fun to live in jeans when you're in high school, not to wear couture. I wear couture now that I'm thirty and go to luncheons every day."[7]

What seems to underlie Laurie's ambivalence is a fear similar to that expressed by Swanee: that somehow spending the money inappropriately, in terms of either timing or level of extravagance, will lead to a way of life where money and the life-style it buys will unbalance a person's life completely. "I don't judge people by what they have," she continued. "I judge them by how they *handle* what they have. I see how they handle a problem, how they handle a wonderful gift, how they handle a lot of money, how they handle a death."

The Hunts' attitude toward money and the life-style it made available to them is closely tied to what could be called the psychological legacies the children and grandchildren have received: their inheritance of the Hunt identity and the complex set of interpersonal relationships that go with being a Hunt.

"If I had my own way I would prefer that my name never appeared in print again," Ray said in a 1977 interview. "But I'm realistic enough to know that there will be times when it's going to appear." "I love not having my last name be Hunt," said Laurie in 1987, "because people have to like me first, and maybe they'd find out who I was and maybe they wouldn't." "I'd rather meet someone without their ever knowing my last name," said June.[8]

In Texas, in New York, even in London or Heidelberg, to be a Hunt is to be noticed, to be examined, and often to be judged. Many of H. L. Hunt's children and grandchildren are comfortable with their last name and identity: by 1987, neither Caroline, Helen, nor Swanee was using a married name, each having chosen to return to being a Hunt; Hugh Lee had finally declared himself to be Hugh Hunt once and for all; and none of the men born to the name Hunt ever mentioned any desire to be anything else. But across the generations and families, there is a feeling—expressed in different ways by different people but consistently present nonetheless—that being "a Hunt" has its negative side.

One problem with the Hunt identity is simply that it draws a great deal of press coverage; Hunts tend to make good copy. "There were times," Swanee recalled, referring in particular to the period after her father died, "when I would feel terribly intruded upon. At one point I got so mad that I took a magazine and crumpled it up and threw it across the room. That doesn't happen to me anymore. I sort of take things in stride."9

As a consequence of the number of stories that have appeared about the Hunts, they have begun to assume a certain automatic identity in the eyes of many people outside the family. In a 1987 letter, Herbert's son Bruce presented a different view, saying that while his uncles are colorful and independent, "they do not bear any resemblance to the J. R. Ewing type that the media likes to portray." Rather, he said, they were simply people who had strong traditional values and who preferred to lead quiet, unpublicized lives.10

Because of the irreversible history of media coverage, by the late 1980s it had become almost impossible for family members to be seen as individuals. "People just assume that if you come from a certain family that obviously your values are off," said June.11 And it was as individuals that the Hunts wanted to be seen, if they were to be looked at at all.

On the other hand, even the most individualistic Hunts have a tendency to stick together. If the residences of the "first-family" Hunts are plotted on a map, they tend to cluster tightly: one of Caroline's sons lives in a house two doors from Herbert's home; half a dozen other family members live only a mile or two away. Very few Hunts from this part of the family, including the married daughters, have moved from Dallas, much less Texas.

Another indication of the family's tendency to stay united is the amount of time they spend together. Not only do groups of Hunts frequently have offices in the same building, but also they frequently socialize with one another. An article about Caroline and her financial empire described how she had emphatically invited Margaret,

Bunker, Herbert, and Lamar out to pick tomatoes on one of the family farms with her and how they'd all turned up.[12] Laurie described in an interview how happy she is to go to a luncheon or committee meeting and see one of her cousins there: they have a camaraderie, like sorority sisters. When she sees a cousin across the room, she knows she'll have someone to talk to, someone she'll feel utterly comfortable with.[13] Perhaps the feeling some family members have ultimately begun to develop is that, after all the family has been through, in some respects no one else can truly understand them.

How have the individuals from the three families related to one another after the interfamily lawsuits, jockeying for asset control, and forced interactions were over? Just as in the years following Hunt's marriage to Ruth, when family members were learning to adjust to a new family arrangement, it has depended on the individuals involved.

After Frania's out-of-court settlement of her claims, a settlement finally completed during the early 1980s, she and her children tended to have little or nothing to do with the other Hunt families. Hugh was living, far from everyone, in Maryland; Haroldina, while functioning as, in one of her daughter's terms, "a whole person," spent most of her energies handling her immediate family's needs as best she could. But as the third generation began to mature to adulthood, there began to be a possibility that some of them would want to explore and reconstruct their Hunt heritage, even if they were not prepared to think of themselves as Hunts in the way their half-cousins did. In 1986, for example, one of Haroldina's daughters started to become acquainted with Swanee, who was about fifteen years older than she was. It began because the two were interested in similar social issues and in the steps women could take to address social problems. The two liked each other and had things in common; the fact that they had a common heritage was only a part of getting to know each other.

Of the two families that continue to be centered in Dallas, each group tends to have its own world, which does not interact consistently with that of the other group. Lyda's children mostly live in Highland Park; Ray and June live in more distant suburbs. The first family attends Highland Park Presbyterian Church; Ruth and June go to First Baptist. Even in the case of Ray's family and Bunker,

Herbert, and their sons, whereas both groups are in the energy business, they tend to be involved in different deals in different parts of the world; both groups consistently go out of their way to differentiate their business holdings from one another. Caroline and her children also make statements of differentiation when their business dealings are confused with those of Herbert and Bunker. Although there are stories of occasional conflicts between members of the two families—one observer said that Margaret's daughter Lyda, who was active in the Dallas business community, never acknowledged the presence of her half-uncle Ray when the two attended the same meetings—generally the two groups seem to have adopted a live-and-let-live philosophy.[14]

Despite their basic separation, however, there seems to be a tendency among the younger members to be interested in the relatives the older generation—particularly some of Lyda's children—prefers to ignore. And some things that may have been extremely painful to Hunt's own children are almost taken for granted by his grandchildren's generation. Caroline's son Stephen, for example, recalled how he "always" knew about Frania and her children; it wasn't a big secret, or, by implication, a big issue. He could understand what the older family members had to deal with, easily seeing how some of them might have had "a whole lot of resentment" and how it would have been "very, very hard for some members of the family to ever get over that." But this is not the situation for him.[15]

As they have achieved distance from H. L. Hunt and his behavior, what seems to have happened for the younger Hunts is that they have looked at their slightly older relatives, especially those from each other's families, and identified with them. They have developed a sensitivity to the older generation's problems and what they worked through, and even, in some cases, have slightly idealized their elders.

In a way this is not surprising; there is a kind of romance enhanced by distance. Whereas Helen, for example, knows exactly how her older sister, June, sees the world and copes with it, she knows her half-sister Caroline less well and can identify with her only on a less intimate level. Consequently, Helen can say that she loves June, but that she sees Caroline as a real model, admiring particularly her success in throwing off her shyness and anonymity and moving into a world of action.[16] Similarly, Lyda's grandson Stephen, who frequently sees his uncles and cousins at church or at the country club, knows perhaps only too well what their foibles and weaknesses are as they deal with attorneys, judges, and lawsuits. On the other hand, he only occasionally sees his half-uncle Ray and more frequently reads or hears what others have to say about him. This slight distance leads Stephen to think of Ray as having had a "tough deal" and how Ray's weathering his problems has led him to become an outstanding leader in the community and in the business world, one whom Stephen obviously admires.[17]

Finally, there is the most basic, and yet in some ways most telling, of Hunt's legacies. Have Hunt's children and grandchildren inherited his best qualities as a human being, his abilities to enjoy life, succeed in the world, adapt to new situations? Or have they inherited his unwillingness, even inability, to face his own problems and drives and confront them in a way that would benefit both himself and those he loved?

As a group, Hunt's offspring have turned out to be remarkably healthy, both psychologically and physically. The most dramatic problem that has surfaced, and one that certainly cannot be taken lightly, is the incidence of mental illness, as evidenced in Hassie and Haroldina.

On another level, most of Hunt's children and grandchildren seem to have been able to hold jobs and take on financial responsibility (though sometimes with limited success) and to fulfill the other traditional objective of marrying and having a family. The one group that seems to have run into the most trouble in the latter area are Hunt's daughters. Caroline has been divorced twice, Helen and Swanee once each. Of Hunt's daughters' children, two of Margaret's children have been divorced, as has Caroline's daughter; Margaret's third child has never married. The daughters' attitude toward ending unsuccessful marriages is in marked contrast to that of Hunt, who developed his own unconventional answers to marital shortcomings, answers that never included divorce.

Still, many—perhaps even most—of the Hunts seem to be happy. Bunker and Herbert, under enormous economic and legal pressure, still have lunch at the Petroleum Club and attend the Cattlemen's Ball—the premier Dallas social fund-raiser—rather than hiding out on a distant family ranch or behind the walls of their Highland Park homes. Caroline, recently divorced, looks first at the opportunities her independence is giving her, rather than at the loss of companionship she has experienced. Ray commits himself to big civic and business undertakings but keeps them balanced with his well-protected and satisfying private family life. Swanee has made peace with her wealth and found a way to give it meaning in the context of her social values.

It was one of the Hunts who provided what might be the real key to the individual family members, what makes them tick, and what keeps them going. "All of us are people of our convictions," Helen said in a 1987 interview. "We're all proactive, not passive. Dad," she added, "would be proud of his kids."[18]

NOTES

AS the following notes indicate, I used a large number of published sources to obtain data about the Hunts. Particularly valuable were Stanley Brown's biography, *H. L. Hunt; Texas Rich*, the somewhat broader story of the Hunts by Harry Hurt; and H. L. Hunt's two autobiographies, *Hunt Heritage* and *H. L. Hunt: Early Days*. In addition, I consulted dozens of magazine and newspaper articles about various family members and interviewed seven members of the family in-depth; I also communicated with several other family members more briefly. Background material for the Hunt story was drawn primarily from books about the history of the oil business and from interviews with people familiar with the industry and its key players. All specific sources are as given.

INTRODUCTION

1. "Southwest has a new crop of super rich," *Life*, April 5, 1948; "The land of the big rich," *Fortune*, April 1948.
2. "Fighting to Rescue the Family Fortune," by H. John Steinbreder, *Fortune*, January 5, 1987.
3. "Bunker Hunt's Savvy Sister," by Roy Rowan, *Fortune*, October 5, 1981; "The Wealthiest Woman in America," Thomas C. Hayes, *New York Times*, October 26, 1986.

CHAPTER ONE

1. The details of Hunt's life in chapters one to seven are largely drawn from his autobiographies: *Hunt Heritage*, by H. L. Hunt (Dallas: Parade Press, 1973), and *H. L. Hunt: Early Days* by H. L. Hunt (Dallas: Parade Press, 1973). Other information is from *Texas Rich*, by Harry Hurt III (New York: W. W. Norton, 1981), and *H. L. Hunt*, by Stanley H. Brown (Chicago: Playboy Press, 1976).
2. *Hunt Heritage*, p. 8.

3. The account of Hunt's game of *cancoon* plus other gambling activities of this period appears in "Just Plain H. L. Hunt," by Tom Buckley, *Esquire*, January 1967.
4. *Hunt Heritage*, p. 19.
5. Sam Forte, resident of Lake Village, quoted in *Texas Rich*, p. 44.

CHAPTER TWO

1. "Just Plain H. L. Hunt," *Esquire*, January 1967.
2. *Life in the Oil Fields*, by Roger M. and Diana Davids Olien (Austin: Texas Monthly Press, 1986).
3. *Hunt Heritage*, pp. 42–43.
4. "Just Plain H. L. Hunt."
5. *Texas Rich*, p. 63. Information in next paragraph is from the same source.

CHAPTER THREE

1. Most of the information regarding Frania Tye is drawn from newspaper accounts of her testimony and depositions in the case *Lee* vs. *Hunt*, which took place in Shreveport, Louisiana, January 9–16, 1978, particularly a series of pretrial articles in the *Shreveport Times*, December 3–5, 1977, and coverage of the trial and its aftermath in the same paper, January 10–15 and January 18, 1978.
2. Descriptions of Hunt's activities during this period are drawn from *Texas Rich*, which also recounts the *Lee* vs. *Hunt* trial in detail.
3. Hunt describes his involvement in the East Texas oil fields in *Hunt Heritage*, chap. 6, "The Greatest Boom in History." There are many other accounts of Dad Joiner and H. L. Hunt. See, for example, *Saga of Wealth: The Rise of the Texas Oilman*, by James Presley (Austin: Texas Monthly Press, 1983); *The Last Boom*, by James A. Clark and Michael T. Halbouty (New York: Random House, 1972); *East Texas Oil Parade*, by Harry Harter (San Antonio: Naylor Co., 1934); and *The Greatest Gamblers*, by Ruth Sheldon Knowles (New York: McGraw-Hill, 1959).
4. See, for example, Hurt's account in *Texas Rich*, pp. 85–89.
5. *Hunt Heritage*, p. 85.
6. *Ibid.*
7. Hurt describes Hassie's childhood in *Texas Rich*, p. 62.

CHAPTER FOUR

1. Hunt discusses the flexible workweek in *Hunt Heritage*, p. 55.
2. Hunt discusses his efforts in support of an oil-depletion allowance in *Hunt Heritage*, pp. 63–68. He makes his case for federal regulation of the oil-and-gas industry on pp. 48–53.
3. One of the few places in his autobiographies in which Hunt discusses his wife, Lyda, and their children is *Hunt Heritage*, pp. 92–94, where he talks about living in Henderson with Hassie and in Tyler.

4. *Fifty Years: The Golden Anniversary Book*, by Frank Bronaugh (Tyler, Texas: Texas Rose Festival Association, 1983). The festival over which Margaret reigned is described on pp. 11–14.
5. See Frania Hunt's testimony in the *Shreveport Times* and other papers, and *Texas Rich*, for details of this period.
6. Hunt describes a wide variety of his investments in *H. L. Hunt: Early Days*. See, for example, chap. 5 and 6, on farm and ranch investments.
7. Frania Tye's court testimony, see note 1 for chap. 3.

CHAPTER FIVE

1. Most of the information on Ruth Ray's relationship with H. L. Hunt is drawn from *Texas Rich*. See also *Dallas USA* by A. C. Green (Austin: Texas Monthly Press, 1984), p. 126.
2. Hunt discusses Ruth's family in *H. L. Hunt: Early Days*, pp. 13–17 and 29–31.
3. June discussed her upbringing in articles in the *Dallas Times Herald*, May 9, 1971 and August 6, 1977; Helen, in the *Dallas Morning News*, December 22, 1985.
4. Details of Hassie's problems are drawn from "An American Fortune," by L. J. Davis, *Harper's*, April 1981, from *Texas Rich*, and, especially, from *H. L. Hunt*.
5. Information on Hassie's youth is from the author's interview with Caroline Hunt in 1987.
6. Information on Bunker, *ibid.*
7. The Dallas social scene is discussed in *Dallas USA* in chap. "Social Games, Art Games, Pretty Gains." Information on Hunt's attempts to join society appears in *Texas Rich* and in *H. L. Hunt*.
8. Hunt recalls his gambling on horses and his handicapping system in "Just Plain H. L. Hunt." See also Hardy Burt's article on Hunt in *True*, December 1960.
9. "Just Plain H. L. Hunt."
10. Jimmy the Greek described his gambling relationship with Hunt in his autobiography, retold in "The Greek Speaks: Many Listen," *Dallas Morning News*, July 13, 1975.
11. A complete history of Hunt Oil's exploration can be found in *The History of Hunt Oil Company* (Dallas: Hunt Oil Company, 1984), written and published on the occasion of the company's fiftieth anniversary.

CHAPTER SIX

1. Hunt describes his original plan in *H. L. Hunt: Early Days*, pp. 86–87. Other information on Hunt's actions appears in *Texas Rich*, p. 153.
2. *H. L. Hunt: Early Days*, p. 88.
3. *Hunt Heritage*, pp. 107–125.
4. *H. L. Hunt: Early Days*, pp. 73–76.
5. Hunt describes *Facts Forum* in chap. 10 of *H. L. Hunt: Early Days*. Almost every article about Hunt during the era of his political activities discusses his political philosophy. See L. J. Davis's "An American Fortune," *Harper's*, April 1981;

Houston Chronicle, October 18–23, 1964; "Portrait of a Super-Patriot," by Robert G. Sherrill, *The Nation*, February 24, 1964.

6. *H. L. Hunt: Early Days*, chap. 10.
7. An account of the wedding appeared in the *Dallas Times Herald*, November 26, 1957.
8. Hunt's interest in religion and his resultant actions are described in *Texas Rich* and *H. L. Hunt*. His developing views are detailed in his writings from this period: see, for example, *H. L. Hunt: Early Days*, chap. 13, "We Must Be First in Defense."
9. Besides his autobiographies, Hunt wrote *Alpaca, Why Not Speak, Fabians Fight Freedom, Hunt for Truth, HLH Columns, Right of Average, Alpaca Revisited, Old Letters-to-the-Editor, Constructively, H. L. Hunt*, and a few other works. All were privately published by various Hunt entities during the 1960s, focused on his political and social beliefs, and were available through LIFE LINE.
10. "Just Plain H. L. Hunt."
11. *Ibid*.

CHAPTER SEVEN

1. *H. L. Hunt: Early Days*, p. 128.
2. *Ibid.*, p. 112.
3. *San Antonio Express News*, September 15, 1968, a reprint of a feature article by Larry L. King that first appeared in the *Los Angeles Times West Magazine*.
4. "Just Plain H. L. Hunt," *Esquire*, January 1967.
5. *Hunt Heritage*, p. 124.

CHAPTER EIGHT

1. General information about Hunt and his family during this time is from his autobiographies and from the biographies *Texas Rich* and *H. L. Hunt*.
2. Caroline Hunt discussed her life in a number of interviews: see "Hotel Developer Needn't Hunt for Secret of Business Success," by Blair Corning, *Sunday Express News*, July 4, 1982; "The Heiress as Innkeeper," *Town and Country*, August 1983; "Caroline Hunt Schoellkopf," *Excellence*, April 1984; "Caroline Hunt Schoellkopf," by Marty Primeau, *Dallas Morning News*, August 21, 1984; and "Caroline Hunt Schoellkopf," by Carolyn Farb, *Interview*, October 1984. Additional material is drawn from the author's 1987 interview with her. All excerpted materials are from these sources.
3. Margaret granted brief interviews to the *Dallas Times Herald*, on September 21, 1975, and the *Dallas Morning News*, on September 28, 1975, after she became president of the Dallas Women's Club. She also was interviewed by the *Dallas Times Herald* on October 14, 1979, in her role as cochairman of a Dallas charity benefit event.
4. All of Caroline's descriptions of her mother are from author's interview.
5. "Profiles of Lamar, Herbert and Bunker Hunt," *Dallas Morning News*, August 21, 1984.
6. *Fifty Years: The Golden Anniversary Book*.

7. Miss Hockaday was speaking on the occasion of her retirement, *Dallas Morning News*, November 15, 1946. Also see *Dallas USA*, pp. 194–195, for a description of the school from a later perspective.
8. Caroline's description of this period of her life is drawn from author's interview.
9. Margaret's role in Hunt's business is described in *Texas Rich*.
10. "The Heiress as Innkeeper," *Town and Country*, August 1983.
11. Letter from H. L. Green to H. L. Hunt, November 17, 1972, reprinted in *Hunt Heritage*.
12. Author's interview with Caroline Hunt.

CHAPTER NINE

1. For articles concerning Frania Tye's depositions and court testimony, see n. 1 for chap. 3.
2. Information about the family in Great Neck is from the author's 1987 interview with Charles T. Bradley, now of Tulsa, Oklahoma.
3. Martha Kreeger's recollections appear in the court records of *Lee* vs. *Hunt*, as reported in newspaper articles cited above.
4. Hugh (as Hue) Hunt testified in the Shreveport trial; most of the information about the Lee children's relationship to Hunt and his other families is based on his testimony, as reported in newspaper articles cited above.
5. An informal history of Frania Lee's life in Atlanta appeared in a feature article, "Claim by Atlantan Surprises No One," by two society writers, Yolande Gwin and Raleigh Bryans, *Atlanta Journal*, January 12, 1978. Quoted passages are from this article.
6. Information on Howard is from author's interview with Charles T. Bradley.
7. *H. L. Hunt* briefly discusses Hunt's relationship with Helen Lee.
8. Hugh Hunt and his identity problem are discussed in *Texas Rich*.

CHAPTER TEN

1. Caroline discussed her early married life in the interviews in *Town and Country* and the *Dallas Morning News* (see n. 2 for chap. 8), and with the author in 1987.
2. "Caroline Hunt Schoellkopf," by Marty Primeau, *Dallas Morning News*.
3. Author's interview with Laurie Sands Harrison in 1987.
4. *Hunt-Bunker and Allied Families: A Genealogical Study with Biographical Notes* (New York: American Historical Co., 1946).
5. *Texas Rich*, p. 170.
6. Like Margaret, Herbert Hunt has maintained a low public profile and granted few interviews. He did discuss his geology degree, as well as other topics, in "A Talk Fest with the Hunts," by Roy Rowan, *Fortune*, August 11, 1980. See *Texas Rich* for additional information on Herbert.
7. *The History of Hunt Oil Company*, section entitled "1954–64." All quotations about the company are from this history.
8. Author's interview with Ray Hunt in 1987.
9. Information about Bunker, Herbert, and Lamar during this period is from *Texas Rich*.

10. The stories of Lamar's early love of and involvement in sports are from feature articles about him, including "The Lamar Hunt Story," by Ron Boyd, *Unique*, the magazine of the *Dallas Times Herald*, April 18, 1984; "Sports Profile: Lamar Hunt," by Sally Wilson, *Dallas Morning News*, April 24, 1983; "Lamar Hunt: Is the Force with Him?" by Wayne Kalyn, *World Tennis*, June 1982. See also "The Outsiders" in *The Rich Who Own Sports*, by Don Kowet (New York: Random House, 1977). Some of the stories about Lamar appear in more than one source.
11. *History of Hunt Oil Company*, p. 39.
12. See "An American Fortune," by L. J. Davis, *Harper's*, April 1981; *Texas Rich*; and *H. L. Hunt* for descriptions of Hunt's actions on Hassie's behalf.
13. *Texas Rich*, p. 171.
14. Caroline's observations concerning her mother are from the author's 1987 interview with her.

CHAPTER ELEVEN

1. Author's interview with June Hunt in 1987. The following material is based on this unless otherwise noted. For additional information on June, see her book, *Above All Else* (Old Tappan, NJ: Fleming H. Revell, 1975).
2. The employee's description appears in *The History of Hunt Oil Company*. The Dallas writer is Frank X. Tolbert, *Dallas Morning News*, April 4, 1948. Hunt himself quoted Tolbert's article, which he said was based on "one of the best interviews, and possibly *the* best, I ever had," in *H. L. Hunt: Early Days*, p. 66.
3. Author's interview with Helen Hunt in 1987. The following section is based on this source unless otherwise noted.
4. Hunt's son Ray and daughters Helen and Swanee referred to this side of him in interviews with the author.
5. Swanee Hunt discussed the two younger girls' childhood in an interview with the author in 1987. The following section is based on this source unless otherwise noted.
6. *H. L. Hunt: Early Days*, pp. 13–17 and 29–31.
7. *Dallas Morning News*, December 22, 1985.
8. Author's interview with Ray Hunt in 1987. This is the source of the following section except as otherwise noted.
9. "How to Live with a Difficult Mate," interview by June Hunt and Jan Silvious of Ruth Hunt, available on tape from Hope for the Heart, distributed by Cornerstone Christian Outreach, Dallas, Texas.
10. *Ibid.*
11. *Texas Rich*, pp. 108–109; *H. L. Hunt*, pp. 142 and 163.
12. Tape recording of June Hunt presentation entitled "Trials: God's Purpose Our Response," undated, distributed by Hope for the Heart.
13. Author's 1987 interview with June Hunt.
14. "Trials: God's Purpose Our Response."
15. The information about Ray at this time is from *Texas Rich*.
16. *The History of Hunt Oil Company*, p. 47.

17. "June Hunt reflects on singing for God," by Helen Parmley, *Dallas Morning News*, April 15, 1985.
18. *Texas Rich*, p. 193.
19. Information about the family and the First Baptist Church is from the author's 1987 interview with June Hunt.

CHAPTER TWELVE

1. A history of the oil-exploration business up to the 1980s can be found in *Saga of Wealth*. Additional information was provided by Glenda Smith, Statistics Editor of *Oil and Gas Journal*, Tulsa, Oklahoma.
2. Information on Bunker Hunt's involvement in Libya is based primarily on *Beyond Greed: The Hunt Family's Bold Attempt to Corner the Silver Market*, by Stephen Fay (New York: Viking Press, 1982), chap. 1; *Texas Rich*, chap. 9 and 13.
3. The story of Lamar's entry into professional football appears in *The Rich Who Own Sports*, pp. 77–88, and in *The Other League*, by Jack Horrigan and Mike Rathet (Chicago: Benjamin Co./Rutledge, 1970), chaps. 1–3.
4. "Sports Profile: Lamar Hunt," by Sally Wilson, *Dallas Morning News*, April 24, 1983.
5. *The Other League*, p. 16.
6. Lamar's description of this story was in "Of billionaires, money and deals, deals, deals," by James McCrory, *San Antonio Express News*, February 25, 1975.
7. *Dallas Morning News*, April 24, 1983.
8. *The Other League*, p. 20.
9. Information on Libya and the foreign oil companies is based on *Oil and Turmoil: America Faces OPEC and the Middle East*, by Dankwart A. Rustow (New York: W. W. Norton, 1982), especially pp. 134 ff.
10. A Hunt associate quoted in *Texas Rich*, p. 320.
11. A biography of Norma appeared shortly before their wedding in the *Dallas Morning News*, January 15, 1964. Additional information appeared in "Tournament time looms large in Hunts' lives," *Dallas Times Herald*, May 7, 1978.
12. *Dallas Morning News*, April 24, 1983.
13. "Hunt Still Believes," by John Meyer, in the *Dallas Times Herald*, July 22, 1979.
14. The history of professional soccer, including Lamar's role, is based primarily on *The American Encyclopedia of Soccer*, Zander Hollander, ed. (New York: Everest House, 1980), supplemented by articles about Lamar cited above and author's 1987 interview with former Tornado associate Tom Meredith.
15. Norma Hunt discussed her husband in the articles in the *Dallas Times Herald*, May 7, 1978, and the *Dallas Morning News*, April 24, 1983.
16. Most of the information on professional tennis, including the WCT, is based on *Tennis: A Professional Guide. The Official Handbook of the U.S. Professional Tennis Association* (New York: distributed by Harper & Row, 1984). Other sources are as noted.
17. "Lamar Hunt: Is the Force with Him?" by Wayne Kalyn, *World Tennis*, June 1982.

18. "Hunt's influence is being felt on American sports," by Mark Whicker, *Dallas Times Herald*, August 7, 1977.
19. "The Lamar Hunt Story," by Ron Boyd, *Unique*, April 18, 1984.
20. This observation about Lamar appeared in *World Tennis*, June 1982.
21. "Wimblewhat? Asks Lamar," *Dallas Morning News*, March 16, 1972.
22. Lamar's losses in tennis are referred to in the articles in *World Tennis* and *Unique* and in an editorial by Rod Humphries in *World Tennis*, January 1984.
23. See articles in the *Dallas Morning News*, January 15, 1968, June 1, 1969, October 15, 1969, and January 22, 1970.
24. *Dallas Morning News*, January 24, 1970.
25. *World Tennis*, June 1982.
26. *The Rich Who Own Sports*, p. 84. See *Texas Rich*, pp. 330–331, for an account of Lamar's house purchase.
27. *Unique*, April 18, 1984. On how Dallas views the Hunts, see *Texas Rich* and *Beyond Greed*.

CHAPTER THIRTEEN

1. See *Texas Rich*, chaps. 9 and 11; other information is drawn from author's interviews with family members, except as noted.
2. Author's 1987 interview with June Hunt.
3. Hill is frequently mentioned in *The History of Hunt Oil Company* as a participant in various undertakings.
4. See, among other sources, *Texas Rich*, pp. 263–264.
5. June discussed this situation in *Above All Else*, chap. 7, "God's Timing—Watch Out!" Information on other incidents in June's life is from this source unless otherwise noted.
6. Author's 1987 interview with Helen Hunt, the source for this section except as noted.
7. Author's 1987 interview with Swanee Hunt, the source for what follows except as noted.
8. An account of Helen's wedding appeared in the *Dallas Morning News*, August 3, 1969.
9. Swanee's wedding announcement was in the *Dallas Morning News*, May 24, 1970.
10. *Dallas Morning News*, December 22, 1985.
11. *Ibid.*
12. *Above All Else*, p. 67.
13. Author's 1987 interview with June Hunt.
14. *Ibid.*
15. *The History of Hunt Oil Company*, p. 47.
16. Author's 1987 interview with Ray Hunt.
17. *Ibid.*
18. The interview in *Playboy*, August 1966, is quoted in *The History of Hunt Oil Company*.

19. Information regarding Hunt's involvement in the company and in other areas is from *The History of Hunt Oil Company* unless otherwise noted.
20. Hunt's decision to pull out of the Alaska and the Santa Barbara deals is from the author's 1987 interview with Ray Hunt, as is Ray's description of Hunt's "sixth sense."
21. Developments at HLH Products are described broadly in *The History of Hunt Oil Company*, pp. 50 and 68, and in more detail in *Texas Rich*, pp. 182–186, 276–283.

CHAPTER FOURTEEN

1. A thorough description of the wiretapping in which Bunker and Herbert were involved appears in *Texas Rich*, chap. 12, "The Wire-Tap Caper," which is the source for much of the information in this chapter. See also *Beyond Greed*, pp. 25–27; "The Hunts Play for High Stakes," *Business Week*, February 17, 1975; "Hunt's billions" by Ann Crittenden, *San Antonio Express News*, January 20, 1980.
2. Information on membership of the Hunt Oil board was provided by the company.
3. *Texas Rich*, p. 359.
4. *Texas Rich*, p. 358.
5. Some typical Dallas observations on the Hunts appear in "The Hunt Brothers," by Bryan Wooley, *Dallas Times Herald Magazine*, May 4, 1986.
6. Among the many articles about silver in the world economy and the Hunts' position in particular, see "High Stakes in the Silver Game," by A. F. Ehrbar, *Fortune*, December 17, 1979; Ray Rowan's "A Talk Fest with the Hunts," *Fortune*, August 11, 1980; and "The Silver Scam," by Alan Trustman, *The Atlantic*, September 1980. The broadest sweep of articles appears in appendices to the records of government hearings after the crash of the silver market; for example, see the report of the House Subcommittee on Commerce, Consumer and Monetary Affairs, May 23, 1980. See also *Texas Rich* and *Beyond Greed*.
7. "Commodities Corner," column by Richard A. Donnelly, *Barron's*, April 8, 1974.
8. The history of the Hunts' involvement in Great Western United is discussed in *Business Week*, February 17, 1975, *Texas Rich*, pp. 328–329, and *Beyond Greed*, pp. 69–73.
9. Two notable obituaries were those by Martin Weil, *Washington Post*, November 30, 1974, and William F. Buckley, Jr., *San Antonio Light*, December 9, 1974.
10. The basic stipulations of Hunt's will are described in "Challenge Clause Put in Hunt Will," by Don Mason, *Dallas Morning News*, December 4, 1974.
11. Author's 1987 interview with Ray Hunt.
12. *Texas Rich*, pp. 353–354.
13. See *The History of Hunt Oil Company* and "This Hunt does his homework," by Toni Mack, *Forbes*, September 14, 1981.
14. *Forbes*, September 14, 1981.
15. "The Hunts Play for High Stakes."

16. "The Smartest Hunt," by Toni Mack, *Forbes*, December 29, 1986.
17. Author's 1987 interview with Ray. This and *The History of Hunt Oil Company*, chap. "1974–1984," are the sources for the following observations about the changes in Hunt Oil.

CHAPTER FIFTEEN

1. The history of the Hunts' soybean investments is told in *Texas Rich*, pp. 363–365, and in more detail in *Beyond Greed*, pp. 73–78.
2. *Beyond Greed*, pp. 72–73.
3. *Texas Rich*, p. 365.
4. The Sunshine Mining deal is discussed in *Beyond Greed*, pp. 191–192.
5. The progression of Bunker's suits in the Libya situation is described in *Beyond Greed*, p. 24; *Texas Rich*, pp. 395–396. The final resolution of his legal actions is described in "Judge says Hunt owes $41 million" in the *San Antonio Express-News*, January 26, 1984.
6. "Waiting for gold and silver to fall," *Business Week*, September 24, 1979.
7. *Beyond Greed*, especially chaps. 5 and 6.
8. "The Silver Scam," by Alan Trustman, *The Atlantic*, September 1980.
9. The broadest account of the Hunts' futures dealings and market reactions to them is in the report of the May 1980 House Subcommittee hearings and in *Beyond Greed*. See also "High Stakes in the Silver Game," *Fortune*, December 17, 1979, and various articles cited in the hearings, including "Everything Has Silver Lining for N. B. Hunt," *Washington Star*, January 10, 1980, and "Crippled U.S. Silver Market," *New York Times*, March 1, 1980.
10. See n. 9 and newspaper coverage from March 28, 1980, including "Silver Drop Shakes Hunts' Empire," *New York Times*, March 28, 1980; "A week that shook Wall Street," *Dallas Times Herald*, March 30, 1980; and "Silver's Slide Bloodies Only Hunt Brothers," *Wall Street Journal*, March 31, 1980.
11. See, for example, "CFTC Launches Probe of Silver," *Washington Star*, March 31, 1980, House Subcommittee hearings report, *Beyond Greed*, and *Texas Rich*.
12. House Subcommittee hearings.
13. "Hunts bare financial souls in statements," by Allen Pusey, *Dallas Times Herald*, May 28, 1980.
14. "A Talk Fest with the Hunts," by Roy Rowan, *Fortune*, August 11, 1980.

CHAPTER SIXTEEN

1. "Hunts bare financial souls in statements," by Allen Pusey, *Dallas Times Herald*, May 28, 1980.
2. "Hunt Still Believes," by John Meyer, *Dallas Times Herald*, July 22, 1979.
3. *The American Encyclopedia of Soccer*.
4. Lamar described the location problems in the *Dallas Times Herald*, July 22, 1979.
5. Author's 1987 interview with Billy Phillips, former Tornado player.
6. Author's 1987 interview with Tom Meredith.

7. See "The NASL: It's Alive But on Death Row," *Sports Illustrated*, May 7, 1984, and "Pro soccer's last kick?" *Fortune*, June 15, 1985.
8. This and preceding information is based on Wayne Kalyn's "Lamar Hunt: Is the Force with Him?" *World Tennis*, June 1982.
9. *Ibid.*
10. *Ibid.*
11. Editorial by Rod Humphries, *World Tennis*, January 1984.
12. *Ibid.*
13. "The Lamar Hunt Story," by Ron Boyd, *Unique*, April 18, 1984.
14. *World Tennis*, June 1982.
15. *The Rich Who Own Sports*, p. 87.
16. *Dallas Morning News*, April 24, 1983.
17. "The Insiders" column, by Jane Wolfe, *Dallas Morning News*, February 2, 1987.
18. Author's 1987 interview with Caroline Hunt, unless otherwise noted.
19. *Town and Country*, August 1983.
20. *Dallas Morning News*, August 21, 1984.
21. *Ibid.*
22. "Caroline Hunt Schoellkopf," *Excellence*, April 1984.
23. "How America's Richest Woman Keeps Busy," by Marguerite Michaels, *Parade*, March 27, 1983.
24. *Town and Country*, August 1983, and *Interview*, October 1984.
25. *New York Times*, October 26, 1986.

CHAPTER SEVENTEEN

1. The trial information is based on on newspaper articles, note 1, chapter 3, and on Harry Hurt's observations in *Texas Rich*.
2. Author's confidential interview with attorney involved in the case.
3. See the *Atlanta Journal*, June 4, 1962, for Helen Lee Cartledge's obituary and accounts of the accident.
4. Some of the legal jockeying following the announcement of the settlement was reported in articles in the *Shreveport Times*, May 23, 1978, and June 4, 1980, and in the *Shreveport Journal*, October 21, 1983.
5. Information about Ray Hunt and his sisters is based on author's interviews with them, except as noted.
6. *Dallas Morning News*, December 22, 1985.
7. Kreiling's involvement with his half-brothers-in-law is reported in *Texas Rich*.
8. *Dallas Morning News*, December 22, 1985.
9. *Annual Report 1985: The Hunt Alternatives Fund*.
10. " 'The other' Hunt seeks to stay out of limelight," by Mike Cochran, reprinted in *San Antonio Express News*, October 18, 1981.
11. The actions of Ray Hunt and Hunt Oil Company during this period are described in *The History of Hunt Oil Company*.
12. "This Hunt does his homework," by Toni Mack, *Forbes*, September 14, 1981, describes a number of Ray's diversifications.

13. "Ray Hunt's Wealth of Influence," by Robert M. Feinstein, *Dallas Times Herald*, July 5, 1987.
14. *The History of Hunt Oil Company*.
15. "The Smartest Hunt," by Toni Mack, *Forbes*, December 29, 1986.
16. "Houston City magazine attracts three bidders," by Michael Weiss, *Dallas Morning News*, December 20, 1986.
17. *Forbes*, December 29, 1986.
18. *Dallas Times Herald*, July 5, 1987.
19. *Forbes*, December 29, 1986.
20. Author's interview with Ray Hunt.
21. *Ibid.*
22. *Dallas Times Herald*, July 5, 1987.
23. *Ibid.* and "Ray Hunt balances time, power and privacy," by Cheryl Hall, *Dallas Morning News*, October 9, 1977.

CHAPTER EIGHTEEN

1. "A Talk Fest with the Hunts," by Roy Rowan, *Fortune*, August 11, 1980.
2. "Despite Setbacks, a Still Larger-Than-Life Texas Family," by Richard W. Stevenson, *New York Times*, August 30, 1986.
3. "Hunts cited for silver deal," by Allen Pusey, *Dallas Morning News*, March 1, 1985; "Hunts seek secrecy for civil proceedings in silver trading case," *Dallas Morning News*, November 16, 1987.
4. *San Antonio Light*, January 26, 1984.
5. Information on the history of Great Western appears in *Beyond Greed*, *Texas Rich*, and "The Battered House of Hunt," by Ford S. Worthy, *Fortune*, April 1, 1985.
6. *Fortune*, April 1, 1985.
7. The demise of Great Western and its affiliates can be traced in newspaper accounts beginning on October 7, 1984, when an Associated Press article reported that banks were taking losses on GW loans. Subsequent articles appeared in the *Dallas Morning News*, March 1, 1985, *San Antonio Express News*, March 8, 1985, *New York Times*, March 22, 1985, *Wall Street Journal*, November 1, 1985, and August 15, 1986.
8. "Quiet Series of Sales Ended Bid to Corner a Market," by Edwin Finn, Jr., and Allanna Sullivan, *Wall Street Journal*, October 3, 1985. An excellent summary appeared in a December 10, 1986, *Dallas Morning News* article, "Sizing up the Hunt empire," by Todd Vogel.
9. This attitude and the Hunts' changing behavior is described in *Fortune*, April 1, 1985.
10. "Offshore drilling site at heart of dispute," by Todd Vogel, *Dallas Morning News*, August 26, 1986.
11. "Sizing up the Hunt empire," by Todd Vogel, *Dallas Morning News*, December 10, 1986.
12. "Six Hunts sue 23 banks," by Todd Vogel, *Dallas Morning News*, June 25, 1986.
13. "Lawyers for the Hunt Family Have a History of Stirring Up Trouble," by Leonard M. Apcar *et al.*, *Wall Street Journal*, September 15, 1986. Also see "A

Texas-Size Legal Brouhaha," by Richard W. Stevenson, *New York Times*, September 4, 1986.

14. "Bank files counterclaim," by Todd Vogel, *Dallas Morning News*, July 17, 1986, and "22 banks countersue," by Michael Weiss and Gary Jacobson, *Dallas Morning News*, July 29, 1986.
15. "New Hunt Charges," by Thomas C. Hayes, *New York Times*, July 30, 1986.
16. "Big Oil Venture of Three Hunts Files for Bankruptcy," by Thomas C. Hayes, *New York Times*, August 30, 1986.
17. A good summary of this series of events appeared in "Trouble in a Texas empire," by Phillip Harper, *Dallas Times Herald*, August 31, 1986.
18. "Hunts Seek Disqualification of Judge, But Barefoot Isn't Walking," by Leonard M. Apcar, *Wall Street Journal*, September 8, 1986, and "Hunts Again Fail to Oust Sanders as Judge on Suits," *Wall Street Journal*, October 17, 1986.
19. These events are detailed in *New York Times* articles appearing on September 2, 3, 4, 8, and 12, and in the *Wall Street Journal* on September 5 and 8, 1986.
20. "Hunt Brothers Keep Foreclosed Land in the Family," by Leonard Apcar and Paul Duke, Jr., *Wall Street Journal*, October 8, 1986.
21. "New Lawyer for Hunts Not Aiming to Settle," *New York Times*, December 12, 1986.
22. "McCabe/Gordon, Ex-Hunt Lawyers, Decides to Dissolve," by Lawrence Ingrassia, *Wall Street Journal*, May 8, 1987.
23. "Hunt Lawyer to Get Fee Despite Limits," *Wall Street Journal*, January 16, 1987.
24. "Hunts' Plan to Drill in the Gulf Runs Into Stiffer Opposition from Lenders," by Leonard Apcar, *Wall Street Journal*, December 23, 1986.
25. "Placid investors reach funding accord," by Walter M. Rogers, *Dallas Morning News*, January 29, 1987.
26. "Sanders removes self from Hunt lawsuit," by Dudley Althaus, *Dallas Times Herald*, May 28, 1987.
27. "Battling a Billion-Dollar Debt," by John A. Jenkins, *New York Times Magazine*, September 27, 1987.
28. First reports of a deal were in "Hunts to offer deal to lenders," by Walter M. Rogers, *Dallas Morning News*, September 5, 1987, and "Hunts may offer to sell two firms," by Rogers, *Dallas Morning News*, September 9, 1987. The deals were off according to "Hunt lawyers cancel meeting after press leaks," by Rob Fixmer, *Dallas Times Herald*, September 10, 1987. The firing of First Boston was reported in the *Wall Street Journal*, November 2, 1987.
29. *Dallas Times Herald Tuesday Business Magazine*, October 5–11, 1987.

CHAPTER NINETEEN

1. "A Dallas industrialist sees gold in the silver screen," by Jane Sumner, *Dallas Morning News*, August 25, 1985.
2. "Profile of Alinda Hill Wisenbaker," by Mark Seal, *Dallas Morning News*, October 10, 1983.
3. "Battling a Billion-Dollar Debt," by John A. Jenkins, September 27, 1987.

4. Author's 1987 interview with Laurie Sands Harrison.
5. "The Lamar Hunt Story," by Ron Boyd, *Unique*, April 18, 1984.
6. Author's 1987 interview.
7. Author's 1987 interview. This is also the source for quotations that follow.
8. Ray Hunt was speaking in the *Dallas Morning News*, October 9, 1977, Laurie Sands Harrison and June Hunt in 1987 interviews with the author.
9. Author's 1987 interview.
10. Private communication to author.
11. Author's interview.
12. *New York Times*, October 26, 1986.
13. Author's interview.
14. Author's interview with a Dallas businessman.
15. Author's 1987 interview with Stephen Sands.
16. Author's 1987 interview with Helen Hunt.
17. Author's interview.
18. Author's interview.

INDEX

ABOUT THE AUTHOR

Ardis Burst grew up in Dallas, Texas, during the days when oil was king of the economy, every eligible politician was a Southern Democrat, and high culture was a shopping trip to Neiman-Marcus. She spent twenty years outside Texas; while away, she earned an M.B.A. at Harvard Business School, worked in marketing and management consulting, and wrote her first book, *The Management Game*. She now lives in San Antonio with her husband and two young children and is a full-time writer.